HAPLY I MAY REMEMBER

BY CYNTHIA ASQUITH

Novels:
The Spring House
One Sparkling Wave

For Children:
Everything Easy
I Wish I Were You

Anthology:
She Walks in Beauty

Plays:
No Heaven For Me

Drawing of the author by Norah Brassey.

CYNTHIA ASQUITH

HAPLY I MAY REMEMBER

And dreaming through the twilight
That doth not rise nor set,
Haply I may remember,
And haply may forget.
                    Christina Rossetti

LONDON
JAMES BARRIE
1950

First published in 1950

135|

MADE IN GREAT BRITAIN

Printed by
The Chiswick Press

Bound by
Hunter and Foulis Ltd.

CONTENTS

ILLUSTRATIONS

AUTHOR'S NOTE

THE letters at the beginning of this book show how it came to be written. The inconsistency I mention in the second of these letters explains, if it does not excuse, its present publication.

C. A.

LETTER TO C. A.

I can comprehend but I cannot condone your reluctance to embark upon an autobiography. It seems to me an excellent suggestion. Setting aside for a moment the value I place on such a book, and ignoring also its interest as the revelation, direct or oblique, of striking and already legendary personalities, such an autobiography would I think be of inestimable value and interest to those born later because of its recording of a world in flux by a mind equipped to detect significance in change.

Things to you familiar, would be to others illuminations; values to you taken as self-evident might come as redeeming surprises to those bred to another tradition.

How and where were you born? Into what manner of family and circle? How bred? To what conventions? When and how did you either abandon these conventions or find them by common consent abandoned?

"Into this world was I born—in this manner was I bred. I remember those about me, my Father, my Grandfather, my Mother, my Grandmother, my step-Grandmother . . . I remember those who tended them, their habits of life. I remember the communities of which they were the leaders. Thus-and-thus did they comport themselves, and have me taught to comport myself. I remember what they read, and what they read to me. I remember the goings from one house to another, and the different people of each . . . and how they changed as I grew up into an appreciation of the talk about me. I remember how we, my brothers and my sisters, were dressed. I remember what gave us pleasure, the toys, the games, the childish 'treats'."

xi

There's the first exercise in autobiographical memory.

"I came to a realisation of (say) George Wyndham in this way—and I remember him thus . . ." "Wyndham was of the Henley circle in letters and I met Charles Whibley." "In that pair of over-lapping circles were some strange contrasts—Wyndham, Whibley, Arthur Balfour. As legends they have become thus, but I recall them thus."

There's another exercise.

"You have read a life and many reminiscences of J. M. Barrie—but I knew the man. This was the man that I knew." "You have read many analyses of D. H. Lawrence. But I knew the man. This was the man."

"The stage! But who should know the stage better than I? This was the way of it. . . . And then the stage was overladen by the Theatre. This has been the Theatre that I have known . . . and this its adornments and disgraces."

"Whose writings opened windows in my mind? Well, the chief of the inletters-of-light, or of new darknesses, were these——"

"I have been so many things and people, but when I was the mother of sons I felt thus and thus, remembering what I had felt when I was the daughter of parents. . . ."

"When I myself, mine own self, my very self, became a woman, I looked upon the reigning beauties, the 'lovelies', and felt this about them. . . . And I remember them thus. . . ."

"How came I to write? I will tell you. . . ."

"Yes, I have twice seen an order of society shattered by war. I thought then of it otherwise, but now I think of it thuswise."

"Protestants, Papists, lovers of Pan . . . this is what happened to my soul (if I have a soul) and this was why—and whether I was moved by somebody's skill with prose or by a mystical experience, who shall say—but thus it was with me. . . ."

"The tone of the time? It has come to me in these ways."

"Talkers? I have met so many—so different—all so good in their ways. My own kind of talk? This kind of talk, as I recall X, and Y, and Z talking it."

"Painting and the other presentational arts? These are my tastes and they were formed thus, and they have changed so. . . . But let me tell you of painters, and how it was with me when I sat to A and B and C."

Those, very hastily, are the specifications that I would have you to work to.

I plead with you to remember that it is the familiar things which demand to be remembered. The shape of the nursery knives and forks—the manner of response to a tenant's greetings—the relationship of the rector to the sexton—what you called your uncles and aunts—and all that side of normal life. For the unfamiliar will tell itself.

REPLY

You do crack the whip. I had no idea you were such an impresario. I wish I hadn't told you of that publisher's offer. Why should I write a book about myself? May I remind you that paper is very scarce? At this juncture in its lunatic history, surely one of the things the rationed human race can most easily go without is a book about Cynthia Asquith?

Why after a long career of oyster-hood should I prise my own shells open? You say my autobiography or memoirs—I really don't know which word I find more distasteful—"would be of value and interest to those born later because it would be the record of a world in flux by a mind equipped to detect significance in change". Certainly lack of "change" is the very last complaint we can bring against our epoch. But, is an *inward-looking* eye well equipped to be a good observer of extraneous things?

You demand a "human document"—I forgive the cliché—but, surely, if on the one hand I am too un-objective to write discerningly of others, am I not on the other too inhibited—sorry to borrow from the jargon you detest—to write revealingly of myself?

You say I have met so many "good talkers". That's true, but alas! the ability to convey why talk was good is one of the rarest of gifts. I have known "interesting people" well? Yes, but I am not a summer-up. The more I see of a person the less can I see the wood for the trees (who was it said "Look well on a man the first time you see him—for you'll never see him again"?). The only people I ever see in distinct outline are the merest passers-by. Isn't it exactly those who are most familiar to us—certainly those we love—whose psychological physiognomy we see least clearly? We see it far too subjectively. In every relationship

I am conscious of doubling the parts of Pygmalion and Galatea; I make and I am made.

Don't we all to suit our moods, our hopes, our anxieties, continually refashion our intimates until virtually we cease to be able to separate them from ourselves?

So much for my ability to delineate personality. Moreover, where relatedness or circumstances gave me the privileges and penalties of, so to speak, seeing both sides of the tapestry; a certain squeamishness (my forbears would have called it delicacy, an author's heaviest handicap, my descendants call it inhibition) would forbid my portraiture being anything more than the most superficial impressionism.

Surely to write a good autobiography one must set a higher value on writing than on personal relationships? No doubt, anyone primarily a writer can, will and must do this. But I do not take myself seriously enough as an author to feel any obligation to sacrifice reticence, a luxury that admittedly no real artist can afford.

Anticipating my evasive wriggles, you plead that it is "the familiar, concrete things that demand to be remembered", e.g., the kind of knives and forks (why this special interest in cutlery?) one used in the nursery—a nursery itself indeed having now become almost a museum piece—"what one wore, what one ate and so on". But although, in the dictionary sense of the word, I am surely very far from young, there are, I would remind you, still alive and yet able to hold a pen, persons who used knives and forks even more antique than those my own childish fingers wielded.

Possibly, indeed, my chief objection to the whole project is the feeling that to embark on any reminiscing book is deliberately to turn your face towards the past; whereas I—smile as widely as you like—shall, I suspect, even if, which heaven forbid, I live to be ninety, still be expectant. I am an incorrigible looker-forward. To concentrate on memories would surely be to recognise with what a rush the horizon is now closing in and therefore inevitably to begin to feel as old as I am. This, by your leave, I do not yet intend to do.

I need not say I'm glad you should think me capable of a

book worth reading; but remember few other people possess
to anything like the same degree your enviable and stimulating
—what shall I call it—curiosity—inquisitiveness? No, I'll be
civil and call it "human interest".

But don't think that I do not know that what really prompts
your whip-cracking is the aching nostalgia of one not quite
brave enough for this Brave, New World.

Re-reading your letter, I see a more personal argument,
indeed a prescription. You say that I am the better—as who is
not?—for mental exercise, and you remind me that crosswords
are not enough. *Touché.* Therefore, since you say you like
getting letters from me, and since you are easy to write to—
non-conductors being quite as operative through the post as in
conversation—may I suggest a compromise? Shall I in my
return letters undertake to try to answer as many of your
questions as I choose? If by skilful and, let us hope, painless
cross-examination, you extract any worth-while material, then
when I am dead—since die I suppose I must—*literally* dead,
mind you, you yourself with the consent of my executors, can
publish a book compiled from these letters.

Since consistency has never been one of my faults, and with
advancing years, no doubt, reticence as well as memory fails, it is
quite possible—indeed very probable that you will be able to
persuade me to let it be published during my life-time. Even
so, I think letters are the right form for a book such as you
demand from me—it's so much easier to write when you aim at
a particular target—and this method should save it from the
ponderosity of some deliberately undertaken autobiographies.
Flitting at random between first and second childhood, I can
dip into the river of time at whatever point I choose.

Remember, I have no intention of telling the story of my own
life, and naturally I reserve the right to reply "no, that
question I can't or won't answer". There must be deference to
the sensibilities of the living. There are also graves on which I
will not "peep and botanize" to order.

I see your demands include "letters from interesting people".
Your surmise is right. As a hoarder I do out-vie the most
assiduous squirrel. But, alas, I have not yet rid myself of the

hampering fear of ridicule, and therefore absolutely refuse to expose my dear self to the charge brought against so many she-autobiographers of publishing "testimonials" to themselves.

Another point: you, as a fellow offender, know that my letters will be clotted with quotations. To keep these out, gate-crashers as they are, would be a great strain, an unnatural effort—indeed a pose. So, their eviction must be left to your own indiscretion.

One thing more occurs to me. Though unlikely, it is not inconceivable that a fit of Benvenuto Celliniism might seize even me, so that, just as he threw all his furniture into the flames rather than see his furnace fail for lack of fuel, I too, in the white heat of writing, might sacrifice valued property in the way of sanctities.

Should this happen, and should the book be a posthumous one, I leave it to my executors to take out anything that they think my own judgment, when cool, would not have included. . . . Your other letter has just reached me. Very well, since you undertake the post of target, I await your first questions. How you will regret this strange compact! Respite for you, of course, there will frequently be—blessed interludes, the while I groan in the Doldrums—but I warn you that though I may forget much, "Haply I may remember!"

C. A.

STANWAY

As this is not the story of my life—that, don't forget, I declined to undertake—but just memories of people, places and moods, there is no reason to keep to chronological sequence. You might find a great unbroken chunk of childhood rather indigestible. I warn you, I'm not like Arthur Balfour, who, when questioned about his childhood, said all he could remember of it was "having very tired legs after walking!"

My difficulty will be to sift my memories.

First I propose to take three houses, each part of the background of my early life, and, letting my memory run backwards and forward across the years, try to describe their very different atmospheres and tell you some of my associations with them. My own discrimination will probably not be a sufficiently fine sieve. Sharpen your blue pencil.

The three houses are Stanway, my very own home—the core of the world so it seemed to me—where naturally my roots are deeper and more widely spread than anywhere else; Gosford, the Scottish home of my father's father; and Clouds, the Wiltshire home of my mother's family.

I'll begin with my own home, though how to pick and choose among all the memories—layers upon layers of memories!— that at the mere name of Stanway begin to stir and throb, I cannot imagine. Even had I, immediately I grew up, left Stanway for ever, it would still be the haunt of a myriad unfading remembrances, as to all of us must surely be the place where, living through the timeless dawn of life, we first opened our eyes on grass, trees and sky; first "felt through all our fleshly dress bright shoots of everlastingness"; first perceived the eternal sigh and the eternal laugh. Oh that intense insecure felicity of childhood! Those wild oscillations from one

I

extreme to another! One moment seized by such joie-de-vivre that, like a puppy scampering over fresh snow, I must jump over my shadow; the next, "drooping, woeful-wan"—dissolved in tears. *Why* I wept I never could say, and it was not for want of asking ("cuttlefish", my mother called me).

All I knew was that inexplicably—appallingly, existence its very self had suddenly become a pain.

So far from being merely the starting-point of my life, Stanway remained till only a few years ago the background to which I constantly returned. Because I did not, as the queer expression then went, "marry a country-house", my husband and I usually spent a large part of his holidays—and barristers were fortunate in the length of their holidays—in my old home. Consequently, Stanway has been the stage on which, willy-nilly, I have in succession played so many different parts—infant daughter, younger sister, only child, elder sister, daughter-of-the-house, married daughter, sister-in-law, aunt and mother. Far the most difficult part is that thrust upon you in the phase of life when, discomfortably sandwiched between the older and the younger generation, you suddenly find both simultaneously dependent on yourself, and must watch and try to help the pathetic gradual reversal, the Changing of the Guard, in the relationship between parents and children.

I remember the panic—I had always hated responsibility—with which I first noticed in those so long at the family helm, unmistakable signs of a wish to shift the responsibility, and with how sharp a pang I came to realise that she on whom I had so long, so heavily leant, now needed support herself—alas, how little I was able to give!—on the downward slope of the hill. In my mother's case, the common lot was accelerated and emphasised by sudden lameness, so that the physical change was painfully impressed on my very hearing by the altered sound of her step—that step once so memorably light, for whose approach I used in babyhoood so longingly to listen—

> "Oh Youth . . .
> What strange disguise hast now put on
> To make believe that thou are gone?"

But for the cruel arthritis that crippled her, my mother, I think, would have remained as young in effect as she remained in spirit. The light of youth was still in her eyes.

All my life I shall remember the shock—never have I felt so much inclined to hit an unintentional offender!—of the first time I heard her spoken of as "A dear *old* lady!"

Perhaps even queerer was the insidious change in my relationship with my father. Was it possible that the alarming, alluring, disquieting being, after whose captious approval I had always strained, from whose usually unspoken but occasionally painfully perceptible criticism I had always shrunk, should now look to me for guidance—actually defer to *my* judgment?

Absurd fusion of the phases of life that just when in my thoughts the name "Grandpapa" began to displace that of "Papa"—so much mellower had he grown, that grandfather-hood seemed more natural to him than fatherhood ever had—I should simultaneously recognise in my own feelings towards him sentiments almost maudlinly *maternal*!

Was it because Stanway was so steeped in memories of my own childhood—memories too vivid for any later experiences to over-lay—that I always found it so particularly difficult to play there with becoming dignity, or indeed at all convincingly, any of the more responsible rôles for which I found myself cast? As *"Aunt* Cynthia", I fear, I acquitted myself very badly—constantly letting down what I should have regarded as my own side. Try as I would, I could never help taking the children's part against their unhappy nurses and governesses; and thanks to my shameless practice of warning youthful delinquents of the approach of those set in authority over them, I was to my discredit, but not to my displeasure, nicknamed "Aunt Ca-vee"!

It was, so to speak, only in inverted commas that I could see myself as a mother or aunt. This failure to feel myself a "responsible person" made me wonder how many others suffered from a similar lack of conviction in the rôles for which they found themselves cast. The "Papa" and "Mamma" so convincing to my own childhood? To them, too, had parent-hood seemed an ill-fitting, uneasily worn fancy-dress? . . .

I'll tell you later how Stanway first fragmentarily impressed itself on my infant mind. To begin with I'll describe it with as much objectivity as I can. You need not be afraid of being Baedekered. I'll be brief.

Stanway is a typical small village on a foot-hill of the North Cotswolds. Its "mansion", as the villagers still call the house, originally the summer residence of the Abbots of Tewkesbury, had become a private house at the time of the dissolution of the monasteries. Because our home was confiscated Church property, someone, needless to say, was kind enough to tell me before I was five that a curse lay on my family. In our case, she added, the curse must surely be doubled, for it was into the hands of the Tracys that the house had fallen, and William Tracy had been one of the four wicked knights who had murdered St. Thomas à Beckett on the altar-steps of Canterbury Cathedral. Poor misguided William Tracy! It was said that yearly on the anniversary of his crime his horse's hooves were heard clattering along the road as desperately he rode in search of a priest who would shrive his tormented soul. I remember the thrill, three parts fear, one part elation, with which I would hear the knell-like local saying, "The Tracys, the Tracys, the wind in their faces."

How came Stanway into my father's family? When, in the eighteenth century, its heiress, one Susan Tracy, married the Lord Elcho of the day. Her husband died before his father, but the property went to her son, the sixth Earl of Wemyss. That is all you shall hear of my forbears.

The house is built of time-tinted golden Cotswold stone. Approached through the arch of the beautiful Inigo Jones Gatehouse, the west front of the house with its four wide sixteenth-century gables, numerous mullioned windows, and one huge oriel, closely overlooks the village church and the huddled graves of the rude forefathers. The southern wing faces a lawn skirted by a wood of yew trees that makes a dark background in the spring for the brief, shimmering, waxen glory of a large magnolia tree. Queened over by the great tulip tree, the eastern lawns stretch out until the ground rises in a sudden steep bank up to the long wide grass terrace that

4

was once a pond and is still called the canal. From the "canal", you climb up, up, up, until you reach the queer stone building called the pyramid (the "Pretty-Maid", I misunderstood its name to be) that has given its name to the entire hill. When I was little, the ascent of the "pyramid" seemed and indeed was an immense undertaking. In later years, whenever there was a spare quarter of an hour to fill, some visitor to lunge, or I just felt the need to let off a little steam, my invariable practice was to race up to its summit and down again—a habit that has left in me the undying impulse to scale any hill I see. Heaven preserve me from arthritis! So long as I am able to stride swiftly up-hill, there are few worries I cannot temporarily out-strip.

The precipitous descent of this garden mountain was ideal for tobogganing; also for its summer variant, "trolleying", a fascinating pursuit for which the architect Detmar Blow designed for my use every conceivable size and shape of wheeled contraption.

From the pyramid you look down on to the house nestling far below in the cup at the bottom of the hill. Blue plumes of smoke rise from its chimneys, and behind it a lovely line of— but enough! I'm no landscape painter, and I don't imagine you to be avid for detailed descriptions of scenery.

I remember some visitor saying, when I was about seven, "How lucky you are, Cincie, to live in such a beautiful place!" No tribute could deepen my allegiance to my home, yet it gave me acute pleasure to hear it praised.

I cannot remember anyone who didn't fall under the spell of Stanway, and feel its peculiarly strong atmosphere—the very air of the place seems thicker and more still than elsewhere —a cloistered, self-sufficing atmosphere that envelops you in a muffling cloak.

The most striking thing about the house is the beauty of the golden hue of its mellowed stone softened by centuries' growth of silver and yellow lichen and thickly clustered over with great masses of magnolia and clematis leaves. More than any other building I know, the house seems to have a face—an actual countenance with an expression that changes like that of a living creature. At times, it looks withdrawn into itself, utterly aloof, benign; at others sheltering and steeped in memories, as though its golden walls had participated in the joys and sorrows of all the generations who have lived within them and were still ready to throb in sympathy with their descendants. I once heard Burne-Jones's daughter, Margaret Mackail, exclaim, "The very stone of the house looks as if it would bleed if you scratched it!"

As a child I loved my home precisely as one loves a human being—loved it as I have loved very few human beings. I could never go away without a formal leave-taking. "How are you?" I would ask on return, gazing up at the gabled front to absorb its beauty like a long, lovely draught, and I fancied that it smiled back a welcome. My besetting fear was that one day I should come down the Cockpit Hill and find the house in flames. Once, when I saw on a placard in London, "Earl's Mansion Burnt to the Ground", I was much too frightened to buy a newspaper.

I don't know in which of its aspects I thought the house most beautiful—glowing like a golden hive in the sunshine; sad and gentle in the twilight, or stern and shiveringly strange under the "cold fruitless moon". Claimed by the moonlight, it looked wan and remote, as though, so I used to fancy, palely repudiating any kinship with those who lived beneath its roof.

Almost as much as the house, I loved its beautiful satellites, the giant beech-trees that, now gilded by the setting sun, now silvered by the moon, towered all the way up to the pyramid. Though in the daytime these trees were all friends with whose branches I was on familiar climbing terms, at night they became awesome mysteries to be worshipped. Determined to overcome my fear of the breathing darkness, but quiveringly alert to all its little furtive rustling sounds, night after night I would force myself to walk under the overshadowing branches to the very top of the hill. . . . Silence, except for the far, far away bark of a lonely dog. . . . Then, startlingly as though voicing all the vague eeriness of the night, would come the hoot of an owl—a sound I still never hear without a strange stirring.

With a shiver, I would turn and hurry back to the shelter of the lamp-lit house. . . .

What attracts most sightseers to Stanway is the magnificent tithe-barn mentioned in the Domesday Book of William the Second's reign and said to be the second largest in England. You would expect the antiquity of this building to be apparent to an eye, yet I overheard an overseas visitor hail J. M. Barrie with the words, "Say, Sir James, when did you build this shack?"

The tithe-barn, the picturesque centre of the village community and the noble setting for every kind of entertainment —cricket lunches, village dances and concerts, political meetings and amateur theatricals—was also our refuge in the wet days of childhood; endless games of stump-cricket were played, and innumerable bruises incurred, on its pitilessly hard concrete floor.

The beautiful little church, close enough to the house to make punctuality practically impossible, at first provided us with the convenient seclusion of a high-walled family pew, a feature swept away, as savouring too much of "privilege", by a vicar ruefully described by his parishioners—to whom change was synonymous with evil—as a "Sad Radical". The long dynasty of my mother's Chow dogs were embarrassingly keen church-goers, and I'm afraid my assurances that in Scottish villages it was the accepted custom for dogs to accompany their masters to worship, did nothing whatever to reconcile our vicars to their regular attendance.

Newcomers struck by the beauty of the outside of Stanway were, no doubt, disappointed by its interior. Expectations of exquisite panelling, chimneypieces and furniture were not realised. Nearly all the original panelling had been removed, and, except for the shovelboard table, the house contained no museum piece. Certainly no one could complain of "period tyranny". Much of the furniture was cumbrous Jacobean; most of the upholstery William Morris. Nor had the house undergone any fashionable redecoration. Neither frozen in the past nor flexible to change, it remained a gradual living growth —a thoroughly lived-in home, where nothing was ruthlessly discarded and little that was not personal was ever added.

Very occasionally a local decorator would be called in to renovate, but never to innovate. We loved the restful shabbiness and gentle, dignified dilapidation of our home. Any so-called improvement would have been passionately resented. We would not even have wished any of its flittering bats—the chase of whom with billiard-cues was a favourite sport of my brothers— to be dislodged; nor its swarm of rats and cockroaches.

Even those visitors discerning enough not to wish to see Stanway redecorated, would, I cannot doubt, have welcomed some modernisation in its standard of comfort. To sleep in one of its picturesque four-poster beds was admittedly an adventure, and the penetrating cold of the house—the draughts were unnumbered—had to be felt to be believed. I remember my uncle Evan Charteris,[1] a very civilised being with a highly developed sense of comfort, complaining that on one visit he had been put into a bedroom—a very small one—with no less than five doors, all so ill-fitting that the converging draughts were like five spears.

The walls between the bedrooms, some of which, because of their double inter-communicating doors, were constantly used as passages, were so thin that occupants could not help overhearing any curtain-lecture delivered in the adjoining room. Single guests burdened with a sense of honour felt they ought to sing or whistle to apprise the adjacent couple of this dangerous audibility.

Electric light was not installed in Stanway until some years after I married. Oil lamps—extremely dangerous, so often were they overturned in what Father Vaughan denounced as "Bear-fighting in Country Houses"—lightened the darkness of the sitting-rooms, but in our bedrooms we had only candles, which greatly added to the excitement of forbidden readings-in-bed. At the sound of approaching steps, I would bring my book down with a bang on the little flame, flattening the wick; but a tell-tale tiny red spark—let alone the stench of tallow— invariably survived to betray me.

The darkness of the house made a walk through its disused

1 Sir Evan Charteris, K.C.

shrouded bedrooms a pleasurably frightening childish exploit. Some of the rooms were vaguely reputed to be haunted. Boards creaked; water-pipes gurgled; furniture cracked; bats brushed against one's cheeks. For some time, my regular evening ritual was to force my solitary self to make the eerie round of the spare bedroom wing of the house in pitch darkness.

Cold though the house may have struck visitors, there was in those days no shortage either of fuel for fires, nor of willing hands to lay them. Personally, I enjoyed the sense of scurrying through Siberian regions to reach a blazing fire.

The house, a Liberty Hall both to children and to dogs, however deficient in luxury, had all the ease of spaciousness, for none of the rooms were cluttered up. There were plenty of deep chairs and well-worn sofas to sprawl on and—greatest of all comforts to children—the sense that there was not much to be afraid of spoiling or breaking.

Most of the pictures were merely paltry portraits of wholly undistinguished Tracy ancestors, who must, I think, have patronised itinerant portrait painters artistically much on a par with the Happy Snap photographers of the seaside resorts of to-day. These works of art were, however, pleasantly framed and not without a certain period pathos.

The only room in the house in the least formal, not in its style, which was a pot-pourri of many ages—its ceiling being reputedly Tudor, its gilt mirrors Queen Anne—but in atmosphere, was the drawing-room. In this, partly because as well as a room it was also a passage, we seldom settled either to read or to talk to any one person in particular, but here, when we were many, we assembled for round-games or dancing.

The great feature of the hall is the huge Oriel window with its hundreds of latticed panes, so mellowed by time that whenever the sun shines through their amber and green glass, the effect is of a vast honeycomb and indeed at all times and in all weathers of stored sunshine.

The hall was the heart—in winter, despite its fire of ox-roasting blaze, the ice-cold heart—of the house, and the splendid setting for diverse entertainments, innumerable cricket lunches and teas, school feasts, Christmas trees and private theatricals.

Here it was that, while treading the boards, my uncle George Wyndham, stamping his foot, suddenly turned to the aghast audience and glaring at an unfortunate mother, fulminated the terrible threat, "Unless that baby is taken out at once, I shall stop acting!"

Here too, in untellable tension were quiveringly produced two plays especially written by J. M. Barrie for my two sons, their five cousins and their grandfather; but of that undertaking, from the strain of which I have not yet, some twenty years later, quite recovered, I'll tell you later.

The windows of the dining-room, originally the servants' hall, were so high that nothing but the sky could be seen through their yellowed panes. Once a neighbour newly arrived in the district and most anxious to make an impression on his first visit, tried to electrify the company by saying, "Those high windows remind me of when I was in prison." Unfortunately, my mother was at that moment much too preoccupied in counting the number of spoonfuls of coffee to put into the machine in which she always made that beverage at the end of the meal, to take in the, as he had hoped, sensational nature of her guest's conversational gambit, and her family were all still too young or too socially inept to register any appropriate reaction. His one social trump-card thus thrown away, the crestfallen guest subsided into a dejected silence from which it took all my mother's deftness to coax him. That coffee-machine often provoked uncontrollable fits of family giggles, for my mother never failed to preface her coffee-brewing by the often laughably unnecessary appeal, "Now, *please*, don't any of you say anything interesting while I'm counting." The wild improbability of any guest then at her table disobeying this flattering enjoinder never made her omit it. It did, however, make her family giggle.

In the square room adjoining the dining-room, called by the staff—ironically, it seemed, for never was a room less private—"His Lordship's Room", we assembled before meals, and at any hour of the day pulled out some of its very readable books. The dust on those in the Old Library—mostly eighteenth-century sermons—was seldom disturbed. Here we played turbulent games of Ping-Pong and Puff-Ball, for both of which we invented revolting variations. Substituting our mouths for bats, we blew the ping-pong balls under the net. Similarly impelled the little cork used at Puff-Ball whirled wetly round the board. The most spectacular player of mouth Ping-Pong was "The Professor", Sir Walter Raleigh, whose respiratory organs seemed able only to inhale, not to exhale. His effect was like the suction of a vacuum-cleaner. Invariably the ball disappeared into his mouth. "Lost ball!" we would cry.

Practically everything in this unassuming knock-about room was restfully ugly. The chairs were very comfortable, and from their capacious depths you could without rising tell the time by the church clock. You could also see callers drive up to the door and decide—though unfortunately the process of decision was seldom unobserved—whether or not you were "At Home". Being the ante-room of the dining-room, it was, because of my mother's incorrigible unpunctuality, the scene of frequent parental impatience. My father, constitutionally punctual—morbidly so, we thought—and endowed with an excellent digestion, was always ready for the next meal. At the first boom of the gong, which usually had to be what was called "sounded" several times, he began to pace up and down the room. In five minutes he would be champing. "Where's your Mother?" he would ask accusingly, detachedly, as though she were a connection for whom I alone was responsible and had for some nefarious purpose incarcerated in a cupboard. Usually the butler, his face an impassive mask, suavely answered for me, "If it please Your Lordship, Her Ladyship has just gone up to the pyramid with Master Cymru." (Cymru was a chow-dog.)

This information did not please his ravenous Lordship, and pell-mell into the dining-room the assembled guests, however much they would have preferred to await their hostess, would then be driven like sheep.

One famous sufferer from my mother's unpunctuality was the unfortunate vicar, who, on his first visit to Stanway, arrived for dinner to find himself—my father was away—alone in this waiting-room with my Uncle Evan, who was then staying in the house. The very shy vicar obviously had come primed with a supply of puns and anecdotes, just sufficient, he reckoned, to carry him through dinner. As the minutes ticked inexorably by and no one else appeared, he was obliged—my uncle said he had never seen greater distress on any face—pun by pun, anecdote by anecdote, to discharge all his precious stock of social ammunition. Before his hostess arrived, the poor man had fired off the very last shot in his locker, and once he had said grace, could think of nothing else to say—nothing whatever.

The Old Library, almost the only room in the house with not more than one door, was reserved for the use of authors or Cabinet Ministers in need of seclusion.

Of all the rooms in the house, my mother's sitting-room— the "Bood-War", as the butler called it—is for me the most richly imbued with memories. Among its myriad happy associations, I remember it as the most propitious setting for general conversation, an art my mother so much loved and was so admirably qualified to preside over.

What, besides the indispensable quality of charm, and her insatiable interest in her fellow creatures, so well equipped Mamma for her favourite rôle of an informal chair-woman, who could always put debaters at their ease and stimulate good talk? For one thing, I think, an unusual alliance of wisdom, impartiality and sympathy, with a delicious naïveté (she loved to be laughed *at* as well as with; in fact, in a manner that was almost arch, invited banter) and also because as a talker she, the least self-centred of attractive women, was herself utterly without competitive spirit, her object being, so to speak, not that wickets should fall, but that as many runs as possible might be made off her bowling. How good, without ever appearing to interrupt, she was at insisting that anyone who wanted to talk should get his turn; those who really preferred merely to listen (and believe it or not, dear fellow egotist, such persons *do* exist!) she would leave in peace; how well she knew exactly when and to whom to send an inviting lob, and at what precise moment, by deftly serving another ball, to change the subject before, not after, the rally began to die down. It was never in the least difficult for her to change the subject because it was natural for her mind to fly off at a tangent.

Another stimulating quality was that, while intensely interested in almost any conceivable point of view, she was herself singularly without any settled opinions of her own. Do you remember the mental attitude commended by Keats—"The mind should be a thoroughfare for all thoughts, not a select party"? This exactly describes the ever-open-door hospitality of my mother's mind and made her the ideal hostess for so many guests with the most divergent views. Herself impartial almost to a fault, she delighted in the prejudices of others. Nor did she mind how vehemently or how extravagantly these might be expressed. She did, however, always contrive to keep the conversation from becoming over-heated.

Despite the icy blasts that pierced the leaden panes of its two great mullioned windows, the thought of long winter evenings in that boudoir warms me with the memory of glowing, winged hours when, as a very young girl, I was privileged to hear so many brilliant talkers—now at their serious, now at their nonsense best—debate with a zest, a gaiety, a courtesy and mutual appreciation that one at least of the traditionally hostile "Younger Generation" found enthralling, entrancing—even exalting....

Arthur Balfour, Walter Raleigh, George Wyndham, Harry Cust, Charles Whibley, H. G. Wells, Evan Charteris, Hugh Cecil, Maurice Baring, Lady Desborough—here, at random, are the names of a few of those (of some of whom I will, later on, if you wish, try to tell you individually) whose faces, as I write, rise before my eyes; whose voices and laughter I can hear again; while now with tempered heat they earnestly discuss some burning question of that day; now, like verbal ballet-dancers, glide, twist and pirouette in airiest fancies; now rollick in fantastic exuberant nonsense. I remember how the hours flew, and how much I used to dread the dispersing sound of "that tocsin of the soul—the dinner-bell".

You must not, for one moment, suppose there was anything pretentious, precious or even deliberately serious about these "symposiums", as we used to call the tournaments of wit and wisdom over which our mother presided with her triple wand of charm, tact and sympathy. Nothing could have been more abhorrent to the protagonists than that conception of social intercourse once expressed at Stanway by Mrs. Sidney Webb to—of all people in the world—Arthur Balfour, "Don't you agree with me, Mr. Balfour, that the only excuse for a dinner-party is that it should end in a committee?" I can still see the expression—flabbergasted is the only word—on Arthur Balfour's usually benign face, for once utterly drained of its famous "affability". (How furious he was to hear this epithet had been applied to him!)

My mother's wish—one I wholeheartedly share—that, whenever the number of guests at meals permit, the whole table should talk together, made her bemoan the deplorable growing (now surely full-grown?) habit of guests whispering together in couples. Again and again, in the persevering hope of getting all her fish to rise simultaneously, she would cast a conversational fly. Unfortunately one inveterate duologuer—would-be soliloquists are less difficult to control—can ruin all attempts at general conversation. I know no severer trial of the manners than to have to try to appear attentive to the drone of your immediate neighbour when you are straining your ears (surely they must sometimes be visibly pricked?) to listen-in to good talk at the other end of the table. Whenever the company is not more than eight in number, should not the hostess always try to keep the talk general?

I used to tell Mamma that the baffled expression of her face when guests balked her of general conversation by their refusal to comply was like a tantalised dog's pleading in vain for a stick to be thrown.

The least exclusive person I have ever known, Mamma, though so well able both to attract and to appreciate the most sought-after guests—those considered the greatest social prizes—was not in the least dependent on such company. No one ever suffered fools more gladly. As for every possible variety of what her family called "Freaks and Funnies", she positively delighted in them.

No specimen of the human race seemed without interest to

her. It must, indeed, be admitted that the catholicity of her hospitality was at times a severe domestic trial to my father, whose social appetite was much less hearty. By no means a match that could strike on any surface, he, poor man, could be excruciatingly bored. Did Mamma—her children would ask one another—by her kindness to others, indulge her own capacity for vicarious enjoyment at too great a cost to her husband? A nice ethical point. Stanway, after all, was his home as well as hers—in point of fact, it was to him that the house belonged.

By her hospitality to guests who bored him (and boredom can be real suffering) was she as one who, in her own pleasure at feeding a hungry bird, gives little thought to what the worm in its beak undergoes?

Whether it seems a case of "Poor Worm", or—should someone rescue the worm—of "Poor Bird" (deprived of his meal) depends entirely on the point of view. A soft heart has two sides to it, inevitably often at variance one with the other. The more active half prompts one to give positive happiness; the more negative, an equal determination to prevent suffering. When, as alas, must often be the case, these two impulses conflict—some obey the dictates of one—some of the other. Of which is the Kingdom of Heaven?

Undoubtedly, many of my mother's guests were invited to Stanway exclusively for their *own* sakes. No one could possibly suppose them to be there for anyone else's, and a taste for their company was not easy for either host or fellow-guests to acquire. I was acutely conscious of my father's boredom. For one thing it afflicted him with deafness. "What? What?" he would bark. There is no other word for it—a purely rhetorical "What?" Repetition of the utterance was the last thing he wanted. Then after two or three of these alarming barks, his face would grow perfectly square, his eyes—a very grave symptom—become quite glazed.

When bored beyond endurance, but not as sometimes to the point of inertia, he would counterfeit an attack of hiccoughs and with a mumbled apology exit hurriedly, handkerchief to mouth. This extreme measure was welcomed by his family, for

a   15

usually about five minutes later a loud chortle of laughter would be heard, almost invariably followed by a spell of fine weather, during which halcyon period I would call him "Sunny Jim". (I refer, of course, to a time long after I had outgrown my initial shyness of him.)

Whatever my father's sufferings while actually undergoing boredom, it should in defence of my mother be remembered that there was not one of her social vagaries that did not, when in time it became a fully matured memory, ultimately afford him great enjoyment by providing him with the raw material for a good story.

Sometimes when his sufferings were at their height, I would remind him to take a long view and remember with what invaluable ammunition he was being supplied.

I'll give you two extreme examples of my mother's tolerance. One was a certain muddle-headed windbag, on whom I will confer the initials H.D. Overflowing with utterly impracticable social schemes, he was also deplorably "psychic"—a gull, I think, rather than a fraud. Wet or fine, indoors or out, H.D. invariably wore a mackintosh that would have shamed a scarecrow. That was his own affair, but his addiction to the "digitated" socks in which he played tennis without any shoes to conceal these horrors, we regarded as a public offence. H.D., why, I cannot tell you, invariably referred to his body—and he often referred to it—as "My Tea-Cup". "They have been exceedingly kind to my Tea-Cup here," were his opening words to my father when on his return from abroad, the host found this unprepossessing stranger well settled into his home. As though their respective rôles of guest and host were reversed, H.D. in his revolting digitated socks (unconcealed, for he wore only sandals) was gracious enough to receive my father on the doorstep. Never had I heard Papa's "What?" more loudly barked out than at this stranger's declaration of gratitude for kindness to his "Tea-Cup".

H.D. brought with him a professional medium—quite the grossest and most opaque-looking woman I have ever seen—and endless séances were conducted in the old library. The "Control", a spirit alleged once to have inhabited the body of

Voltaire, who communicated with the "earth-bound" through his medium, required to be baited with a diet of garlic and pineapple, so both these amenities were placed on the table destined to be "turned". My father was what would now be called "allergic" to the smell of garlic, the stink of which pervaded the whole of his house. The supply of garlic was supposed to keep its potency, but the pineapple—no small expense—had to be fresh each day.

Many of the messages transmitted to members of the house-party while, with fingers interplaited, they crouched for long pitch-dark hours in a circle round the garlic-garnished table that was rapped and was periodically heaved and occasionally even "turned" by the hefty medium, were far from complimentary.

The opaque medium refused to admit either my future brother-in-law Raymond Asquith or myself to any of these devout séances, a mark of disfavour we both took as a very pretty compliment. Asked by one of the company to transmit some message to a friend in Australia, the garlic-battened spirit excused himself on the grounds that the "wires of wireless" (then new to the world) made communication too difficult!

What finally put even my mother off H.D. was when his ideas on the ascendancy of Mind over Matter prompted him to tell my eight-years-old brother, Yvo, then precariously poised on the edge of the roof, that if only he had sufficient faith he could jump down the forty feet or so to the ground without any risk of bodily harm. This incitement to suicide was too much for Mamma, and, as a guest, H.D. was relegated to the past, from which as an almost mythical memory he provided invaluable fuel for my father's wit. In his letters he constantly assured Mamma that "in the spirit" he was still at Stanway; but in the "Tea-Cup", thank heaven, he came no more.

My second example was a connection of my mother's— elderly and whiskered—whom I will call Aunt Gussy. She certainly was a star-turn farcical performer on the Stanway stage. Invariably gowned in Eton Blue, with, precariously skewered to her wig, a toque of the same colour, trimmed either with red cherries or with cornflowers, Aunt Gussy had an

archness of manner I have never seen off the stage of a costume-
play. I cannot remember that she ever actually carried a fan,
but the Peep-Bo coyness in her brandy-ball eyes suggested the
kind of ogling best carried on across the manipulated flutterings
of one of these aids to fascination.

With my father—no matter how little response beyond a volley
of barked-out "What? What? What?"'s it might evoke—her
manner, hinting at some delicious shared secret, was particularly bridling. For him, too—pulling out a special stop in her
lisping voice and with the same "You and I are so different"
innuendo—she always gave a great display of soulfulness, a
malady for which my father's tolerance was very low. Fortunately Aunt Gussy had, I won't say a gift, but a great yearning
for painting in oils. The fact that she also had some mysterious
infirmity referred to as her "Game Leg" gave me an idea, for
which my father was passionately grateful. I told her that the
Stanway view pronounced by all artists to be the most paintable
could be enjoyed only from the bench on the very summit of the
pyramid. Leaning heavily on my shoulder, and propelled from
behind by her tiny husband, she creakily made the great
ascent and declared herself in agreement with her fellow-artists.
Yes, clearly, her duty to Art, herself, and her host was to
immortalise so fair a prospect. Obviously this painful climb
could not be undertaken more than once a day, but first thing
every morning until the end of her generous visit I assisted
Aunt Gussy's arduous pilgrimage to this point of vantage.
There, unflaggingly daubing her canvas, she would remain
until dusk fell. A judicious admixture of some tiny criticism
with copious praise prevented her from considering her master-
piece finished until the very eve of her departure. Meanwhile
the labour of carrying her meals up to her eyrie was willingly
undertaken by relays of fellow-guests. Never before had I
been in such high favour with my father, now rid of his would-be
captivator until dinner, by which time she was too sleepy
from eight hours in the open air to be at her most provocative.

It was under the weight of Aunt Gussy that one of the always
touch-and-go old four-poster beds finally collapsed. Telling us
at breakfast of this curdling mishap, her husband, chronically,

I think, a trifle dazed by his matrimonial good-fortune, ended up with the words, "Really, it was only by the greatest *bad* luck that dear Gussy was not suffocated!"—a happy slip of the tongue that delighted the simple sense of humour proper to my fourteen years.

Besides her toleration of individual guests, my mother showed great courage and skill in her triumphantly successful mixing of what might well be expected to be the most incompatible ingredients. For instance, she thought nothing of entertaining H. G. Wells and the local bishop (both of whom unfortunately were poisoned by the fish provided the first night at dinner) at the same house-party. Wells—but that may have been the fish—did show some signs of embarrassment; the bishop none whatever. My father, I remember, appeared ill at ease at meals, but this was not because of the incongruity of his guests but because he could not remember upon whom, when a bishop was present, the host should call to say grace. Should it be the Prelate himself? Or his chaplain? Or the Stanway vicar? In this matter of grace-procedure, his nerve had been broken since the day—the occasion must, I think, have been the Induction of a new vicar—when from every side of the table several reverend guests simultaneously lifted their voices in petition to be made "truly thankful" for what they were "about to receive".

Besides her house-parties, my mother gave daring entertainments to the neighbourhood. Successfully combining neighbours and tenantry, and waving her hostess's wand, she would make all her guests play ridiculous games on the drawing-room floor. Infused by her own liveliness, old and young, stout and slim, rich and poor, willingly submitted to being blindfolded and to various other indignities.

Though, undeniably, Mamma did on occasions set herself no easy task, there was, I think, no social ice that, given time, she could not break. How thick the ice could be before she got to work on it, I, because of her deplorable unpunctuality, had only too good reason to know. My sufferings in early youth when I was obliged, "supported" only by my father, very often in no holiday mood and impatient for his fast-cooling soup, to receive the most whimsically assorted guests, was social torture as acute as any shy girl could well undergo.

Once, in a specially Circe-like mood, my mother decreed that an impending dance should be in fancy-dress. For this gala occasion, my father was cajoled with the utmost difficulty into an eighteenth-century costume of apricot satin. Considerable physical exertion, as well as wheedling, was needed to get him into this fancy dress, for he had recently stoutened, and during his investiture the seams of his gorgeous coat were strained to bursting point. However, with that unfailing punctuality so much deplored by his family, he was fully arrayed some time before the hour appointed for the guests to arrive. Even then, he showed a tendency to jib, but we coaxed him downstairs, and as the hour approached, closed round to prevent a last moment retreat. At the first jangle of the front door bell, he made a bolt for the passage, but we cut off his escape. The door was flung open. The local doctor announced. To our horror he entered the room not, as we expected, in the guise of Buffalo Bill, a Bandit, Pierrot, Red Indian, Clown or Chef, but irreproachably turned out in the conventional evening dress of the day!

When three more guests, all men and each in mufti (my mother had forgotten to put "Fancy Dress" on the invitation cards) sedately entered, my father stampeded from the room and in highest dudgeon flat-footedly, reverberantly stumped upstairs to his bedroom. . . . A quarter of an hour later my mother, dressed as an Egyptian Queen, blithely tip-toed into the room. I told her what had occurred. She looked momentarily distressed, but was soon too busy welcoming her guests to concern herself with anything outside the room.

"Has Papa laughed yet?" she found time to ask me between the third and fourth figures of the Lancers. Through the ceiling I could feel the thunderstorm atmosphere overhead. Did she really suppose I had ventured into my father's room? Later on, however, I was prevailed upon to take him a propitiatory glass of champagne. The situation upstairs surpassed my worst imaginings. My father, who had a most enviable capacity to fall asleep the very instant his bald head touched the pillow, always went straight to bed whenever, which was very often, he could think of nothing better to do; but, unable without assistance to doff the tight finery—in which in his efforts to extricate himself he had burst every seam—he had on this occasion not been able to seek his usual solace. Repeated tugs had broken the bell-rope, but—so busy was the staff—broken it in vain. It took me a long time to release him from his satin bondage. Scissors had to be used.

Meantime he had gulped down the glass of champagne. To my inexpressible relief, the glum square of his face suddenly relaxed—it was like seeing the sun burst through clouds—and before long a rich "Ha-ha-ha" shattered the tension. After this blessed recovery, he allowed himself to be persuaded into ordinary evening dress, and in his most charming form came downstairs to join the company—even with utmost affability taking part in Sir Roger de Coverley. . . .

You may well ask why I, one of a family originally seven in number, claim to have played the part of "only child"? Because so wide a gap separated me from the next daughter that I was the only child left at Stanway after the death of my little brother Colin and when the Big Boys, as my elder brothers, Ego and Guy, were always called, were away at school.

Of my sister Mary's impending arrival, I had no idea whatever; a state of unenlightenment that must, I am sure, seem astounding and probably somewhat shocking to any parent or child of to-day. But so it was. I do not even remember any coy allusions to a stork or to gooseberry bushes. "We've got a surprise for you, Cincie," said my governess one October afternoon when I was eight years old, and that, I assure you, was my very first intimation of an utterly changed home. I remember the thrill of astonished delight with which I first saw, lying in the crook of my mother's arm, the exquisite tiny creature with long pencilled eyebrows (like mouse's tails, I remember thinking them) and dark lashes that already swept her cheeks. A Beauty from the cradle, Mary shows no sign whatever of relinquishing this rôle.

Less than a year later my youngest brother, Yvo, was

born. Green-eyed, and with a disproportionately large head, he at first seemed to us as ugly as his sister was beautiful; but this engaging puppy ugliness soon blossomed into alert, sensitive, swiftly flushing, shiningly fair good looks. "Doomed to know not winter, only spring"—but I'll tell you about Yvo later.

A few years after Yvo, Irene, the last of my mother's seven children, was born. With her stormy eyes and lovely sensitive mouth, "Bibs", as she was immediately and irretrievably nicknamed, had from infancy the look of an "old soul". Preternaturally articulate, she showed at an astonishingly early age the remarkable gift of expression that makes her so wonderfully able to communicate to others the complexities of her own thoughts and emotions. Born to "haunt, to startle and waylay"; then, as now, she had in talk the faculty to exhilarate, illuminate and perplex; now with exuberant, fantastic, almost Surréalist funniness; now with the tortuosities of hair-splittingly subtle analysis.

To return to the reopening of the nursery, brought up as I had been with brothers instead of with sisters, I had never had much truck with dolls, but this large, live doll of a baby-sister, who was constantly given a bath in real water and had real hair to brush, was a marvellous plaything.

Far sooner than was fitting or can have been welcome to the pupil, I took an eager and active interest in my little sister's education, and I'm afraid Mary's first lessons were by no means all Reading without Tears. Later on, naturally, there were times when I found the rôle of elder sister irksome, and the after-tea institution, then known as "The Children's Hour", a duty I would occasionally have preferred to shun. My own lessons ended, I wanted to be free to read to myself or run wild in the garden. Practice soon made me ingenious at devising Children's Hour occupations that allowed me plenty of respite. It was a long time before Mary or Yvo saw through the "Let's Pretend" game of who could get to sleep first and stay asleep longest. A night journey was the best setting for this popular form of make-believe. For quite half an hour at a time, both children would lie with screwed-shut eyes, rhythmically breathing, outstretched on the sofa, leaving the self-appointed Ticket-Collector free to read her book in peace.

In the cricket field too, where I often wanted to be at leisure, not necessarily to watch the game but to enjoy myself with my own contemporaries, I hit on a most successful ruse for disencumbering myself of my unsuspecting little brother and sister—a slow race (prize one penny) round the railing of the cricket field, the rule being that, as in a slow bicycle race, the competitors must always keep just on the move. Even so, this race would take them off my hands for quite half an hour, and then, more often than not, they were eager to enter for a second.

Being without any companion of my own age during term-time, I was always eager for contemporaries to play with. A friend with whom for many years I enjoyed the greatest fun was Viva Smith, a daughter of my father's land agent, a man of much personality and shrewdness, who knew reams of Shakespeare by heart. For years on end, Viva and I played a thrilling serial game—a glorified, elaborated version of Follow-My-Leader, called "Perries" (derivation—peril). By some feat, either of skill or of physical or what we called "moral courage", preferably both, you gave your opponent a lead. If she failed to follow it, you were one up until the tables were turned. Vying with one another either in foolhardiness or in effrontery, Viva and I perpetually tried to go one better—or, as our elders thought, one worse than the other. Examples of physical "Perries"? To venture on to some hitherto unreached branch of a tree or point of the roof; break our record high or long jump; or climb on to the back of a recumbent cow. Moral "perries" were really competitions in outrageous cheek, such as trespassing in the houses or gardens of strangers; ringing front door bells; reversing signposts so that the traffic was misdirected off the main road into a cul-de-sac; sticking labels on to the backs of policemen, and so on. Two of my more out-of-the-way victories were poking my face into a bee-hive (I escaped with only two stings) and taking a bite out of a jellyfish!

The upper regions of Stanway comprised a fascinatingly mysterious no-man's-land between the tiles of the roof and the ceilings of the attics. Here, blinded by cobwebs, choked with dust, our cheeks brushed against by bats, we would crawl in the merest glimmer of light for what seemed miles and miles. Because once or twice our feet, preceded by a cascade of plaster, came through the ceiling of a housemaid's bedroom, this was a strictly forbidden sport. So great, however, was the lure of this and other prohibited areas that long after I myself was old enough to know better, the younger members of the family continued to enjoy them—a fact recorded in the following extract from that excellent letter writer, "Nanny" Cliffe:

"But what I do want to ask our Dear Ladyship that is, to write certain things down for the dear children what they are not to do, it will save a lot of worry and they are thoroughly bent on doing like they did before, and will do it so they say. It seems stupid to have to do so, but on the whole I feel it will be best; the chief things are, if I may name them, getting out on the roof, or between the ceiling and the plaster, climbing the garden wall after the fruit or going down to the cellars where the furnaces are, another is to go bathing in the pond without your permission, I think these are the chief ones I can think of now and I know quite well they are bent on if not particularly told from you."

I don't know which entertainment most dismayed our visitors—being conducted for a perilous tour over the roof or for a dark, dusty crawl in between it and the ceiling.

Among my Stanway playfellows were Mary and Eleanor, the two daughters of the architect, Sir Arthur Bloomfield, who lived in the famously picturesque village of Broadway. I went to tea with them practically every week and we revelled in highly ambitious dramatic undertakings. Stage-struck as I was, their mother, Lady Bloomfield, had immense glamour for me. Not only was she beautiful and able to recite with intense emotion and some technique, but she was rumoured, however vaguely, to have some actual connection with the professional stage. She demanded great versatility from her amateur company. My own parts ranged from Elaine the Fair—Elaine the Lovable, and the Lorelei, to the rugged Miles Standish,

24

brave Horatio, and the noble Brutus, with frequent revivals of
my representation of Britannia Ruling the Waves.

To my admiration and envy, Mary Bloomfield leapt into
fame, not, as we had hoped, as an actress, but when on being
presented at Court, she (what a superb "Perry"!) yelled, "Votes
for Women!" and rushed at by Court officials, was scuffled out
of the royal presence. . . .

Though, as a child, I on the whole preferred unorganised to
organised games, I had an absolute passion for cricket, and
bevies of girls from the village came to practise it with me. This
roused my vaulting ambition. I resolved to be the first to
captain a women's eleven against Australia! For this dazzling
dream I designed the badge we should have embroidered on
our blazers.

It was, indeed, pathetic how less than no foundation was
needed for the most towering castles in the air to rear themselves
in my imagination. I could never walk up the paltriest hill
without seeing a vision of myself scaling Mount Everest. As for
swimming—an exercise for which I had no aptitude whatever—
one lesson, and I saw myself half-way across the Channel!

To return to my cricket: I had one quite hefty leg stroke
indiscriminately applied to all balls, however ineligible. I
could throw in with considerable force and more often than not
in the intended direction, bowl over-hand, then, however
gently performed, an unusual accomplishment for a girl; and
I was an intrepid fielder, eager to incur rather than to escape
spectacular bruises. In spite of these qualifications, my
yearning ambition to distinguish myself sensationally in what I
called a "real" cricket match was never realised.

Oh! the agony I suffered the day an elegant grown-up girl,
whom I thought what we then called "affected"—a term often
loosely applied to anyone who happened to be unlike myself—
came to play in one of our mixed matches. She was ridiculously
over-dressed, even—disgusting creature!—*scented*. It never
crossed my simple mind to suppose that in such fashionable
flummery she would be able to play at all, and I was prepared
to be scornful. Imagine my feelings when the unwomanly
creature stayed in three hours and made a hundred and two

not out! (My own top score in a "real match" was only twenty-two.) Wildly applauded, and metaphorically as well as actually carrying her bat, she approached the pavilion. My prayer that she might drop down dead was not granted, but it was some comfort to learn that for three days after her triumph, muscular stiffness kept her in bed.

Though I took these mixed matches with deadly seriousness they were, of course, wholly farcical affairs. Considerable ambiguity prevailed as to how much "chivalry" should be accorded to women, then greatly encumbered by their far from sensible clothes, and so much less Amazonian than their descendants of to-day. There was, nevertheless, a more or less accepted convention that at least the first two catches patted up into the air by a woman's bat should be dropped as convincingly as possible. My father, who seldom took the field was, however, much more concerned with his own cricketing averages than with feminine sensibility. When he consented to play he liked to get people *out*. That was the object of the game, wasn't it? In one memorable match, just as his hands were in the very act of smugly closing on a little pat-ball catch, an absolute "sitter" off his own bowling, my brother Guy, chivalrously disposed, saw fit deliberately to cannon into his father to make him drop the catch. So great was Papa's dudgeon at being thwarted of a "Caught and Bowled" that with infanticide in his heart he stumped off the ground, and square-faced and glassy-eyed, flumped into the pavilion. It was not until nearly five minutes later—his admirable sense of humour was always liable to these terrifying temporary suspensions—that to our intense relief the frustrated bowler's laugh, a rich mellifluous "Ha! Ha! Ha!", rang out from the pavilion.

I can't tell you with what palpitating suspense we would sometimes wait to see whether or not my father was going to laugh; how anxiously after some possibly miscarried joke or any real or supposed affront we searched his face for an incipient smile, in our trepidation almost, as in a boxing-match, counting out aloud, and what music when we heard it was the preliminary chortle that heralded the explosive laugh—so rewarding a laugh when it did come, that it was worth taking considerable risk to try to ring so intoxicating a bell. Grandchildren too were one day to vie with one another in the ringing of that bell, but they, I think, ran considerable less risk of failure than their parents had done.

Whether or not a particular joke would amuse him, depending, as it did, mainly on his mood of the moment, was no more predictable than the weather. Certainly, some of the "stunts", as such things were just beginning to be called, he encouraged would have been forbidden by most fathers. Of one horrid trick of my own—filling my mouth with Eno's Fruit Salts and in a very passable imitation of an epileptic fit, writhing and foaming on the floor, I once gave an impromptu performance in the crowded "Lounge" of a large hotel. Deeply distressed by what seemed to them so sad as well as so utterly revolting a spectacle, the residents were terribly shocked when, with what they took to be the most extraordinary callousness, my father roared with laughter. When they realised the whole deplorable affair was a joke, they were outraged.

I cannot doubt that our neighbours thought some of the parlour tricks performed for their benefit peculiar. Among them was an elaborate, long-drawn-out imitation of sufferers on a rough Channel crossing. Oddly enough my father found this very simple form of humour extremely diverting, and often acted as Impresario to this star turn of Guy's and mine. In retrospect it certainly does seem a curious source of parental pride. It was, however, the only way in which I ever remember his showing me off!

Country Neighbour: "Does your daughter sing, Lord Elcho?"

Papa: "No, thank God! But she can do a Channel crossing."

Visitors had to suffer dogs gladly as well as children. I don't want to be a dog-bore, but to give any idea of Stanway without some mention of the Chows that unto the third and fourth generation ruled my mother's life, is quite impossible. I can never remember being able to enjoy an uninterrupted walk with her. Chows are indefatigable sportsmen, and invariably disappeared, so that the air would be rent by Mamma's shrieking the name of some variety or other of oriental porcelain. Neither did she ever sit through a single meal, but perpetually sprang from her chair to add some succulent tit-bit, often wrested from my plate, to her dogs' own sumptuous dinners. My husband complained that, because Pina preferred her meat without condiment, he was never allowed to have with his helping of lamb the mint sauce to which he was so particularly partial!

The misdeeds of our Chows ranged from visitor-biting to sheep-murder, the last an extremely costly sport, for the bereaved farmers claimed huge compensation. The punishment was even worse than the crime, the corpse of the victim being tied to the assassin's neck for four days. Though the hideous sight on the croquet lawn where this sentence was carried out put me off mutton for life, it seemed never to take even the edge off the sportsman's appetite for the living animal.

The tolerance developed in most of her guests towards her lawless dogs was a great tribute to my mother's charm. Some, however, received with snarls by her Chinese sentries, remained unconverted, and failed to take any intelligent interest in her dissertations on the monomaniacal devotion of Chows for one individual—an idiosyncrasy supposed to justify any degree of inhospitality.

Arthur Balfour acquired sufficient what Horace Walpole called "dogmanity", to satisfy the most dog-ridden hostess. Once, on entering a room where he was enjoying a tête-à-tête with the then reigning Chow, I overheard him exclaim with the utmost solemnity, "Oh Ching! My fluffy Ching! I *am* so devoted to you! No one knows how greatly I love you!"—an impassioned declaration acknowledged by the merest flutter of the plumed tail. Some guests were more captious. Lord Hugh Cecil, I remember, complained that once when he had been cajoled into reading aloud, he was, book in hand, driven from room to room, and in each room (four, I think, the number was) some dog at the sound of his uplifted voice had immediately been sick.

As sons and daughters-in-law joined the family, the dog situation worsened. Everyone brought their own dog, but could not imagine why anyone else's could not be left in its own home. Dogs-in-law is the trickiest of relationships....

Ponies and horses loom large in all early Stanway memories. Of all things, riding was what gave me most delight, and hunting was sheer ecstasy. In no way was I more disobedient than in failing to return for afternoon lessons when a morning-off had been conceded, and from the age of twelve to fifteen my matrimonial ambition was to marry a M.F.H.

Between rides I spent hours in the stables, over-feeding the horses with sugar and carrots, and concocting my own idea of a bran-mash, derived from reading *Black Beauty*, a classic that inspired a violently aggressive missionary phase, prompting me when in London to unloose the bearing reins with which the horses of the fashionable were then tormented. The horses were grateful; their haughty cockaded coachmen indignant.

One of the sharpest pangs of my life was the realisation that my pony was not, as in my innocence I had supposed, a child-horse who would grow as I grew, and be able to carry me all through my life, but was already quite old, and certain to die while I was still young. One day, too, there was the anguish of seeing an old favourite put up to auction. This suggests some sensational decline in the family fortunes, but was, I think, only because I had out-grown my mount.

Talking of family fortunes, our finances, so inconsistent did they seem, were puzzling to a child. Though, since we lived in a large house amply staffed and almost continuously full of visitors, there must, according to present day standards, have been a considerable amount of money, yet I cannot remember a time when finance was not an ever present worry to my parents. There was always talk of the necessity for "retrenchment"— sometimes even, desecrating thought, of the letting of Stanway, and in most ways we were brought up most unluxuriously. Our horses, all of them definitely eccentric, were obviously "bargains". The standard of warmth and comfort in our bedrooms would not nowadays be tolerated by the most un-assuming staff. With the single exception of my father, every member of the family invariably travelled third class. (A story of Ego's was that when one day he met both his parents at the station, Mamma emerged from a third class carriage carrying a book called *The Soul*; Papa from a first-class carriage carrying a book called *Her Soul*!)

Pocket money? My allowance, subsequently raised to one shilling, was for many years only one penny a week. In those days plenty of trash could be bought for a shilling at the village sweet shop, but there was no idea that confectionery should be part of a child's staple diet, and my average consumption of sweets was far less than the present ration.

My clothes? My habit was seldom costly; neither could Polonius have condemned it as "gaudy". In summer, I usually wore coloured linen smocks; in winter knitted woollen jerseys and brief serge skirts. In those days stockings were uncompromising in colour; either just black or just brown. Except for evening wear, when they were silk and glorified by ornamentation called "open-work", mine were made of thick, ribbed worsted. If I changed for tea, it was usually into one of my Roumanian blouses, woundingly—I thought them lovely—described by some wag as "Balkan Atrocities".

Unless I happened recently to have been a bridesmaid, my wardrobe included no especial provision for gala occasions.

Out-of-doors a coloured beret, made either of cloth or of velvet, was usually crammed on to my head, from which, plaited into a great bell-rope of a pigtail, my tangled mane of hair, parted in the centre, hung floppeting down my back far below my waist.

As the eldest daughter, I was spared having to succeed to the outgrown garments of sisters, but, hard though I was on my clothes, Mary wore my cast-offs for many years after my marriage. "Our-Poor-Dear-Miss-Cincie-As-Was" said Nannie Cliffe, who disapproved of my father-in-law's politics.

Unlike most girls in their teens, I did not in the least want to grow up, and stubbornly resisted all attempts to put me into Young Ladyish clothes. If I must be hampered by that odious badge of femininity, a skirt, at least let it remain as short as possible! Despite all warnings that, if persisted in, such folly would make my large feet "spread", I refused to be shod in anything less yielding than rubber-soled canvas sandshoes.

Stanway

Drawing of Mary Wemyss, the author's mother, by Violet Rutland.

Stubborn as was the battle over my footwear, it was nothing to
the war over the decree that I must "go into" real stays or, as
they were more genteelly styled, "corsets"—appalling boned
contraptions lacing up the back and fronted with dreadful
mysteries called "busks"! In determined attempts to overcome my die-hard resistance and force me into these—to my
mind symbolical as well as actual—horrors, the then Mistress
of my Robes dastardly carried off the dear, old, boneless stays
of my childhood. Rather than be thus coerced, I three times
rescued these threadbare garments from the refuse-heap on
which they had been flung. Obliged to take them off at bed-
time, I concealed them each night in some different hiding-
place. Alas, one fatal morning they were discovered inside my
pillow-case, and forthwith consigned to the flames. My boats
thus literally burned, I was left without anything to which to
fasten the suspenders of my stockings, and in those unenlightened
days, it was not, except at the sea-side, considered decent to be
bare-legged. No hope for it now! Either I must stay in bed or
else encase myself in the loathed corsets. Thus was I cabined,
cribbed, confined. . . . That was the beginning of the end.
Shades of the prison house now rapidly closed upon the growing
girl.

To return to the Stanway finances. Though for entertaining
and largesse my mother could no doubt have done with bound-
less wealth, few women can ever have spent less money on themselves. I can scarcely remember her even buying so much as a
book, let alone an ornament either for herself or for her house.
I don't believe she ever used any scent more costly than
lavender or rose-water, and I have no doubt most of her
friends thought she spent far too little on her own clothes.

Neither, except in cigars, had my father expensive tastes. He
was not, like other members of his family, a collector of
pictures, china or furniture; and would—for "thou shalt love
thy neighbour as thyself" was not the behest he found most easy
to obey—I'm sure, have been well content to spend much less
money on entertaining. No, as far as his children could make
out, all he wanted money for was to have plenty of it to lose!
This one exception was, however, an all important one; his

D   31

early catastrophic losses on the Stock Exchange having financially crippled him for life. . . .

Besides the day-to-day occupations of riding, trolleying, "Perries" and so forth, life at Stanway was enlivened by the local events that brightly if sparsely punctuated the slowly revolving year. Winchcombe—sometime capital of Mercia and our nearest town—had an annual Agricultural Show, the excitements of which included horse-jumping; prodigious prize bulls with rings in their noses; and, in an exceedingly stuffy tent, my own father making a speech to carousing farmers who, flushed and stertorous at the end of a Homeric luncheon, enthusiastically applauded him by banging on the table with the butt-ends of their knives, and then—how my daughterly heart swelled with pride!—with one accord lustily sang "For he's a jolly good fellow!"

When next, on some more private occasion this "Jolly-Good-Fellowness" of my father's, so unanimously acclaimed by the farmers, was much less conspicuous, indeed obviously under eclipse, I would hum under my breath the opening bars of that rousing chorus; this invocation to "Good-Fellowness" being, I imagine, more to reassure myself than with any admonitory ambition.

Even more entrancing than the Agricultural Show were the Flower Shows, appreciated not so much for their display of prize blooms and pantomime pumpkins, but because, to stimulate attendance, the horticultural attractions were reinforced by "All the Fun of the Fair"—coconut shies; shooting galleries; swingboats; earringed gipsies with clay pipes telling fortunes, and—greatest of all delights—glittering with brass and revolving strips of mirror, and ear-splittingly blaring out its metallic music, a Merry-go-round! Though each rapturous "ride" cost only one penny, in one crowded hour of glorious life I spent five shillings without once dismounting from my gallant grey. . . .

Enough for now of these trivial fond records; but as the background of that Edwardian girlhood of which you want me to tell, you will hear plenty more about Stanway and some of its neighbours. Later on too, if you like, I will tell you of the many summer months when it was the temporary home of J. M. Barrie. Now I'll describe some of the villagers.

I think the density of Stanway's own atmosphere, combined with its—in those pre-motor-car, pre-telephone days—cut-offness, fostered the growth of idiosyncratic personalities. The village was rich in "characters", whose corners—entrancingly queer corners—never even began to get rubbed off. Pertaining to one place only, rooted like trees, their personal relationships were few, simple, inevitable.

The most spectacularly picturesque figure—no artist but Rembrandt could have done justice to his rugged visage—was old James Prew, who after untold years as a mere "helper" in the stables, was suddenly presented with a coat and a cockaded hat; the outward and visible sign of his elevation to the rank of coachman. As a family retainer, dear Prew was the most extreme survival of feudalism I have ever seen; some of his demonstrations of that out-worn attitude of mind being very shy-making for those he so devotedly served. "Get out of Her Ladyship's way! Get out of Her Ladyship's way!" he would cry, cracking his whip, when my mother—I can still see the expression of acute embarrassment on her face—drove in or out of the inn stable-yards at Winchcombe or Broadway.

Somehow or other—local legend whispered it was in the saw-mill the accident had occurred—Prew was alleged to have lost every one of his ten toes, a rumour that gave him a sort of John Silver-esque glamour. His shambling, hobbling gait was unforgettable. The whirling windmill action of his long scraggy arms seemed an attempt to make up for the disablement of his nether limbs.

No man can ever have been less suited to his occupation. Except when they were safely inside the stables, he was terrified of all horses. They might have been so many ravening wild beasts. "Don't loose him! Don't loose him!" he would shout at anyone about to mount or drive the gentlest cob.

On the other hand, when they were in the stables he regarded his charges as there not to earn their keep, but merely as so many pets to be cosseted. "Crool! Crool!" he would protest at the suggestion that a horse who had been driven or ridden one day should be taken for another gentle outing the next.

As for people who voluntarily placed themselves on the backs of horses, he thought them too foolhardy to be considered sane. I could never come home from the quietest ride, without his giving fervent thanks for my safe return.

"Thank you, Miss Cincie! Thank you! Safe home again. Safe home *this* time." His words were few, but each raucously repeated at least ten times and with the intensity of a Greek chorus. As for going out hunting, it was like being seen off to the front. Like a watcher who with very little hope scans the horizon for a missing ship, with one hand shading his eyes and desperate anxiety delving seams in his face, he would stand on the look-out at the stable gate for hours before there was any likelihood of our return.

Prew and his wife, one of the best friends of my childhood, lived in a little gabled cottage near the church, an abode with a peculiar unanalysable fusty smell, a fascinating wheezy harmonium, and framed photographs of all my family standing thick as the tombstones in an overcrowded cemetery.

Mrs. Prew was full of charm, but lacked skill in housewifery— her ceaseless complaint being that since her last move, made some twenty years ago, she had "never got straight".

In the early days of cars, Prew's great delight, one frequently enjoyed—was to go to the rescue of some stranded motorist. "Horses is best! Horses is best!" he would intone in a triumphant chant. "I never did hold with they newfangled things."

Prew, the most anachronistic being I have ever known, died as defiantly un-brought-up-to-date as he had lived. A pathetic instance of his unsophistication was a number of uncashed cheques found after his death in his cottage. Every summer at the end of his tenancy of Stanway, Barrie had told me to give Prew to whom he was devoted a present of £5, and each year I had written out a cheque for that sum. Alas, the poor old fellow, whose wages had always been paid in coin, had never known what to do with the mysterious slips of paper!

Another memorable figure, thick and slow of speech, and heavy in movement, was Wynniatt, the village carpenter. My mother once met him walking up the village with the intent expression of a tight-rope-walker on his whiskered face, and his empty hands held up in front of him at some distance apart from one another. "Would Her Ladyship please not to speak to me?" he muttered, "I be carrying the measurements of a door."

Wynniatt's wife was in charge of the village post office, where her gift for paraphrase provided us with fascinating problems in the way of telegrams. Then there was the red-faced postman who once trudged all the weary eight miles of his beat arriving on the stroke of the appointed hour—but without his letter-bag!

In my childhood, a "Village Idiot" seemed to be an inevitable feature of every parish. In "Our Sally" Stanway possessed a spectacular example. Nothing at all like her could now be seen outside an institution, but in those days she, like others similarly afflicted, was devotedly cared for by her mother. A visit to Sally was a recurring ordeal of my childhood, for enough of the "Lady Bountiful" tradition survived to make it still the custom for us to go, feeling rather feudal, from cottage to cottage carrying to each two wicker-work covered china jars, one filled with meat, the other with pudding. Our visits to Sally's home gave me terrible nightmares.

Another duty that punctuated the years of my childhood with horror was my monthly visit to a Dickensian workhouse, where, conducted the ghastly round by the matron, I dispensed tea, sugar or snuff among the "paupers", as all those unfortunate enough to "Come On to the Parish" were then invidiously called. The grimness of this hideous, God-denying institution was indescribable. In bare, scrubbed, carbolic-breathing rooms, furnished only with backless, wooden benches, huddled, dehumanisingly garbed, men in one ward, women in another, the incongruous, mutually antipathetic inmates, some the victims of mere mischance, others of their own follies. Self-respecting, hard-working citizens, there only because they were no longer strong enough to work and had no relatives willing or able to support them, rubbing shoulders with lifelong wastrels who had been in and out of prison until no longer physically fit to break the law. Imbeciles too! The blankness of the bare walls was broken only by framed regulations headed

in huge type by the words PUNISHMENTS FOR RE-
FRACTORY PAUPERS.

I wish I could show unconvincible pessimists, who deny that
Social Reform has achieved any improvement, that workhouse
of my childhood, an institution where the only chance of
preserving any individuality was to be a physical freak. The
one cheerful "pauper" able, indeed, to cut quite a figure, was a
quarter-witted man, born with a third thumb, a distinction
he loved to exhibit to visitors. One had to try to counterfeit
admiration, even envy, but in reality that extra thumb was an
object of haunting horror to me. I used to dream my own
hands had sprouted superfluous digits.

Upstairs, the utter bleakness of the wards where the bed-
ridden lay in long close rows, seemed to present old age and
illness as punishable offences. The grimmest sight I ever saw
was one Christmas Day when crackers had been provided, and
the well-meaning matron had crowned the pitiable head of each
of her charges with the mockery of a paper cap!

Children seldom divulge their dreads. No one ever suspected
the effect those visits to the workhouse had on me; nor why it
was that I so often re-read *Oliver Twist.* . . .

One more sketch must be added to my very incomplete
gallery of Stanway characters. Harry Last, the gamekeeper,
was a wonderfully picturesque corduroyed figure whose gallant
encounter in early youth with a desperate gang of poachers had
invested him with a glamour he never lost. The first time I
saw him, he was lying in the Cottage Hospital, a wounded hero
with I don't know how many rounds of shot in his arm.

Last had immense charm both of appearance and manner.
He was uncompromisingly reactionary in politics and voiced his
violent prejudices with a trenchancy of speech that made him a
most diverting companion.

Apart from his prowess as a very redoubtable gamekeeper,
he also cut a gallant figure in another important sphere. A very
keen and spirited, if scarcely a correct player of cricket, the
daring impetuosity of his disposition made him so prone to
run out other more steady players that he was seldom allowed
in before the ninth wicket had fallen, when his hit-a-boundary-

or-get-out style of batting either promptly brought the innings to an uproarious close or provided a spirited sting to its tail.

The Stanway cricket field, where from first to last I must have watched thousands of matches, was the summer centre of village life—the battle-ground on which local patriotism seethed. It was a great attraction to neighbours who, from far around, came in large numbers to sit beneath the shade of its trees, applaud the game and partake of the Gargantuan teas provided for the cricketers either in the barn or in the hall.

One of the most enthusiastic spectators was Madame de Navarro, before her marriage the actress, Mary Anderson, world-famous for her beauty. Despite her regular attendance at matches, and her having for many years entertained Barrie and his cricketing eleven, the *Allahakbarries*, in her house in Broadway, Madame de Navarro remained engagingly ignorant of the rudiments of the game that she always persisted in calling "Crickets". One instance of this invincible ignorance was her question: "But do tell me, why do *eleven* men play against only *two*? It does seem so very unfair!" Another time when Barrie told her during a single-innings match that she need no longer watch as his side had already passed the other side's score, she said hopefully, "Yes, but you still have several *more* men to go in, haven't you?"

From time to time the Stanway cricket field was honoured by sensational star turns; Jessop cracking ball after ball over the tops of the towering elm trees, or the Australian Test Team giving an exhibition game. Comic relief, too, was frequently supplied by mixed matches in which the men were handicapped by having to bat with broomsticks instead of bats and to field left-handed.

In gratitude for many hours of enjoyment, Barrie presented the Stanway cricket club with a fine pavilion. Until then a disused railway carriage (third class) had done duty. It was an irony of a kind to which he was well accustomed that his generous gift should somewhat spoil the lovely village cricket ground for himself. Perhaps it made it seem too much like Lord's. For me, too, this new grandeur impaired the old unassuming charm. In any case by that time the memory of matches played long, long ago, and of players who would play no more, now seemed to come between one and the game of the moment.

Though a heavy toll was levied of its stalwart sons, the First World War had in other ways seemed very remote from the drowsy village of Stanway. There had then been no wireless to pelt country people with bad news; and I do not think any enemy aircraft was ever sighted or heard in Gloucestershire. The chief outward and visible sign of a changed world had, indeed, been the cricket field, hitherto so well-trodden and carefully tended, where, through the long slow years of war, the un-mown grass rose higher and higher, dandelions flourished, and, instead of the crack of the ball and the shouts and the laughter, silence smote on the air.

When, at long last, the grass was again mown and village cricket resumed, it was something of an ordeal to steel oneself to go and watch the new players. Nowhere had my brother Ego, who for many years had captained the Stanway eleven, seemed more intensely alive than on that cricket field. Harry Last I am sure spoke for many when at the end of that first post-war match, he so feelingly said to my mother—"Ah, how I missed that brown head and those long swift legs that swallowed up the ground, and the quiet, strong voice, and the patience, kindliness and tact that considered everyone's feelings." . . .

When, you ask, did Stanway cease to be the background of my life? In 1937, at the sudden death of my mother, followed so closely by that of my father.

Some weeks later I went "home"—for by that name I still thought of Stanway—to go through my mother's papers. Every sight, every sound, every scent jabbed a thousand memories alive, yet the house seemed already to have gone cold. Then, and then only—since so long as one parent with whom you have kept in close touch still lives, your childhood, no matter what your age, can never be quite done with—did I for the first time in my life feel really grown-up—desolately grown-up. The sense that from now on there would no longer be anyone, so to speak, behind me, was almost like physical dizziness. It was as though nothing now stood between myself and the vast neutrality of the sky.

The "Elder Generation"? Invidious, sundering appellation! Was it by that estranging label that we, till so recently—so it seemed to us—ourselves the "Younger Generation", would now be appraised? The "Handing On of the Torch"! Had that responsibility devolved on us? . . . If we disagreed amongst ourselves, to what higher Court could we now appeal? . . .

When, only two years after the death of my parents, the Second World War began, Stanway's fate was singularly fortunate. Instead of being requisitioned, it was leased by the Misses Kerr-Saunders, who ran it as a secretarial college for girls. Much loved and admirably cared for, in their hands it again became what it so long had been, a golden hive humming with young life.

At intervals throughout the long years of the war, I travelled from Sussex to Gloucestershire just to assure myself by a glimpse of its golden face that all was well with Stanway—that in a shattered world its timeless benign beauty was still unchanged.

So deeply imbued with the past; so serenely impervious to the present; the memory-laden thickly-charged atmosphere re-enfolded me. Reality faded away.

CLOUDS

CLOUDS, the house where I was born, a home so to speak, made to measure instead of inherited, was about as unlike Stanway as possible. Designed for my grandfather, Percy Wyndham, by the architect Philip Webb, and finished in 1885, it was only a few years later burnt to the ground by a housemaid leaving a lighted candle in a cupboard. Within three years, however, the house had been rebuilt brick by brick.

I remember Clouds as a large, happy abode full of light and air, with a smell all its own—compounded, I think, of cedar wood, beeswax and magnolia-soap; and in the spring time, fragrance from the gorse that blazed on the Windmill Hill would drift in through the open window. It was because I was born at Clouds that I was named Cynthia (the Moon).

I always loved staying at Clouds. No sooner had I been hugged in the hall and plomped on to the weighing-chair—we were always weighed both on arrival and departure—than I felt happy and at ease. This was because of my enchanting grand-mother, Madeline Wyndham, to us always Gan Gan. To no children can so-called old age have been more radiantly presented. With her lovely white hair, glowing cheeks, shining eyes and open-armed welcome, she radiated love, and her spirit warmed the whole house. When I first came on the lines:

> "an old age serene and bright
> And lovely as a Lapland night"

I thought of her. Not that the word "serene" applied. She was far too vibrant, too vulnerable. What and where are the "cockles of the heart"? Whatever, wherever these may be,

I am sure Gan Gan warmed them. In her glowing presence everyone felt at their best and most natural.

Clouds was alive with dogs—cushioned baskets accommodated grinning fox-terriers in every room—and the whole place was an aviary. Resplendent peacocks strutted to and fro on the lawns, halting every now and again to draw themselves up and display in fully outspread fans the preposterous beauty of their feathers—a dazzling sight, though scarcely sufficient compensation for the discordant cries that, especially in the early mornings, assailed the ears of guests invited to Clouds for a "rest". Even at an age when one was comparatively indifferent to noise, the voices of those peacocks used to make me wonder why nature had not provided me with a pair of ear-lids as well as eye-lids. From a wired enclosure against the house, African Jackasses shrieked with mirthless laughter; doves flew about the rooms, and from miles around wild birds flocked to the bounty far-flung after each meal by Gan Gan, just as spiritually hungry human beings gathered to feed on her vitality and the generosity of her nature. Simple, spontaneous, the least didactic of women, Gan Gan never seemed consciously to help or to exhort. That would have shown an awareness of the shortcomings of others and of her own superiority; for this she was much too unself-conscious, too utterly devoid of self-righteousness. Yet what power she had to help! To quote her son, George Wyndham—"She helps unconsciously, just as a mountain helps those whose horizon is too limited, by leading them to lift up their eyes." Most of us can grieve with our friends; few fully share their joys; but Gan Gan's grey-green eyes would literally shine with vicarious happiness.

I saw her only in "beauty o'er snowed", but I cannot believe that she can have been lovelier in youth than she was in her untampered-with old age.

In my memory Gan Gan is always drawing, painting or enamelling, and I heard many good judges call her a "born artist". Though she was such a devotee of the pre-Raphaelites —many of whom, Burne-Jones in particular, were great personal friends—her own work, instinctively impressionist, was curiously before her time.

Except for her charity and hospitality—both quite uncurb-able—Gan Gan's greatest extravagance must have been gratifying her love of beautifully bound books. Thousands of her favourites were specially rebound for her by Roger de Coverley, and she would always put some old friend in new vellum—it might be anything from Bradshaw to the Bible—in your room. Eddie Marsh[1] says he found by his bedside a tiny exquisitely bound book so slim that it could contain only a few pages, and with no name on its cover. When he took it up a printed slip fell out. On it were the words "With the author's compliments". Opening the little book, he found it to be the Lord's Prayer!

I remember how much impressed I was to hear that Gan Gan had been the first woman in England to smoke. If she really were the pioneer of this practice—in those days so inexplicably considered "fast"—she remained a very moderate exponent, never more than three cigarettes a day, one after each meal.

Grandpapa Wyndham made a charming pendant picture to Grandmamma. Snow-white hair; grey top hat, chiselled features, fresh complexion—I never saw anyone so *noticeably* clean—and an exceedingly "droll" (no other word for it!) expression. Possessed of very strong views and abounding in eccentricities, Grandpapa Wyndham was a widely licensed "Character". No one could deny that he was irascible, but the brief explosions of temper in which he could be startingly and most originally out-spoken, were nearly always followed by his leading the burst of laughter against himself. Had his coun-tenance been the sky, a rainbow would often have spanned it, frowns and smiles so constantly overlapped one another. Grand-papa was also extremely obstinate but in the most disarming, harmless and self-amused way. "I *must* do what I like! I *must* do what I like!" he was once heard muttering under his breath.

He was much addicted to the pinning up of a written injunc-tions, but none of them so autocratic as that famous notice seen on one estate, THE CUCKOO MUST NOT SING IN THE WESTERN

[1] Sir Edward Marsh, K.C.V.O., C.B.

woods. Indeed all his rules—for instance that your horse must be walked the last quarter of a mile back to the stables— were perfectly reasonable, and I assure you his grandchildren were anxious to keep them; much more though, I think, because he was so lovable than from any fear of the consequences, for whatever alarm his gusts of anger might cause was so largely neutralised by our complete confidence in the affection on which no child of any child of his own could possibly overdraw.

His love for his family was so clearly not on this side idolatry; his adoration for his brilliant eldest son, indeed, showing itself in a way as comic as it was touching to some, and, I cannot doubt, irritating to others. Acting as self-appointed chairman, the doting father would hold up his hand to silence any other talker who interrupted, or even one that he feared might be about to interrupt the flow of George's eloquence! I'm not exaggerating. Any guest, no matter what his age or note, was liable to be unceremoniously corked by his host. "Shush! Ma'am," I once heard him hiss at Princess Christian, "Shush! George is going to speak!"

At times Grandpapa's intensive love of his own family and its intimate friends ("confidential" was his generic term for those he fully approved) clashed with Gan Gan's all-embracing love of humanity. One Christmas Eve there was a grand explosion. The local carol-singers, who had twice bleated through a mercilessly long programme, and then been copiously regaled at the dinner table, had at long last wiped their mouths, tugged at their forelocks and clumped out of the room, and Grandpapa— good easy man—thought the long awaited time for talk and decanter enjoyment with son George was at length arrived. With a great sigh of relief he re-settled himself in his chair. Alas, instead of, as was expected of her, rising to lead the ladies to the drawing-room, Gan Gan, her eyes blazing, her face flushed with defiant concern, declared she must invite the singers to return "to sing Good King Wenceslas just once more" and— since, as in their carol, the snow lay all around and "the frost was cru-ell"—some more soup must be hotted up for them. "It wouldn't", she added, "take more than ten minutes. . . .".

This was too much for Grandpapa's already over-strained Christmas spirit.

"Damn my soul, Madeline!" he exploded, overturning a glass of port as he sprang from his chair. "If you say one more word about those carol-singers, I shall have to send them all to Hell!"

There was a silence followed by nervous suppressed titters.

The absolute seriousness of Grandpapa's tone had made my six-years old self take what he said quite literally. . . . How, if Gan Gan *did* say another word—and of course she would! Wasn't her obstinacy on behalf of others famous?—how would he carry out his dreadful declaration? With pounding heart, I awaited some supernatural co-operation. . . . Time stood still. Not until Grandpapa himself burst into a loud guffaw, did I realise that his terrifying threat had been merely rhetorical.

My relief was not untinged with disappointment.

Grandpapa, they told me, was both an assiduous landlord and magistrate and had sat for many years in the House of Commons. None of this impressed me. No, what I considered the real feather in his cap was his having been Master of the Hounds! A treasured family story often told by its "hero" himself was of the time when my father, a man never quite so unhappy as when in the saddle, was courting my mother. Because she was the daughter of the M.F.H., he felt himself obliged to escort her hunting. One afternoon at the end of a hideously good run, he was congratulating himself that at last the long day's sport was done—weren't those wretched hounds just about to be whipped-in—if that was the correct term? Yes, blessed sound! His prospective father-in-law blew his horn to that effect. Now only the long jog, jog home—oh, the stitch in his side!—sundered him from hot bath and poached eggs.

Imagine his horror when, descrying a fox, the keen daughter of the M.F.H. stood up in her stirrups, waved her whip and yelled, "Tally-Ho! Tally-Ho!" Great Heavens! was the whole ghastly business to be set going again? "Shush! Miss Mary. Shush!" shouted her gallant suitor, trying, so she alleged, to

stifle her cries with the Jaeger comforter he should most certainly
not have been wearing! . . .

Grandpapa had made a golf course on the Wiltshire Downs,
to which we would often drive in a brake to have luncheon
with the players in a small hut built of furze. Long, long talks
over veal and ham pie, méringues and Château Yquem; and
after coffee, made in those pre-thermos days on a spirit-lamp,
Mamma would read aloud *The Shropshire Lad*, then newly
burst on the world.

We always went to Clouds for Easter, a festival kept by Gan
Gan with as much ceremony—hundreds of eggs hidden all
over the garden and the house—as Christmas. Each year there
was a family party, augmented by two or three other guests, of
whom Arthur Balfour was always one. Thanks to the super-
stition against sitting down thirteen to table, "little Cynthia"
would sometimes be kept from bed to make a fourteenth at
dinner, not an unqualified treat, because after soup and fish I
was supposed to leave, and it was embarrassing to have to get
up from the table, and very tantalising to miss, not only dessert,
but also a certain ritual that I considered quite Grandpapa's
star turn in the idiosyncrasy line—his habit—can it ever have
been the custom?—of, so soon as he had gobbled his savoury,
filling his mouth with water, flinging back his head and
with a sudden loud roar gargling into his finger-bowl! Never,
not even when I became old enough for "Late Dinner" each
night, did this fascinating sting to the tail of the meal lose its
thrill for me. But Grandpapa's gargling was by no means my
only entertainment at Clouds' dinners. I loved listening
to intensely interesting discussions between Arthur Balfour,
George Wyndham and other brilliant talkers, and was
often very sorry when the time came to leave the gentlemen.
One prolonged debate I particularly regretted not being
able to hear to its end was an argument on the Reforma-
tion, an event considered by George Wyndham—on this
point diametrically opposed to Arthur Balfour—so great a
calamity. How I envied my privileged mother who, contrary to all usage, was often invited to stay on in the

dining-room after the other ladies of the party had left for the (with)-drawing-room.

Another frequent Easter guest was Sir Oliver Lodge, on whose huge dome of a forehead, as though it displayed a ponderously ticking tape-machine, the process of thought seemed to take on actual visibility. Impressive, but perhaps a little lumbering in talk—a propounder, not an exchanger of ideas—this distinguished professor could never "chip in". There had to be a pause, before he could enter into the conversation. Yes, as a talker his technique was decidedly that of someone who can play a game with a sitting but not with a moving ball. Sometimes at the Clouds dinner-table I, a silent spectator, felt as though I were watching a game in which one solitary golfer strayed from the golf course, had somehow got involved with three agile players on the tennis court. As though perpetually about to "drive off", Sir Oliver would continue to address some to me invisible ball, while, volleyed and half-volleyed off the racquets of the others, the ball I did see flashed backwards and forwards across the net. Sometimes the rally would end before Sir Oliver had so much as played a single shot. Whenever this looked likely to happen, my tender-hearted mother, always a solicitous chairwoman, would raise her eyebrows in concern, at which Arthur Balfour's ineffable courtesy would surge up. Flinging down his racquet, so to speak, he would stop the game in mid-rally and turning himself into the most considerate of caddies, build up an inspiring conversational tee for Sir Oliver. Then he would virtually shout "Fore!"

Uncle George would submit to this muzzling with as good grace as possible, but I must admit that being arrested in full cry did make him look very like a kettle about to over-boil— a kettle, if you can imagine such a thing, filled not with water but with red wine.

A naturally deferential little girl, I had an affectionate respect for Sir Oliver, but to my childish self-esteem he was quite as diminishing as Gan Gan was enhancing. Having a dozen children of his own, perhaps when away from home he did not care to see any other little boys or girls about. In any case, even if children must be seen, surely they need not be heard?

George Wyndham's father and mother.

George Wyndham.

Imposing as Tall Agrippa, Sir Oliver, complete with black-board and chalk, often gave lectures to the house party. Acting as bright pupil-teachers, Arthur Balfour and George Wyndham plied him with intelligent questions on electrons, cyclons, and wireless telegraphy (then only in process of discovery) while the rest of us gaped in respectful mystification. Once Ego, Guy and I, wishing to hear part of a lecture, without incurring any obligation to sit it out, had hidden ourselves under the piano. In trying—crawling like Red Indians on our stomachs—to make our escape from the room we overturned a screen causing a terrible disturbance. Sir Oliver was not amused. Book in hand, he approached processionally and, looming over us—I can see him now, he looked so Jehova-ish—pointed without a flicker of a smile to the door through which, like whipped dogs, we fled.

Sometimes instead of lecturing, Sir Oliver would read aloud to the house party, particularly, I remember, Tennyson's "Enoch Arden" and—versatile man—the then little-known plays of Bernard Shaw. The plays were read with the air of one consciously flinging open doors and windows into other people's minds; the poem with intense feeling. Long before he arrived at the line: "And when he died the little town had seldom seen a costlier funeral" my childish sobs were providing a running accompaniment to the stately cadences of his fine voice.

Shakespeare's truism, "There never was philosophy could cure the toothache", was painfully illustrated the terrible day one of Sir Oliver's molars gave him trouble and, his mighty brow now seamed with suffering instead of with thought, the Great Man strode up and down the hall while women twittered around him with cloves soaked in hot oil, wads of cotton wool steeped in port wine and other bootless remedies.

The morning when, in a game of Hare and Hounds, I thrust my hand through the glass of a swing door, all but severing my wrist, poor Sir Oliver as the Scientist at the Breakfast Table was dragged away from his kedgeree to arbitrate between two maids who—one advocating hot, the other cold water—were pulling me between the two of them as though I were a Christmas cracker. Asked for his verdict, the Man of Science

E

47

looked immensely sapient and after long deliberation split the difference with the pronouncement "lukewarm". Fortunately (for I'm sure Sir Oliver's vast knowledge included nothing so trivial as the "Pressure Points", and on the balance I have immensely enjoyed my life) the artery in my wrist had just— only just—been missed.

These Clouds days were before Sir Oliver became an ardent spiritualist, thereby converting so many others to the same belief, because—so argued his disciples—he had a "Real Scientific Mind". Later on Sir Arthur Conan Doyle's influence carried similarly irrelevant weight. Confusing him with his immortal creation, readers credited the author himself—in reality an engagingly credulous man—with the most penetrating detective powers. How then could such a man be imposed upon? Cross-examined by Sherlock Holmes, what possible chance could a fraudulent medium have?

Two great contributors to my enjoyment at Clouds were my cousin Dorothy Carleton and my godmother, Fräulein Schneider, the German governess of my mother's childhood, who had saved my life in the fire; Bun, as Fräulein Schneider was always called, stayed on at Clouds until the war of 1914. Year after year this great lover of England, whose Teutonic exuberance and intense appreciativeness made her intoxicating company to children, would return from a brief visit to the Fatherland, and rattling a box with a slit in its lid, naïvely invite us all to contribute to the battleship then being built from subscriptions collected by the women of Germany. A curious thought that for several years of my childhood I in all innocence dropped one of my precious pennies down that slot!

One more shake of this kaleidoscope of Clouds' memories shows me a lovely, very girlish-looking aunt singing with taste but not much voice to her own accompaniment on a gaily beribboned guitar. This was my mother's youngest sister, Aunt Pamela, who after the death of her husband, Lord Glenconner, a brother of Lady Oxford's, became the second wife of Sir Edward Grey.

But enough of these burblings. You must be champing. Don't I know your only interest in Clouds is as the home of your hero, George Wyndham? Do you remember that first time we met when you didn't know I was his niece and you were almost shocked to hear me call him "*Uncle* George"! It had been so long since I'd so much as even heard his name mentioned that I thought him forgotten, and I can't tell you how pleased I was to hear you say you thought him "all that a Renaissance Prince could possibly have been—brave, cultured, gifted, and good to look on, a scholar who was modest about his learning, a warrior modest about his courage, an orator and writer almost unaware of his extraordinary command of cadence and vocabulary, and a statesman whose only ambition seemed to be to serve the State". In fact you said that in his personality he "exhausted all the superlatives".

Now in return I'll do my best to reinvoke for you the "Uncle George" of my childhood. To begin with, I think he was my first real friend both of the other sex and the other generation. No doubt, though quite involuntarily, he was also a strong influence. How could so eloquent a showman, one so much enraptured by the beauty of the world, fail to tinge a child's view of life?

"Outrageously"—that was how I heard it put—handsome, George (I'll drop the uncle) was the most vital, ardent being I have known. He symbolised zest, positively whirled through life. Impossible to think of him without such words as Spirit, Pulse, Gusto, Panache, Tournament, Troubadour, rushing to one's pen. You often read of, seldom see eyes that glow; his of a deep grey really did seem to smoulder with something of Promethean fire.

As with all memories of childhood, I find it difficult to sift my direct impressions from those I gathered from others. I know I very early realised that this uncle of mine was an exciting person, someone of whom others often talked. I remember overhearing his sometime governess tell mine he had "very mixed blood", for, English on his father's side, he was both French and Irish through his mother, she being a grand-daughter of Lord Edward Fitzgerald, that romantic figure of the Irish Rebellion of 1789 (imagine how thrilled a small child was to learn she was descended from a REBEL!) and of his French wife called La Belle Pamela, the daughter of Madame de Genlis and (reputedly) of Phillipe Egalité. (I remember wondering what on earth "reputedly" meant.)

Later on, of course, I saw much both in George's looks and in his mercurial temperament that spoke of these Irish and French strains. I also remember hearing some visitor say you could "tell at a glance that George had been brought up in an atmosphere of complete love and understanding". This I think was true. Does anything else ever give quite that same utterly unconscious confidence of bearing? Besides this, I gathered— not of course as I shall put it, but in words to the same effect— that he had early hurled himself from the springboard of an appreciative home into a many-sided career; first as a keen soldier; then as both a politician and a passionate votary of literature. Being so doubly dowered doomed his nature to ceaseless conflict between its literary and political sides. Do you remember how he described himself? "I still hope a little, but fear I shall get nowhere riding these two circus horses of politics and literature round the narrow arena of my capacity." Had it been only a simple duel between politics and literature! But, as you know, he was never to lose his love of soldiering, and would always insist on sandwiching arduous yeomanry duties in between exhausting public speaking and ministerial work, or, when not in office, front bench opposition work and shadow cabinets. Also, under the inspiring auspices of his great friend W. E. Henley, he had flung himself with fury into journalism. Above all (yes, I know I'm straying from firsthand memories, but wait a minute) there was his consuming zest for existence itself—never was a greater reveller at Life's feast—his insistence on enjoyment of every kind, including almost every variety of violent exercise; hunting, steeplechasing, polo and strenuous tennis. Then too, whatever the demands on his strength, he would always be eager to sit up talking into the small hours of the night. Hours after I had gone to bed I would hear his voice booming up through the floor from the smoking-room below. What a pity you couldn't have been there to share both the talk and the decanter! You two would have revelled in one another's company, and he would so very much have liked what you wrote of him—"How supreme he would have been among his own beloved romantics of the Pleiades or at the Mermaid Tavern, how welcome and dominant at 'The Club', matching his easy erudition and his effortless flow of words even with that of Johnson and Burke. To have dined and wined and talked with him would have been a career; to have worked with him in administration or soldiered with him another."

Needless to say, he would never deign to make up for late nights at the other end. The delight of the eye was always so much to him and he had such a special love for what he called "the green sky and the cold untainted breezes of the morning", that on a fine day he could scarcely bear not to be up in time to salute the rising sun. In one of my earliest pictures of him, I see him—it is hours before any other grown-up person has so much as thought of leaving bed—running in red rubber-soled shoes round and round the dew-bediamonded garden. Glancing up at my window, he shouts with a wave of his hand, "Come out and join me, Nyncie, and then help me write an 'Aubade' before breakfast." Not wishing to confess my ignorance, but anxious to know in what I was to collaborate, I tried to find the word "Aubade" in the dictionary (that is why I remember the incident) but as I looked for it under the letter "O", I did not succeed. Hours after these early morning scampers and "Aubades", other men would crawl down to breakfast, excusing their yawns on the grounds that George's enthralling talk had kept them from their beds until three or four o'clock.

No public claims on George's time were ever allowed to crowd out private ones, for you were so right when you said that perhaps "above all else he was a great humanist". Certainly it implies much that men as diverse as Arthur Balfour, Cecil Rhodes, W. E. Henley, Charles Whibley, and so many others, should all have loved and esteemed him so greatly. Years after his death I remember Belloc telling me he still missed him more than any other man.

Though the least meddlesome, George was one of the most helpful and inspiring of friends. By over-valuing people to their own good, he would make them all they were capable of becoming. While in his company all his geese (I can vouch for one) did at least try to be swans.

This, a book not of verdicts but only of impressions, is no place to treat of the shipwreck of a brilliant political career to which no limit had been predicted; but if, as is said, George *was* sacrificed to Party considerations, there was—this I can certify—no bitterness in his heart against anyone, least of all against his leader Arthur Balfour, of whom to the end of his life he remained the devoted friend and admirer. Neither—I mention this only because I know how apt people are to think the exuberant and courageous over optimistic—was he, when he became Secretary for Ireland, unprepared for personal disaster. His romantic love of that country did not blind him to its perils. "This land of Sorcery", he wrote, "where through the green and golden witchery comes the piercing appeal of grinding and hopeless poverty, so that like the mermaid in Hans Andersen, I walk on sharp knives" . . . and "Nobody knows better than I do the risk of doing anything in this country . . . I am very happy here. Not that I hope to succeed personally. A man who expected personal success in Ireland would be ripe for Hanwell. But the work is enthralling and the call peremptory."

The call peremptory? That, the sense of an immense debt owed to his country (how could one accept privileges without obligations?) far more than personal ambition—not that he lacked this—spurred him on to the tireless discharge of public duties so much at war with his love of literature and of existence. However little grudged, this sacrifice—never a complete one, for thank heaven he always lived as well as worked to the full—was a fully conscious sacrifice. "I feel like a lark escaped from a vault!" he exclaimed at the end of a stormy session in the House of Commons; and I remember his saying, "I must now shut up the poetry drawer in my head and pull out the political one, in which I must burrow for the rest of the day."

In the years when I knew him I had not yet sufficiently disentangled the actual and contemporary world from that in which I read and dreamed to realise how much out of his own period George was. I seemed to meet him on every page of *Morte d'Arthur*, and Chivalry would certainly have been a good surname for him, but I see now that you are right in calling him a "glowing Renaissance figure". . . .

My own predominating memories of George? In many of the most vivid he is on horseback, for Clouds was in the most glorious riding country and the best rides of my life were with him. How he loved horses! I called him my "Centaur Uncle". (Less accountably he called me his "Nereid Niece".) As I write, I see him—how distinctly—as we canter over the Downs. His raven-black hair streaked with white is blown back, and hat in hand he bends right forward in the saddle to sing into his horse's ear—to him every horse was a Pegasus— until as we break into a thundering gallop, his voice is drowned in the thudding of hooves. Often—too often I thought—our rides would be interrupted by his dismounting to unroll a map, for he had a passionate interest in the English countryside and was always making a real or supposed discovery either of a pilgrims' track or of some remains of Roman civilisation.

A reckless rider, George adored hunting, not for the sake of outwitting the fox; still less from any of that "blood lust" which in these lopsidedly "civilised" days of ours I so often hear alleged to be the only possible explanation for the love of hunting, but just for the sheer physical joy of the thing—the bodily and mental glow: "I hunted for six immortal hours of galloping and singing to my horse when he was tired and I was jubilant. . . . The music of the hounds screaming like silver bells made my blood sing."

Neck to neck with riding memories, come memories of books. I remember how he would arrive with some volume already open in his hand and at once begin to read aloud to me. He loved a companion when he travelled in the realms of gold. Besides so devoutly worshipping at well-established shrines, how happy he was when some new planet swam into his ken! I specially remember his discovery of "Cyrano de Bergerac"; of Francis Thompson's essay on Shelley, and of "The Ballad of the White Horse". Of Chesterton's great poem which warmed him like wine, he said "To read 'The White Horse' aloud is like bathing in the sea or riding over the Downs in a company that becomes good company because of the exhilaration."

One vivid memory picture comically combines both reading and riding. It is of a time when as a child I stayed with him in Ireland in the Chief Secretary's Lodge. Uncle George, about to snatch a day's hunting and already red-coated and spurred, is conducting family prayers while, portfolios in hand, secretaries hover outside the door of the chapel ready to pounce on him the moment he emerges. As he reads the lesson—at the gallop, I must admit—quite unconscious of what his arm is doing he loudly beats on his booted leg with his riding-crop. Almost one can see beneath him the horse he felt himself already to be astride.

In actual output of words, with the exception of Hilaire Belloc, I suppose he surpassed all contemporaries. One day at Clouds, Donald Tovey had played the piano for three hours on end, and despite his great love of music, we had wondered how much the enforced silence had irked George. By a happy chance that very evening he chose to read aloud Browning's "A Toccata of Galuppi's". You won't be surprised to hear that when he came to the line, "I can always leave off talking when I hear a master play", the whole of his audience dissolved in laughter.

Naturally, for inevitably he had his personal as well as his political detractors, there were those who thought George talked too much. He did not go in for special bowling, and like all talkers much more interested in their subject than in what impression they make, he lacked a certain kind of social antennae—did not always take the temperature of the company. But you mustn't think he was in the least like whoever it was who said, "If *other* people are going to talk, conversation becomes impossible!" On the contrary he could be a very good listener, loving not only to infuse others with his own impassioned interest, but also to draw them out.

You asked if he was impatient. At times, certainly, particularly, of course, of interruption, but *not* from love of the sound of his own voice, or from over-keenness to score, but because when he was interested in a subject he could not bear it to be changed. Certain types of people fretted him too—pompous men or fashion-plate women—both very good at wrecking conversation. But don't think he always wanted Big Talk, or to discuss only those subjects nearest to his heart—Shakespeare's sonnets; Roman civilisation; the Springs of Romance and so forth. No, he could talk delightful nonsense—be amusingly flippant. In a house full of superlatively pious people, he said, "I almost expect to find haloes hung up on the hat pegs". Astringent he could be too, and saltily incisive in criticism. Of certain crudely emotional writers he complained, "They know no mean between a weeping willow and a hyena"; and of wilfully obscure poets, "There is all the difference between painting a fog that is beautiful and painting a clear-cut steeple by looking at it through blurred glasses."

Overcharged with ideas as with energy, his talk was perhaps at times a little over-concentrated. I'm told his public speaking had the same tendency. "Dilute, my dear George, dilute, dilute", was Arthur Balfour's advice to him after one of his earliest speeches in the House of Commons.

The sudden death, before he was fifty, of a being so vital that I could never imagine him even so much as asleep, was a dreadful shock. It was as though a great generous blaze at which one could always warm oneself had been blown out. Bereft of all that glow of gaiety, courage and love, the world seemed chilled, the future drained. The capacity to rouse expectation was still so much there; one hoped so much both for him and of him (only two days before his death I had a letter from him all about the joy of being alive). As for that stock consolation, "and now can never mourn a heart grown cold, a head grown grey in vain"; it just didn't apply. *His* heart could never have grown cold!

From a medical point of view, the early death of one so much over-engined that he consistently overdrew his physical account was not surprising. George's high spirits always made him (and others too) mistake exuberance for vigour, and to the last day of his life he over-spent his strength. To an already overcrowded life his father's death had added the responsibility for a large estate, and throughout his brief reign—1911-1913—at Clouds he was unremittently occupied with ambitious schemes for the future—all he intended to do for his tenants and agriculture.

"Some people", he wrote, "inherit an estate and go on as if nothing had happened. I can't do that. I must use all my energy and whatever imagination I may have to get something done that shall last and remain." ...

"Something that shall last and remain"? Clouds has of necessity long since been sold, and little more than a year after his own death his only son, Percy, was killed. I am glad that these two untimely deaths did at least occur in the natural sequence. The loss of his beautiful son—the delight of his eyes and his heart—would, I think, have taxed even his courage and faith.

I remember your asking me what a child "learnt" from Uncle George. I'll try to tell you—not that he was in the very least didactic, but even though he never intentionally taught, no child could be much in his company without imbibing something of the climate of his temperament and mind. Suppose I had never heard him spoken of, never read a single word about him, what would I remember of my own direct impressions? How much should I have inferred of his temperament, standards, code and philosophy of life? It isn't easy to empty your mind of all knowledge acquired later, but I'll try to exhume my, even to this day, still only lightly buried childhood and speak for that self of long, long ago.

To begin with, he gave me a sense of exhilaration—being with him was like breathing mountain air, and I also felt his own determination—loyalty to life, I should now call it—to enjoy himself. "I *must* have fun! Like Shelley I feel annoyed if I'm not happy!" Whether or not he actually told me so, I don't remember, but I certainly gathered that he thought love and courage the saviours of the world, and that if he had a motto, it would be "Courage, Love and Fun". When I first came across the expression "a Romantic", of course I thought of him. That he certainly was both by nature and by training. He never ceased to look with wonder on the world.

Clouds

Politics? I don't remember much actual talk of party politics, yet from him I did somehow imbibe that Conservatism need not, as in my childish ignorance I had hitherto supposed, necessarily derive from complacency with the *status quo* and indifference to the sufferings of the under-dog; for obviously here was one passionately concerned with the bettering of the human lot. No, Conservatism could be based on distrust of glib panaceas and, that jerry-building of legislation, hasty, ill-considered reform. In George this distrust derived from a sense of realism strong enough to prevent his heart from over-balancing his head, and was rooted in such knowledge of history that with keen imaginative insight he saw past, present and future as one continuous growth. Through him I understood with surprise (yes, you may well smile at such naïvety, but remember the Cynthia who is trying to answer your questions is not yet even in her teens) that Conservatism could be constructive as well as obstructive, and that often when it seemed most obstructive it was merely acting as the brake on the wheel, applied not to *stop* the coach's progress on the road to sound reform, but to prevent it, from over-precipitancy, being shattered on its way. The fact that the brake was often undeniably too soon applied and kept on too long did not make it any less of a necessity.

"Tradition" is a word one now scarcely has the courage to use. George—a torch-bearer, if ever there was one—loved the word, and, I think, made me understand its true meaning. How, I can't remember. Probably by some such analogy as that because a structure requires to be added to and restored, you do not necessarily destroy its foundations. When after his death I read in his letters, "Give me tradition to clamp together the loose spars in our hearts and minds. In that way gradually, surely, we shall get a tower rising tier on tier until at last we scale the heavens and strike our foreheads against the stars", some such forgotten image stirred in my memory.

What did I gather of George Wyndham's—what shall I call it?—philosophy of life? Roughly, very roughly, that though most vulnerable to misfortune—how could so loving a heart fail to give hostages to fate?—he was yet a man whom no extremity of sorrow or pain could possibly embitter; largely, I think, because he conceived God as a great artist whose medium was humanity. Without suffering or the dread of suffering, without insecurity, could there be much love in the world? Could there be any need for the beauty of courage and the compensatory power of humour? And without Love, Courage, and Humour, would there be very much in Man worth the creating? Earthly existence, human endurance, were for the grinding out of those three qualities—Love, Courage, Humour.

After George died a friend of his told me she thought his own lines on the death of Robert Browning applicable to himself:

> "This man saw all the world's distress,
> Wondered and shrank from its wrong,
> Knew fear, though his faith was strong,
> Yet he raised his voice ever to bless
> The love his great heart could guess,
> And dying drowned Death in his song."

GOSFORD

I was six, I think, when I first visited Grandpapa and Grand-mama Wemyss at Gosford. I remember the journey there—a seemingly everlasting day in the train with a cage showering birdseed, a nursery maid being sick, and myself eating hard-boiled egg sandwiches and sponge cakes. Then I remember clambering out of the train and being hoisted up into a huge conveyance called the Station Omnibus; someone darting out of a lodge to open the gate into an enclosed park full of shaggy Highland cattle; their wide horns were gilded by the light from our carriage lamps, and I saw steam coming out of their nostrils. At last the horses drew up at an open door and I was lifted out of the omnibus by a tall unsmiling man and plonked down on to a hard white floor. Sleepy and dazed, I stood blinking in the brilliant glare—my first introduction to the magic of electric light—of the "Marble Hall". . . .

I remember stumping up wide shallow steps and then having to pass very close to a ferocious-looking eagle made of stone. The bird glared at me, and I shied like a pony. The bustling, bobbing little person with a bunch of keys jingling at her side, who had welcomed us on the doorstep, now pattered on ahead. (For years I thought this tiny housekeeper's surname, Patterson, was only a nick-name, for she was never seen to walk, but invariably pattered.) We followed her down long narrow corridors hung with pictures, then up, up, up, and into a room called but not in the least resembling a nursery. . . . Then came bread-and-milk, and dreams of that over-impressive eagle. . . .

Next morning I was taken downstairs to be inspected by Grandpapa Wemyss. How like that stone bird he looks! thought I, but like a stag too. And how funny to have *two* beards! (That was how his Dundreary whiskers struck me.) Grandpapa's hands did not, like Papa's, hold a cigar-sceptre, but instead a large purple pencil—one of the "indelibles" with which he indited so many indignant letters to the Papers. Stately and grave, Grandmamma Wemyss sat in another stiff-backed chair close beside Grandpapa's. She was dressed all in black with a velvet bag hanging by a silver chain from her waist. The room was very airless. I felt I couldn't breathe, and oh so shy! Grandpapa was looking at me so intently, and his eyes were very piercing. But he was very, very kind and beautifully polite. He took me on to his knee; called me "Pussy" and invited me to twist his two white beards into one across his parchmenty chin, but all the time I had an oppressive sense of undergoing inspection. Then, pleasant as a warm bath, a delightful feeling flowed over me; the awareness of approval!

Grandpapa pinched my ear, took my hand in his, led me out into the hall and right up to the ferocious bird to whom I was now formally introduced. It was a Roman eagle, he told me, that had once belonged to a clever gentleman called Horace Walpole. ("What a pity", I thought to myself, "Horace Walpole, whoever he might be, hadn't kept the horrid bird!") Then Grandpapa pointed to a number of pictures, most of them of people who seemed to me very insufficiently clad. Many of these pictures I didn't like at all. One I particularly disliked was of a naked man stuck all over with arrows like a pin-cushion with pins. Ugh! From time to time I nodded my head, but what to *say* while Grandpapa went on and on talking to me about the pictures I had no idea! Before long I became uncomfortably aware that instead of attending to what he was saying to me, I was listening only to my own intermediary "Um . . . Umm's". It was very uncomfortable having to look up all this time and the crick in my neck began to be very painful.

"Now, Pussy", said Grandpapa, "you must learn to use those very wide-apart eyes of yours. Tell me which of all these paintings you like best. Take a good look before you answer."

Conscious that a great deal was at stake, I pointed after a

few seconds' hesitation to a picture that took my fancy because, instead of being quite naked like the three ugly fat women Grandpapa called the Three Graces, the lady in it wore a cloak of the loveliest blue. Moreover she had a sweet gentle face, and I liked the rose-garden in which she knelt, and her beautiful fat baby. By sheer good luck this Madonna, one attributed to Botticelli, was Grandpapa's favourite picture—a fortunate fluke that lofted me into lasting favour. His delighted approval of my choice made me glow.

"And what do you intend to do in life with that great big forehead of yours, eh?" asked Grandpapa, adding for the first of many thousand times the peremptory injunction, "But hold your head up, child!" As he spoke, he enforced his words by that trick he had of narrowing his colourless lips into one long straight line and at the same time widening the lids of his stiletto eyes. "Hold your head up", he repeated, "or you'll spoil your looks!" ("Spoil" my "looks"? Was there then something to spoil? darted through my mind.)

Before I had had time even to try to answer Grandpapa's question, I heard a jingly noise. Mrs. Patterson and her keys appeared from nowhere, and with a playful parting pinch of my ear, Grandpapa handed me over into her bustling care. Away almost as fast as the White Rabbit went Mrs. Patterson— pitter-patter, pitter-patter—and I on my short legs trundling after her. I followed her through forbidding-looking regions full of mustn't-be-touched things. At last we were below-stairs, and I began to breathe more freely. Turning one of her keys in a lock, Mrs. Patterson opened a door and I had my first sight and whiff of her famous store-cupboard! After that unforgettable initiation, I had but to hear the music of her jingling keys to re-taste crystallised apricots, pineapple-chunks, almonds, raisins and other deliciousnesses. In the eye of my memory that dear little becapped and beribboned domestic fairy still goes bobbetting ahead down endless corridors, every now and again turning to look back over her shoulder with a beckoning smile at the little girl who trots behind her.

Despite her kittenish appearance, what authority there was

in every inch of Mrs. Patterson's plump little body! This, many well-trained maids had good reason to know. The grand-daughters of the house too, for fond though she was, she was never over-indulgent, and as soon as we began to think breakfast in bed attractive, she made it very plain that she "was not one to hold with any such softness".

What else do I remember of that first visit? A confusion of grown-up persons, many of whom I couldn't remember ever having seen before, but whom I must be sure to call Uncle This or Aunt That. Not all of these—this I was told as though it were reassuring information—were "blood" relations of mine. There was also a Great-Great-Aunt, a marble bath, the thrill of switching the magic lights on and off, and some fascinating old grandfather clocks in which little doors opened every quarter of an hour, and quaint stiff figures emerged and jigged about while twangy eerie music quavered on the air. Then there were long cold walks by a grey winter sea, or through the shrubberies with their "ornamental" ponds. Permeating all else there was a persistent homesickness for Stanway, and a sense of constraint and oppression because in this large un-homelike house, I must always be so very tidy, polite and punctual.

Gosford, neither, like Stanway, entirely old, nor, like Clouds, entirely new, had not been finished long before my first visit. The centre-block, the beginning of an Adam house, with its three huge rooms—drawing-room, dining-room and "saloon" —had been built by my great-great-grandfather. To this Grandpapa added two long wings, one containing the—to a child's eyes—dazzling precincts magniloquently called "The Marble Hall", really of stone and alabaster with a marble staircase. Strangely out of place in Scotland, the outside of the house seemed to implore a blue Italian sky. Silhouetted against the cold grey northern light, the poised Venuses, heraldic lions and swans that ornamented the roof looked shiveringly cold. The view of the Firth of Forth was superb—the coast of Fife opposite, then the queer humps of Arthur's Seat, and on clear days the arches of the Forth Bridge.

Reflected in the glinting foreground, the sunsets, to which the smoke of Edinburgh added a lurid beauty, irradiated the

Author's grandfather, the Earl of Wemyss, with his younger son Evan Charteris.

Drawing of the author by John Sargent.

gold and purple sands, gleaming gulls, black rocks and silver bents of that lovely stretch of coast.

Unfortunately I never went to Gosford at a time of the year to enjoy it as a sea-side, but always in autumn or winter when often for days on end the ravening east winds would make it impossible to stand upright out of doors, and at night they wailed and moaned round the house with the melancholy of all the ballads of the world.

- A peculiar depression—"Gosforditis" we called it—often fell on me at Gosford. Compared with Stanway the house seemed so bleak—so without atmosphere, like a handsome person without charm. The rooms were airless and except with the aid of a long hooked pole, it was impossible to open or shut any of the heavy windows. Out of doors I missed the mossy drowsiness, the green leafiness of Stanway with its great over-spreading beeches. Here, dwarfed and twisted, the trees were cut by the wind as though by a razor.

Much as I often enjoyed myself at Gosford and childishly proud though I was of its size and grandeur, I never felt any real fondness for the place. Probably I instinctively recognised it to be a rival to Stanway; guessed that one day it would be here in Scotland instead of in England that we should have to make our home—quite enough to antagonise me. To some of my cousins the weeks spent at Gosford were, I believe, the happiest in the year; to me it was a place of exile in which a painfully uprooted plant was bedded-out. Yet goodness knows there was plenty to enjoy, not least the sheer size of the house with the glorious scope it gave for Hide-and-Seek. Then there was all the fun with cousins—Mary Vesey, Maurice Yorke and the five Brodericks. As for the schoolroom teas, so much attended by truants from the drawing-room, they were fabulous. Every known variety of Scotch scones!

Besides Mrs. Patterson herself, the hierarchy of the staff comprised other attractive personalities, notably the head housemaid, Anne, in appearance the absolute embodiment of the word "bonny", and with the very best Scottish accent. Poor Anne survived bitterly to deplore the decay of domestic service—"Not one of them gurrrls knows how to scrrrub!" she

F

complained of post-war maids, "and they wastes their time at cross-purposes!" (Crosswords, she meant.)

Though I never got to know him well, I was deeply impressed by the perfectly perpendicular butler. Also by a mysterious dignitary who, though apparently he had nothing whatever to do with horses, was called "the Groom of the Chambers". What this person's functions were, I never discovered, but his title thrilled me.

That perpendicular butler *looked* more irreproachable than anyone I have yet seen, but alas, he had a not uncommon weakness. He "exceeded", and on one occasion betrayed his condition in a memorable way. He went on and on pouring out claret for a dinner guest until, overflowing the glass, the wine gushed on to the cloth and streamed across the table. As no one intervened, the libation continued until the bottle was quite empty and a large purple puddle lay on the carpet.

Far the most valuable element in Gosford life was our wholesome, bracing fear of Grandpapa. Does any child of to-day enjoy that particular thrill—the thrill of awe? I remember it as an experience utterly distinct from that ill-at-easeness Papa sometimes gave me. With Grandpapa you knew exactly where you were. Though some of his rules might seem both peculiar and unnecessary, at least they all had the great merit of being definite—as definite as those of Tom Tiddler's Ground. His wrath was therefore perfectly predictable, and in the straightforward, wholly accountable fear it inspired there was nothing that could possibly damage a child's nervous system. On the contrary, like occasional thunder, it added a pleasurable thrill to life.

Besides those thrills of awe enjoyable even at the time and in retrospect so greatly valued, I owe Grandpapa another debt of gratitude. To feel pride in a relation is agreeable to a child, and I *was* proud of him—proud of his spectacular looks, superb carriage, and of his perfection both of manner and of manners. He really was a master of courtesy.

When I first remember Grandpapa Wemyss, he was already close on eighty, but except for his deafness, the whiteness of his hair, his veined hands and that parchmenty look, his appearance triumphantly belied his years. Until the very end of his life his sight was still sufficiently unimpaired for him to be a good shot, and he always remained alert and supple in movement as well as uncompromisingly upright in carriage. At seventy-nine, more erect than anyone else, he rode in the Jubilee of 1897 as aide-de-camp to Queen Victoria. He learnt to bicycle when he was over eighty, and won a threesome at golf on his ninetieth birthday. Indeed, had he not, while coaching a descendant in the art of valsing, slipped up in his marble hall and been obliged to stay in bed because of an injured hip, I doubt whether even at the age of ninety-six it would have occurred to him that the time to think of dying had yet come.

Born three years before the death of Napoleon, and living till only a few days before the war of 1914-18 broke out, Grandpapa had for one in his particular circumstances undeniably chosen his span of life well.

Powerless to abate his physical strength, age failed equally to impair his vigorous, unintellectual mind. From cradle to coffin he was untroubled by doubt, and his uncompromising principles, derived more from temperament and tradition than from any deep or sustained thought, never moulted a single feather. He sat for many years in the House of Commons as a nominal Conservative, but independence was the breath of life to him and his tendency to condemn all politicians as vote-hunters and to regard any modifications of what he considered principles as base concessions to fear and opportunism, made him denounce all parties with equal violence. Though not a literary speaker—he rarely opened a book—he had a natural turn for oratory; could flame with a fine fire of conviction and was never so happy as when fighting for a lost cause in a minority of one.

In 1859 Grandpapa had headed the Volunteer Movement, raised the London Scottish of which he was Colonel, and become Chairman of the National Rifle Association. The nickname of the "Brigadier", acquired by these activities, stuck to him for life. He continuously bombarded the War Office with inventions—the Elcho boot, the Elcho bayonet, the Elcho military shovel and so forth. Nor was his practical ingenuity confined to military gadgets. A vast variety of golf clubs of most bizarre design were produced. As for his artistic activities, they were legion. He drew, painted and sculpted. Hundreds of Gosford sunsets—described by himself when they were exhibited in London as "Senile, Sunny Sketches"—still survive in coloured chalk.

In the same medium he made several over-life-size unlikenesses of his grand-daughter. Thanks to his unusual method— he literally measured the disproportions of my face with a steel compass, one sharp leg of which was actually pivoted on my nose—"sitting" to Grandpapa was an unusual and far from painless experience.

In early youth, while making the Grand Tour, Grandpapa had collected in Italy for remarkably little money a quantity of very fine paintings. He had a natural flair for a good picture, and there the matter ended. Questions of authenticity and theories as to technique merely exasperated him. When the renowned art critic Berensen visited Gosford and ventured— that, indeed, being what he supposed himself to be there for— to question some of the attributions of the Gosford pictures, Grandpapa was incensed by this, as he thought, presumptuous attempt on the part of a guest to re-label his host's treasures. The doubts cast on the genuineness of his two favourites, the Madonnas imputed to Botticelli and Mantegna, particularly infuriated him.

Similar exasperation met my uncle Evan's well-intended efforts to doctor his father's prose, when, desiring his son merely to point out any possible political or social indiscretions, Grandpapa submitted to his judgment some Memoirs that he intended to publish. Misunderstanding what was required of him, Evan, himself a practised and elegant writer, took immense trouble over his father's manuscript which showed a characteristic independence of what its writer would have called "arbitrary" rules. When the much-loved Benjamin handed back to his father a copiously corrected manuscript, his reward for concerning himself with "split infinitives", "unattached participles" and other such nonsensical niceties was to be called a "damned pedant" and sent flying from the room. I chanced to be in the hall when the would-be mender of split-infinitives was precipitated from the paternal presence. Never before had I had the pleasure of seeing a grown-up person look so discomfited.

Grandpapa was indeed sublimely unhampered by any sense of his own limitations. Besides these Memoirs which are still unpublished—the most morally courageous member of the family (needless to say a woman) was deputed to tell him they must remain so—there was a privately printed volume of verse. Grandpapa had ridden well to hounds; he was also a very good shot. Why then, he asked, should he not be a good poet as well? Possibly his never having read any poetry written by anyone else made the undertaking seem lighter. Alas, no more an original than a derivative poet, his attempts were pronounced to lack the essentials even of verse!

The same freedom from diffidence made Grandpapa engagingly willing to teach all experts their own jobs. Yes, he was always ready to give free advice to any painter, dancer or professional game-player. I remember finding him showing Donald Tovey exactly how he should hold his hands on the piano!

Unlike his descendants, many of whom are inclined to be introspective, ironic, complex, over-sensitive to ridicule and quite as prone to laugh at themselves as at others, Grandpapa Wemyss, in every way what in the jargon he would so much have hated would now be called an Extrovert, was positive and direct. As for his inviolable code of honour, it was quite as simple and direct as his sense of humour. In no way was he more unlike his family than in his sense of humour. He was much addicted to chaff, also to puns—some of these very good —but I don't remember him ever laughing at anything *except* a joke. When his conversation was neither gallant nor denunciatory nor yet facetious, it was largely reminiscent. No degree of dissimilarity between himself and his children could, however, lessen his devotion to them. He had an absolute horror of gambling, and it was a cruel irony that his sons should have had so strong a propensity to harass him in this particular way, but, however much distressed by what he regarded as suicidal folly, he was able generously to forgive what he could not understand.

Very temperate in his habits, Grandpapa liked to impute his marvellous health to natural abstemiousness. He never smoked and cared so little for wine that to the blushing embarrassment of his sons he would urge guests to mix claret and port in the same glass!

What, I think, he found far more difficult to understand or forgive than any moral weakness was that any descendant of his should be one whit less physically erect—he carried his own head like a challenge—than was natural to himself. To ensure bodily uprightness in his own sons and daughters he was said to have put holly under their chins and spikes in the backs of their chairs. Though he never went to such lengths with his grandchildren, I assure you that at the sound of his approaching step we would automatically square our shoulders and draw in our chins.

The great thing was to remember to try never to offend his aesthetic eye. Ugliness, awkwardness, untidiness distressed him so terribly, and for any physical defect or disorder in dress he had an eye like an eagle. "One of your shoulders is higher than the other!" . . . "There's a wrinkle in your stocking!" . . . "Don't eat like a rabbit, child!" and so forth he would bawl at us across the table. These pelted injunctions were not seldom enforced by a vigorous pinch on the soft part of one's arm. I'm sure he had no idea of the strength of his fingers. Those pinches hurt.

Not to dress for dinner would I'm sure have been inconceivable to Grandpapa. Never shall I forget his reaction the evening he found my two brothers in the drawing-room, still wearing the very muddy boots in which they had been out partridge-shooting. "D'you think you're at the Klondyke?" he blazed out.

A martinet? Yes, but how benevolent, magnanimous and just! The more I look back, the more I realise that, accompanied as it was by very real respect, my fear of Grandpapa was one of the emotions of my childhood I should be most sorry not to have known.

Grandpapa was no slave to fashion and certain sartorial

innovations were anathema to him, particularly that, introduced in male attire at the beginning of the century, of turning up the ends of trouser-legs at the ankle. The first step any grand-daughter of his took when she got engaged was to insure that whatever else his shortcomings, the young man about to be submitted on approval should at least not wave this particular red rag in the face of his prospective grandfather-in-law.

Just as anything he regarded as vandalism in new buildings goaded him into public protest, so Grandpapa yearned to be able to denounce physical blemishes. I can still see the expression on his face and how he drummed with his fingers on the table the day three sisters, for whom nature had done little and art nothing, came to luncheon at Gosford. Poor girls! they were in the most unbecoming stage of adolescence—their teeth, complexions and hair all in urgent need of attention. Since courtesy—for these girls were not his grandchildren— forbade any active missionary work, frustration was added to outraged sensibility. I'm sure those girls had no idea what it was that had so much upset their host. But *we* knew! Had we not all suffered the ordeal of sitting immediately opposite him facing the pitiless glare of that northern light, and all of a sudden wondering with which of our faces it was this time and for what particular reason he was so visibly disgusted! Oh, those luncheons in that oppressively vast dining-room, hung with huge still-life pictures of eatables—lobsters, pineapples, boars' heads! Delicious as was the Scotch broth rich with suet dumplings, it was often dearly bought, for the social strain of those meals was great. Most of the visitors, many of them only birds of briefest passage, would either ignore a child's presence or else embarrassingly address it in a perfunctorily jocular or cajoling way. Whereas at Clouds three generations seemed to overlap and harmoniously mingle, at Gosford they were sundered as though Mappin Terraces stretched between, and the atmosphere of the one house seemed as critical as the other was appreciative.

Then there was Grandpapa's deafness, like all deafness treacherous, for though it was so difficult to make him hear any remark addressed *to* him, he was disconcertingly apt to overhear

snatches of talk not intended for his ears. Moreover, whenever
there was laughter he naturally wanted to share the joke, and
you would be obliged to repeat some banality or indiscretion.
Then—jokes repeated out of their contexts being usually so
terribly unfunny—as likely as not he would look sadly un-
amused.

In contrast to Stanway where nearly all the guests were either
dearly loved friends or, however boring to others, enter-
tainingly comical to us, Gosford visitors seemed to assemble
not so much because they particularly wanted to be there or
because their company was greatly desired, but because they
happened to be on their way to the north of Scotland, and
Gosford made so convenient a break to the journey. This gave
the house a rather hotel-like atmosphere. Many of the women
were what, with the austerity of childhood, I vaguely condemned as "Fashionable". Most of the men played—PLAYED!
—what an inappropriate word!—golf, then to my mind the most
inexplicable pursuit. So intolerably tedious did this game look
to me, that I supposed it to be a punishment! I'm not joking.
Honestly, I remember wondering what on earth Uncle Evan
and other players, none of whom *looked* wicked, could have done
to deserve such long sentences as the hours and hours and hours
during which they were, as I thought, condemned to the links.

Long post-mortems were often held over the morning's golf,
and players who had been "off their game" would be plunged
in gloom at luncheon. Some days I think they must all have
been off their game. I remember long silences in which I found
myself listening only to the unpleasing sound of mastication
unaccompanied by talk.

Golf was "played" every day except of course on Sundays.
The strictest Sabbatarianism still prevailed in Scotland, and
anyone seen on the Lord's Day with a golf club in his hand
might well have been stoned. We attended the Presbyterian
Kirk every week. At the end of the service with its long
extemporised prayers, the extremely dour-looking minister
would surprisingly unbend by making his way with extended
hand to where we sat and bursting into a brisk secular chat.

At one time daily family-prayers were held in the dining-room, but this practice was soon discontinued, the wheezy, hiccoughing harmonium that accompanied the hymn-singing of the family, many of whom were tone-deaf, being too much for the gravity of the congregation.

But far the worst giggling scandal at Gosford was that fatal day when the then Poet Laureate, the minute Sir Alfred Austin, kindly suggested reading aloud to the house-party. *Lamia*, he said he would like to read. "But won't you read us something by *yourself*?" civilly enquired one of my aunts, not unnaturally assuming him to mean Keats's poem of that name. It turned out, however, that—as doubtless we should have known—this *Lamia* was not by John Keats but by Alfred Austin! Not an auspicious beginning. Still, there was little excuse for the disgraceful scene that followed.

In the course of the pocket poet's reading, one after another, each member of his audience in turn broke down—broke down so hopelessly that retreat became the only possible course. Biting cushions or with handkerchiefs—wholly ineffectual gags —stuffed into their mouths, one by one a long file of uncles, nieces, aunts and nephews crept on all fours from the room! Coming in to attend to the fire, the butler was surprised to find the tiny poet, who was quite oblivious of the general exodus, impassionedly reading aloud to himself.

My worst social torture at Gosford was having to practise the piano in the drawing-room just when visitors were streaming through it on their way to breakfast. This was awful!. Most of them mercifully hurried past with averted eyes, but the more amiably disposed felt obliged to make some friendly advance. Some would merely give my pigtail a playful tug and feel they'd done their duty, but others would comment favourably on my playing, a kindly insincerity for which they were severely punished by my Austrian governess, who could swallow any praise of her pupil. "I'm sure you would like to hear Cincie play a 'piece'," she would purr. My five-finger exercises would be interrupted and, while coffee, bacon and eggs cooled, there the unfortunates would have to stand while I pounded my way right through "The Merry Peasant".

Unlike Stanway, Gosford had a very definite "Season", and

in contrast to these vast impersonal autumn gatherings—
sometimes with visitors and all their maids and valets there
would be as many as a hundred people sleeping in the house—
I stayed on through long bleak weeks when Squidge[1] and I were
the only visitors. But there were also riotous Christmases with
the house given up to the entertainment of the young, when we
and our cousins had tremendous fun riding in hordes, acting
charades, telling one another ghost stories in the dark and
playing every game except that for which it was made on the
billiard table. The dread of that terrible mysterious offence
called "Cutting the cloth" (I've never seen it committed, have
you?) added immense thrill to these boisterous games.

No child of to-day can conceive the fascination and glamour of
glinting golden money. Grandpapa's Christmas present to his
descendants was always coins in special little envelopes straight
from the estate office. Half a sovereign up to ten years old, and
gradually increasing until when we reached the age of eighteen
and ever afterwards, five golden sovereigns!

You can imagine how much "Perries" were enhanced by the
fear of Grandpapa. Dodging him was as exciting as trying to avoid
a calamitous bunker. Tobogganing down the stairs on tea-trays
was a strictly forbidden sport but one I found it quite impossible
to forego. One day I miscalculated his return from the golf-links
and my tea-tray with myself on it overran his foot at the bottom
of the stairs. This was an occasion on which he had plenty to say.

"Honour thy father and mother that thy days may be long
in the land" etcetera. All I had to do to make myself obey this
commandment was to recall the legend (can it really have been
true?) that in his early boyhood Papa had once actually pulled
away the chair on which Grandpapa was just about to sit
down! What a hero!

One mild escapade that never palled was to hide behind the
curtains and watch the company assemble for dinner, and then
ensconce oneself between the double doors of the dining-room
and listen to the conversation. Greatly daring, Mary Vesey and
I once actually ventured right into the dining-room in our night-
dresses. Our mothers shook in their satin shoes. However, to

[1] Fraulein von Moskovicz, my Austrian governess.

their astonishment Grandpapa was not in the least angry, but affectionately pinching our ears, plied us with almonds and raisins. Had our night attire exposed any bodily defects that full dress had hitherto concealed from him, no doubt his wrath would have been great. As it was he liked the new line of my hair as done, or rather not done, for bed. It gave him an idea as to how it should always be dressed, an idea that became an obsession and was one day to cause me hideous inconvenience. Eight years later, I was waiting, a quaking débutante, all arrayed and beplumed to be presented at Court—the carriage had already been announced and for once Mamma was in time —when of a sudden who should appear in my bedroom but Grandpapa! And in his most zealous missionary mood! He insisted on a radical change in my coiffure which he vehemently denounced as "time-serving" and utterly out of keeping with what he called my "Florentine looks". This attack stripped me of my last shred of self-confidence. I did not want to arrive late at Buckingham Palace. Still less did I want to look con-spicuous, and I could scarcely suppose that "Florentine" was the right thing to look at a twentieth-century English Court. . . .

Though I was only seven when Grandmamma Wemyss died, I can still see her distinctly. She was always in black—she had never worn colours since the early deaths of her two elder sons—and in my memory is never without the black velvet bag of my first sight of her. On her head is a lace cap from which a ribbon hangs down her back almost to her waist, and she wears earrings, tiny golden bells that give out a faint tinkle whenever she moves.

Grandmamma was as erect—no doubt she had need to be— as her husband, and never sat in anything but an absolutely straight-backed chair. Despite her somewhat alarming appearance and reputation for rectitude amounting almost to austerity, she had plenty of lurking playfulness of mind. I remember how the dignity of her face would suddenly ripple into a smile. To me she was always most kind and delighted me on my first visit by saying I read aloud well, and must read the Collect, Gospel and Epistle to her every Sunday.

With her pale wild-rose skin, black hair and large luminous eyes, Grandmamma must have been very beautiful, and the story of Grandpapa's courtship of her thrilled me with its romance. The first time he ever set eyes on her, she was, Juliet-wise, looking out of a window in Naples. He at once procured an introduction. Three weeks later they were married. During all the many years of their married life they were scarcely ever apart. Adoring her devoted husband, Grandmamma Wemyss was always tenderly and tactfully amused by his intransigence and the political solitudes into which it drove him. She was deeply, orthodoxly religious, and had a moral code that would no doubt now be considered as uncompromisingly rigid as her chairs, but she was much more exemplary in conduct than didactic in speech, and no altitude of standard for herself ever made her intolerant or unsympathetic towards others. Re-pressed, and inherently, however unintentionally, stately, Grandmamma like other shy souls welcomed fellow-creatures who were not too deferential to take the initiative. She was lastingly and affectionately grateful to the intrepid Margot Tennant, who, though young enough to be her daughter, rushed her into intimacy by, so to speak, bursting through a door at which others would not have dared so much as to knock.

Seven years after Grandmamma's death Grandpapa married Miss Grace Blackburn, a remarkably handsome woman still under forty. Immediately after this marriage, which was secretly contracted, he was seized with a violent fit of sentimental remorse. Nothing, he declared, would ever persuade him to put another woman in the place of his beloved first wife. Never, never again would he return to Gosford! This situation, apparently a deadlock, was almost as uncomfortable for the whole family as for the principals, but Aunt Evelyn, who unfailingly came to the rescue in every crisis, at once took things in hand. She made her father bring his bride to stay with her in Ireland and gradually persuaded him that his scruples were as morbid as they were tardy and that he must have the courage of his intentions. Before long the marriage, previously only according to civil law, was solemnised in church, and shortly afterwards Grandpapa took the second

Lady Wemyss to Gosford where they lived happily ever afterwards for the remaining fourteen years of his life.

How well I remember the news of that second marriage being broken to me in between the second and third acts of *Julius Caesar*! I was at that time deeply in love with Brutus, and if my informants expected this family bombshell to take my mind away from Rome for one split second, they were greatly mistaken.

To take over the reins of Gosford where everyone had loved Grandmamma, and become stepmother to so large, adult and critical a family can have been no light undertaking, and her success was greatly to the credit of the second wife who looked after Grandpapa admirably and kept him wonderfully happy. Her gift for drawing delighted him, while her classical profile provided his own pencil with an admirable permanent model. As "Granny Grace" she became very much one of the family and under her reign Gosford continued as patriarchically hospitable as ever. When Mary Vesey and I grew up a coming-out ball was given in our honour, and after my marriage my children were most welcomingly received.

Because of political heat   I married at the height of the House of Lords conflict—my engagement to an Asquith had been a considerable blow to Grandpapa, whose nickname for my future father-in-law was the "Robber Chief". A premature rumour of the engagement had occasioned a violent explosion, but, needless to say, once it was an accomplished fact, my future husband—of course dutifully out of the fashion as to the ends of his trousers—was welcomed in the most charming and courteous fashion and at once became a devoted adherent.

Grandpapa died in July, 1914—only just a day or two before the outbreak of the war that he, always a passionate advocate of conscription, had so persistently predicted. . . .

I see no one now alive who can even remotely remind me of Grandpapa Wemyss. I sometimes wonder what, suppose he could now revisit the glimpses of the moon, he would think of our Brave New World. However much distressed by all that would strike him as hugger-mugger, yet quite undismayable, he would, I'm sure, at once vigorously set to work to devise some highly remarkable labour-saving devices for his descendants. . . .

Gosford, as well as Clouds, provided its grandchildren with a dazzling uncle. Evan did not, as George Wyndham did, play a large part in my childhood; but directly I grew up I found his company one of the great luxuries of life. Besides being so extraordinarily amusing himself, he had that intoxicating quick-mindedness that Sir Walter Raleigh, one of the best-loved of his literary friends, described when he quite gravely said to me, "Evan always understands what I want to say long before *I* do!"

Though to his intimates this may not have seemed so very important, one of the qualities that most struck people about Evan was his grace—an effortless grace and elegance that, incidentally giving him that perfection of style for which he was renowned at golf and as a gun, inevitably imbued every move-ment he made and every sentence he phrased. His looks had a rare distinction—a chiselled delicacy that always reminded me of the oriental china of which he was a collector; but this appearance was deceptive; steel determination and persever-ance underlay that porcelain exterior. Though he looked fragile and, indeed, never was robust, his spirit, industry and remark-able versatility enabled him to get through a formidable amount of very hard work as well as strenuous exercise; and yet never to seem too busy, preoccupied or too tired to enjoy the company of the many friends for whom he enriched life.

The truth was that though he had such lightness of touch and appeared to do everything with such ease, he really worked as hard as the most dogged plodder.

How else could he for many years have earned a very large income at the Parliamentary Bar, while holding important administrative posts on the executives of Art Museums, and yet have found time to write in an admirable style, disciplined to the point of austerity, several books that involved no little drudgery of research? Meanwhile he contrived to keep up his reputation as one of the best shots of the day, to excel at games, and to cultivate many friendships.

I think few people can have had the art of living for its own sake to a higher degree than Evan. Many young men equally well equipped for it would have been content just to cultivate this pleasant art. If the proverbial "competence" really be a curse, he had this curse to contend with, and could on a private income reinforced by his charm, taste and social gifts have floated through life quite effortlessly.

He might easily have remained the merest dilettante. Indeed, had he so wished, he could unchallenged have drifted a complete idler on the then halcyon waters of the social world like some admirably well-rigged pleasure yacht. But though he never allowed his labours to interfere with that enjoyment of life at which he was such an adept, he never presumed on his natural advantages. From so agreeable a "traveller 'twixt life and death", no fare could have been exacted, yet he invariably did pay his passage promptly and to the uttermost farthing. Never did he spare himself; least of all at the very end when in direct defiance of doctor's orders he flung himself into Home Guard activities.

I doubt if mere acquaintances, most of whom probably associated Evan chiefly with his rapier-like wit and that curiously characteristic, somewhat startling laugh that many found so "alarming", ever suspected the inflexibility of the standards he set himself. Assuming that so vigilant and alert a sense of humour must interfere with his emotions, some, I cannot doubt, were undiscerning enough to label him "cynical". If so, they had no conception how the "elements so mixed in him"; for if his gay mockery could at times be scathing, his praise was often correspondingly generous. In fact his bump of veneration was unusually large, and to the very end of his life he was capable of surprisingly naïve, indeed almost school-boyish enthusiasms. To him, those he loved were sacrosanct. Had the phrase "The Queen can do no wrong" not already been coined, it would, I'm sure, have sprung from his lips.

Probably not many people gauged the warmth of Evan's heart or suspected how actively kind he could be. I can witness that he was one of the very few who more than once when I told him some friend was in distress, gave me money to hand over *anonymously*.

Evan very often stayed at Stanway. I always rejoiced to hear he was coming, not only for my own sake but because his presence invariably meant that my mother would be happy. No one suited her better. Besides the pleasure and amusement his company never failed to give her, some quality of his invariably soothed her nerves which—for the details of life could sorely harass her—alas, seldom shared the serenity of her soul.

For many years Evan might well have been pointed out as the shining example of triumphantly successful bachelorhood, but when in 1930 he married Dorothy Grosvenor (incidentally a great friend of my own), we were soon made to see how incomplete his life had been until then. We had so long known him amused, interested, successful. Now for the first time we saw him content. They had ten years of shared happiness from which many friends benefited by being allowed to bask in the wonderfully satisfying beauty of the home that her taste made an ideal setting for his famous collection of pictures and ornamental china.

Few men can have defied the arbitrary divisions of time so successfully as Evan. I can hardly remember being even so much as reminded that we belonged to different generations. He always seemed a contemporary, and I don't think that this was because he knew how to bridge the gulf, but rather that no gulf existed.

His approach to life remained so youthful. He had kept not only the enjoyment, but also the scorn, expectancy, curiosity and indignation of youth. This quality of freshness was all the more surprising in one so highly civilised, so delicately fastidious—in every way an Epicure. "Over-sophisticated" some people called him. But here was the happy paradox: cultivation and discrimination wrought no disenchantment. Undulled, undisillusioned, still expectant, he remained one of those whom the Gods love, and as such, despite seventy-six crowded years of life, he died young.

Drawing of the author by Sir Edward Burne-Jones.

Painting of the author by Augustus John, O.M.

SOME PAINTERS

BEFORE bracing myself to the effort of going right back to my first childhood, I think I'll obey that other behest of yours and see what I can tell you about the artists to whom I have sat. But I must call them painters, not artists. They hate that word.

I suppose you would like their sometime model to turn the tables on the painters and draw pen-portraits. This I'm afraid I shall find beyond me, but if in the attempt the years should fall away, and memory waft me back into their various studios, how lovely to be there again!

I love the atmosphere of studios. It's so inspiriting to watch people at work on the very thing they would pay anything to be at—"grinding away", I suppose that is how they would put it, at their greatest delight. How one envies them! What a lovely way of making your livelihood! It is just as though you were paid for reading Catullus or for drinking Claret.

I enjoy, too, the, so to speak, diligent indolence of "sitting" —the agreeable sense of serving some purpose without any exertion. I can sit for hours on end and, except that my hands tend to get St. Vitus's Dance, find little difficulty in what is called "holding a pose". If I were allowed to sit in silence I should have none, but painters always seem to assume that you will fall into a state of catalepsy unless they entertain you all the time.

"I don't want all the expression to leave your face," they explain.

My difficulty is that I can't talk with just my mouth alone. All my other features have to join in and waggle. However, since they were such good talkers, I am glad the artists— painters, I mean—did consider conversation necessary.

Despite its charm, being painted does let the model in for one great ordeal. Sooner or later you are "allowed" a peep at your portrait and then—hideous embarrassment—something must be said . . . what? Admiration, no matter how genuine, is never easy to express. And whatever you *say*, how terribly flat your voice sounds! Do you remember how Queen Victoria pronounced on her portrait when trembling, the artist submitted it to the royal gaze? "We are redder than that," was Her Majesty's only comment.

I wish I could take an invitation to "sit" as a compliment, but alas, artists seldom fail to explain that it is not beauty they seek in a model; still less prettiness—a quality that, indeed, they seem to consider repellent. Far from it. What they like to paint is irregularity, oddity—in fact, let's face it—something definitely freakish! This was trenchantly put to me by Professor Tonks, never one to mince his words, the very first time we met.

"What we like," he said vehemently, "is something QUEER. As for you, Miss Charteris, you should be kept in a glass case for artists to draw",—harsh words, at which my seventeen-years-old self all but burst into tears. For it was not as if I had been destined to be an artist's model. No, at that juncture, my fate—unshunnable as Death, so it seemed—was to acquit myself as well as possible in the ball-room, and, in that arena, unfortunately, I could not doubt that it behoved one to be pretty rather than peculiar.

Having asked me to sit, and so encouragingly explained why they did so, artists then invariably proceeded to abuse me for being so "infernally difficult to do". My mouth, they would complain, was never for two consecutive seconds the same. My adjustable chin, now so short, now so long, also got cursed. As for my respective profiles! They belonged to two wholly different characters (according to McEvoy, one represented Comedy, the other Tragedy) while my full face—and remarkably full it was then—suggested yet a third and wholly different person. "In fact", squeaked McEvoy, in his exasperation snapping his paint-brush in two, "you're not a person at all, but only an emanation!" (He little knew what a disquieting indictment this was to one always troubled by a sense of her own discontinuity. Had not "Catch e'er she change the Cynthia of the minute" been quoted at me until I could have screamed?)

Of my first sitting I have but a very faint and feathery memory. The artist—prepare yourself for an immense shunt in time—was Edward Burne-Jones. I can just remember hearing my mother say, "Isn't it lovely? B.J. has asked me to bring Cincie to be drawn." Then we rumbled along in a four-wheeler to a house in West Kensington called The Grange, where the artist himself welcomed us with a beaming smile on the doorstep. He wore a white studio-coat, but it revealed a peep of sky-blue shirt and a tie drawn through a golden ring. He took us into a vast—at least so it appeared to my eyes—studio in which the many lovely coloured pictures—poems in paint—seemed to a child nurtured on the *Myths of Hellas* and *Morte d'Arthur*, so many illustrations of all her favourite legends.

Entranced, I gaped at the beautiful, drooping, ethereal maidens robed in flowing draperies, and the wan palely-loitering knights in shining armour—all beautiful, all subtly ailing, denizens of some enchanted misty moonlit realm—a realm my conception of which was for many years to tinge my vision of the actual world.

Because in it every single picture was deliberately romantic in subject as well as in treatment, the influence of that studio—one I was very slow to shake off—was to make me look away from, instead of into life for Beauty.

To my disappointment the sitting took place not in this enthralling studio, but in the comparative tameness of a pale, subdued drawing-room that implicitly obeyed Ruskin's dictum that a room should contain nothing that you did not either believe to be beautiful or else know to be useful. Having deposited me in this rarefied atmosphere, my mother, after the dreadful way of mothers, disappeared, leaving me alone with the artist. Straining my memory's eye, I can see his white beard, sad, amused face and large, gentle, blue eyes. Much more distinctly, I hear his very soft yet deep rumbling voice, the tone of which for some inexplicable reason brought into my mind the line, "The Owl and the Pussycat went to sea in a beautiful pea-green boat". At first I was rigid with shyness, but Burne-Jones was so kind and, in a gentle way, so deliciously funny, that I soon felt quite comfortable. Of course I was prepared to like him. Had I not been told of his lovable practice of drawing on the wall delicious pictures of "spression" animals in the corners of the nurseries in his house at Rottingdean, so that any grandchild who was Put-In-The-Corner for naughtiness, should pass a blissful, instead of a tedious quarter of an hour. In those days being Put-In-The-Corner was the stock punishment. I hated it, but how those lucky Rottingdean children must have vied with one another to incur it!

I wish I had been older, for from all I have been told, Burne-Jones was one of the most entrancing of talkers. Even though I was only seven, I remember how the fun in his mind made my own thoughts dance about. I have a vague memory of the intermittent hovering presence of an exceedingly grave but kind lady—very tiny but immensely dignified. This was Lady Burne-Jones. More vividly I remember the coming into the room of a lovely fairy-story apparition—a sprite—with eyes like blue flowers. This was the artist's cherished only daughter, Margaret Mackail, whom I was afterwards to know well, and to love. As witty as she was beautiful—few have had a more individual flavour in talk—she had a magic touch with children. How I loved that institution of hers called a Bad Behaviour Meal at which children must do exactly what they are always told not to do—plant both elbows on the table, gobble their food, talk with their mouths full, and so on.

Margaret Mackail, and her very handsome silver-haired husband, Jack Mackail, pre-eminent Greek scholar, and the most complete walking encyclopaedia I've ever met, were life-long friends of my mother, as their children, Angela Thirkell and Denis Mackail, have been of mine.

My only other memory of that long, long ago sitting is of the embarrassing intrusion of a lady whom I thought odiously gushing. Bursting into the room, she clasped her hands and bleated out, "Oh, what a dear little damsel in white! But she *is* a Burne-Jones!" What she meant I had no idea. Little did I know I was being labelled an anachronism. Just as well—for

the pre-Raphaelite vogue was already well on the wane—
might she have pronounced me born some thirty years too
late. Yes, in the parlance of to-day, I had missed the bus.

That is all I can tell you of a sitting to an artist who, had he
been born five hundred instead of a hundred and sixteen years
ago, could scarcely have belonged to an age more utterly
remote from our own. But I still possess his lovely drawing, and
I find it terribly touching. Indeed, I confess I can scarcely look
at that little girl, all unconscious of her doom—such a podgy
somnambulistic little girl with her curtains of straight hair,
wide wavy mouth, and no nose to speak of—without my eye-
lids pricking.

That first sight of an artist's studio left me an ardent lover of
Burne-Jones, and the moment I acquired a cheque-book of my
own, I rushed out to buy framed photographs of twelve of his
pictures. I then felt a woman of property. At that time almost
my only other possessions were four mounted foxes' brushes.
These cherished trophies of the chase I looped over the frames
containing Sir Galahad, Aurora, the Beggar Maid, and the
Beguiling of Merlin—an almost Surrealist juxtaposition in which
I saw nothing in the least incongruous. . . .

My second studio was G. F. Watts's. To this I was taken by
Grandpapa Wemyss, not as a model this time, but as a devout
pilgrim. While we clopped along for what seemed hours and
hours in a brougham, Grandpapa told me that "Signor", as
Watts was called by his friends, had just celebrated his eightieth
birthday, when he had had eighty candles on his cake. Also,
that he always got up at four o'clock every morning to start his
day's work. I have no clear visual memory of Watts. I only
remember that he looked very frail, wore a black silk skull cap
and, like Burne-Jones in this, if in nothing else, had a white
beard. There was an atmosphere of calm, steady toil in his
large studio. It was thrillingly full of scaffolding, pulleys and
ropes, palettes and oozing tubes of paint.

For some little time the artist painted while we stood at his
side, but to my great surprise Grandpapa, who usually told
everyone how to do their own jobs, did not show him how he
should hold his brush. Instead, he kept on asking his grand-

daughter whether she did not like this and that picture, and which one she admired most. This cross-examination made me almost sick with shyness. I did like the pictures, but had no idea what to say about them. I felt, not for the last time, like a tap that wouldn't turn on. At last I mumbled something about Love and Death being "very nice", but was painfully aware that with the word "nice" I had not hit on the right adjective. The picture of Hope seated on the globe of the world with but one string of her lute still unbroken, I already knew well—at that time there can scarcely have been a schoolroom in England without a photograph of this favourite—and I had long been pleasurably terrified by those two nightmares of Watts's imagination, Mammon, and the Minotaur.

But the Watts picture that moved me much the most was the one of Paolo and Francesca, that hapless twain, condemned to drift for ever and ever through space and eternity. As, however, the lovers were in one another's arms, I at first supposed them, despite their lack of harps and haloes, to be in some strange sort of heaven. Tartly my governess put me right on this point. "They are in Hell", she said firmly. "They sinned."

Now I come to think of it, I could not on that particular day have seen any of the pictures I have mentioned for they were already in public galleries, but by some strange telescoping of memory, in my mind's eye I see them all assembled in that studio.

One picture I did see there was of a lovely flower-strewn creature drifting down a swiftly flowing stream—Ophelia, they told me her name was. What a lovely name, I thought— like a long, long sigh. But when I described "Ophelia" to my mother, she told me the picture was really of Ellen Terry, who had once been the artist's wife. I asked how long ago she had died, and was very much bewildered to hear she was still alive, for of any end to marriage other than death, I had not yet heard—astonishing ignorance to any seven-year-old child of to-day!

Because Burne-Jones was a great friend of my mother's, and Watts a great friend of my aunt Evelyn De Vesci's, family loyalty compelled my cousin, Mary Vesey and myself, to be violently partisan whenever the relative merits of these two artists were discussed, and I think they were compared quite as often and almost as futilely as were Dickens and Thackeray.

I remember how this rivalry made me represss my natural upwelling admiration for Watts. Because I had heard others say so, I would contend that his pictures were "not so much works of art as moral tracts". Most disingenuous of me, for in reality I hadn't the slightest objection to tracts (what child does not enjoy a moral?). As for allegory, I loved it! Had I not been brought up on *Pilgrim's Progress*? Sometimes, driven to attempt almost technical criticism, I would plead, "But look at the beauty of Burne-Jones's treatment of *drapery*". In the last resort I pompously produced my trump card by parrotting a charge often brought against the artist, "Watts is not a great colourist".

My second sitting was to Charles Furse, whose Diana of the Uplands had recently been the picture of the year at the Royal Academy. I sat to him while we were both on a visit to George Wyndham and his wife, Lady Grosvenor, at Saighton Grange. For some mysterious reason I was posed in a glass greenhouse full of ferns, and, though I was dressed in blue and the weather was extremely hot, depicted against a background of snow in a Red Riding Hood cloak—all very puzzling to my eight-year-old self. Except for the greenhouse and my surprise at the snow, I remember nothing of this sitting except how onlookers broke all schoolroom canons by making personal remarks and my utter amazement when the snub nose about which my brothers were always so rude was *commended*!

Except that he had a black beard—evidently a beard was the one common denominator between all artists—I remember nothing about Charles Furse.

"Why do all artists have beards?" I broke my customary silence to ask. "To wipe their paint-brushes on, of course", replied some wag. That was just the sort of joke grown-up people used to make to children.

My next memory of sitting is very vivid. A "flapper" of fifteen, I am precariously posed on a hard stool in a cold room at Gosford temporarily called the "studio". Three people are drawing me simultaneously—my grandfather and two guests of his, the Duchess of Rutland and her daughter, Marjorie Manners.[1] For once I am not in the very least self-conscious. The spectacular beauty of that mother and daughter has startled me out of egocentricity. Their two so different faces enthral me—the mother's still, sculptured beauty, with her superb bone structure and the faintly sinister strangeness of her eyes so deeply set in shadowy caverns; and—in ravishing contrast—the fluttering, wistful, *espiègle* loveliness of the daughter.

Marjorie Manners! I remember no face more difficult to take one's eyes off than hers!

The Inferiority Complex had not yet been christened, but anonymity did not prevent it from torturing me. With her dancing golden-brown eyes, raying lashes, elfin grace and bewitching attire, Marjorie had everything to inflame it. She made me feel a gawky, large-footed hoyden. She was also dazzlingly "accomplished", a word now rapidly becoming obsolete that in those pre-gramophone and pre-wireless days was still very much in use. Yes, without doubt every conceivable fairy godmother had attended Marjorie's christening, each bringing her the gift of some talent. She could sing— across all these years I can hear her voice trill out, "Ah! Love, could'st Thou and I with Fate conspire"—she also had a remarkable talent for drawing and was a devastatingly brilliant mimic. To say that I envied this dazzling being would be an understatement.

Next to the beauty of this mother and daughter, my most vivid memory of that day is the fuss about my coiffure. Hankering after a more fashionable and, I hoped, more becoming effect, I had recently started surreptitiously to fluff out my hair by a process called "backcombing", and, abolishing the centre-parting, had piled half of it on to the top of my head and plaited the residue into what was called a carthorse's tail—a doubled-up affair tied with an immense bow of satin ribbon. But to my chagrin, for this occasion my ambitions to Young-Ladify myself were ruthlessly crushed; my furtively fuzzed-out hair flattened back into the old uncompromisingly severe lines.

[1] Afterwards Marchioness of Anglesey.

"Why ever should you want to make yourself look like everyone else?"asked the three artists—surely no very intelligent question to put to a girl of fifteen.

Other amateurs to whom I remember sitting were Lady Lodge (Sir Oliver's wife), Mrs. Harry Cust, and much later on and with two excellent results to Lady Norah Brassey....

Now I jump to my first "Season", throughout which I sat to Wilfrid de Glehn, an artist—the first beardless one I had met—with whom I'd just made friends. For this occasion Miss Charteris (as I am now called) is in full evening dress, with her never very obliging hair defiantly "back-combed" and heavily laden with ornamental combs. The most atrocious of these were actually of blue enamel!

These sittings in a delightful house in Cheyne Walk were graced by the artist's charming wife, Jane, so much envied for her exquisite profile. They were very pleasant. At first we just talked. This, though enjoyable, was not compatible with the requisite stillness. So Jane read Kipling aloud—his short stories —but my horror over *The End of the Passage* so much distorted my gutta-percha countenance that it had to be discontinued.

Wilfrid de Glehn exhibited one portrait of me in the Royal Academy, and then painted another; but he cannot have been satisfied with either, because instead of, as he had promised, giving one of them to me, he gave me the beautiful watercolour of Venice that you saw in my dining-room.

Towards the end of my first season I sat to Sargent. In his uncompromisingly black and white, forcible—even perhaps slightly blatant—charcoal drawing, finished, if I remember rightly, in two sittings, there was nothing whatever in common with earlier pre-Raphaelitish versions of me.

Mrs. Val Prinsep is alleged to have told her nieces always to read their Bibles before going to dances so as "to give themselves heavenly expressions". Thank heaven, a look of purposed soulfulness was never enjoined on me, but there was, I think, nevertheless a slight tendency among my contemporaries, though of course not deliberate, to look vaguely wistful. "Otherworldliness"? More, I think, as though, in a state of semi-suspension, you lived in momentary expectation of meeting your "Affinity", at recognition of whom you would, with Dante Gabriel Rossetti, exclaim, "I have been here before!"

But there was nothing of the Soul's Awakening, Lady of Shalottish or remotely "Greenery-Yallery" in the surly, sullen, hefty-looking lass of Sargent's portrait. Square-faced as Holbein's Henry the Eighth, she has a most determined jowl; also a distinct, what in Russian fiction is politely called a cast but in plain unvarnished English is a squint, mercifully an outward one.

Large, virile, plethoric, with protruding eyes and a sort of over-boiled, throttled look, Sargent was, in himself as well as in his art, as great a contrast to Burne-Jones as could be imagined. A curiously inarticulate man, he used to splutter and gasp, almost growl with the strain of trying to express himself; and sometimes, like Macbeth at the dagger, he would literally clutch at the air in frustrated efforts to find with many intermediary "ers" and "ums", the most ordinary words.

He gave himself plenty of physical exercise while he drew, for, like a bowler about to deliver a ball, he always took quite a long run at his easel in between every few strokes, and from time to time he broke off to thunder on the piano. When pleased with the way his work was going, he emitted a contented kettle-on-the-hearth noise; when dissatisfied, he repeatedly muttered the word "Demons" under his breath.

Various people came in while I was being drawn. If the artist were obviously fidgeted by their presence, his model was excruciatingly embarrassed by their personal remarks, for I was still afflicted by the hampering self-consciousness that was not to leave me until I was well over forty, I think, when, blessed deliverance, it left me so completely that I now find it difficult —so little memory has one even for one's own dead selves—to make sufficient allowance for its crippling effect on the young. Oh to be young again and NOT shy!

Far the most distracting as well as the most glamorous visitor was Mrs. Patrick Campbell. Enthralling, fantastically witty, and always a most disturbing presence—she used literally to send my temperature up—this beautiful actress, then at the height of her fame, provoked an absolute volley of "Demons'es".

Like one moving to music she made a slow undulating entry and took the centre of the stage.

"Oh, you are trying to draw my golden Frog!" she warbled in that wonderful husky, *troublante* voice. "Isn't she Batrachian?" (She always accused me of having misappropriated the features of a frog.) "Mind you get the preposterous width between her green eyes. They're so far apart that if a fly wanted to go from one to another he would have to take a fly—I mean a cab."

Sargent was not in the least amused by this extravagance, but to his annoyance the "frog" giggled.

"I don't think she's like a frog", demurred some other onlooker, "she's more like a cat—not a hearth-rug pussy, larger and semi-wild, but definitely feline."

"No, no, no! She-is-the-great-Golden-Frog-of-the-Western-World", trilled Mrs. Pat in her best Mélisande voice, her lovely throat rippling up and down like Maud Adams's arms.

The expression on Sargent's face suggested that—just as Dr. Johnson considered a cow, though a very good animal in a field, one to be turned out of a garden—so he thought Mrs. Pat, though a very good animal on the stage, one to be turned out of a studio.

The offender now produced and held up a singularly unpleasing object, a tiny portable dog—a griffon, I think—hitherto concealed in one of her cascading sleeves.

"Wouldn't you like to draw my Pinky-Ponky-Poo?" intoned the actress; her voice, now like the stage-wind in an Irish play, making the words sound pure poetry. "Isn't he be-yoo-ti-ful? He's got Wemyss's whiskers, Balfour's nose and Marjorie Manners's eyes!"

Sargent eyed the so-called dog with great distaste.

"I like *big* dogs", he said curtly.

"If you were a real artist, you would want to draw my lovely Pinky-Ponky-Poo instead of that plump, pale frog", sang Mrs. Pat.

Sargent grunted and drew out his watch. Piqued by his lack of response, Mrs. Pat returned to the charge.

"But my dear Man, you mustn't make my golden Frog's

hair *black*. Can't you see it's the colour of the best marmalade?"

"Demons! Demons!! Demons!!!" spluttered the purpling artist. "Since the er-um medium in which I am *trying* to work is black and white, how can I make Miss Charteris's hair look er-um fairer without making it er-um appear to be *white*?"

At the sixth "Demons", someone firmly led the Prima Donna off-stage. . . .

Decidedly not a comfortable sitting. Nor did I greatly care for the result.

Though Sargent was one of the most likeable of men, I cannot say that I ever felt really at my ease with him, not even after I grew up. His own shyness was too contagious.

That sitting was not my first meeting with him. Some time before I came out, Eliza Wedgwood, who was a great friend of his, had taken me to one of his musical parties.

It was then that I first met Tonks who became and remained one of my greatest friends until his death in 1937. We were never introduced to one another and, goodness knows, our first exchange of words was sufficiently absurd.

It was the first musical party I had ever been to; indeed, it was the first grown-up party of any kind.

"When music sounds, gone is the world I know. . . .?" I confess I was much too distracted by the spectacle of such quantities of human beings packed together in serried rows of gold chairs to be able to give more than half an ear to the music. Suddenly, half way through a concerto I became acutely aware that two men, one very cadaverous, the other very rounded, were staring at me. What was more, as well as scrutinising me they were obviously quite openly discussing me, just as though, instead of being a sentient fellow-guest, I were a picture or a map. What was wrong? My hand flew up to the back of my head to feel if my hair—always an anxiety— had come down. Nothing amiss there. Was there a smut on my face? What girl now alive could believe it, but I was without a pocket mirror. I had, you see, no pocket and I did not carry a handbag. I used to look at my reflection in spoons!

At last the music left off yearning like a god in pain. The two men whose behaviour had so much disconcerted me immediately rose and came up to where I stood against the wall, for I had arrived too late to occupy a golden chair. The tall cadaverous man addressed me. "You simply must sit, Miss Charteris", he said peremptorily.

My vanity winced. The last thing I wanted was commiseration. After all I was not at a *dance*. Why should I be mortified by the sympathy due to wallflowers?

Discomfited, I mumbled something about being "perfectly happy standing, thank-you". Tonks—the cadaverous one— gave the little short bark of a laugh I was to know so well. "I mean you must sit to *artists*", he explained. "To begin with, to me and to my friend, Steer", he indicated his silent, benign-looking rounded companion.

"Steer is the most distinguished painter alive", he added aggressively, almost angrily, as though I were likely to dispute the claim. Unable to think what to say, I produced what I hoped was a suitably deferential mumble.

"Has anyone told you that you are a Pre-Raphaelite, Miss Charteris?" asked Tonks.

Oh dear! With my hair atrociously over-tonged and fashionably, however disfiguringly, "dressed" by an expert, I was trying to pass myself off to myself as quite up-to-date. Yes, I hoped I was looking what would now be called "Edwardian".

It was then that Tonks so warmly congratulated himself on the "queerness" of my face.

To my relief the music began again, and the embarrassing strangers left me to myself.

Ignoramus that I was, I had never heard of Steer, but Eliza Wedgwood told me all about him in the next interval. She also enthusiastically edited Tonks, informing me that besides being a distinguished painter, he was the revered, redoubtable, dreaded and loved master at the Slade. Many people, she added, considered him the greatest living teacher of drawing.

I don't remember when I next saw Tonks, but however long the interval, I should not have forgotten him. Tall, lean and angular, he was an arresting figure. The remarkably high bridge to his nose gave his profile the look of a battleaxe, and from this jutting salient of a nose, deep, flying-buttress lines ran to the corners of his mouth; a grim mouth, but the eyes were kindly. He looked like an anchorite, which indeed was what he was, an anchorite of Art, who regarded painting as a solemn holy craft; himself as its humble dedicant.

His working hours were sacred. Callers would find affixed to his front door the notice in large lettering, "Hours of WORK Midday to 8 p.m." Between those hours very few dared to ring the bell. As soon would I have interrupted a religious service to ask the officiating priest to have a chat.

It was not that Tonks did not enjoy the company of his fellow-creatures. He delighted in it; but to encroach upon his working hours was to rob him of his most precious commodity —time in which to draw and to paint. "I live much alone now", he wrote to me after he retired from the Slade, " and in many ways I like it, not because I do not get pleasure from human society. I do—particularly I like to know what the gifted young are thinking—but because it is the surest way to liberty."

By "liberty", he meant, of course, not leisure, but the utmost possible opportunity for work.

His invaluable housekeeper, Mrs. Gough, gave an amnsing account of how she once infuriated him when, tethered by illness to his bed, he was chafing with impatience at being prevented from getting on with his picture. To console him, Mrs. Gough said, "Never mind, Professor. To-morrow I'll bring you your easel, and you'll be able to amuse yourself in bed."

Bursting with indignation, Tonks started up on his pillow. "Amuse myself!" he fulminated. "Amuse myself!!! Let me tell you, Woman, my painting is not my amusement. It is my LIFE! ... Amuse myself indeed!"

The picture-gallery of my memory holds no portrait more distinct than Tonks's. His angular character was so clearly outlined, so boldly, strongly, economically drawn. "Not quite yourself to-day, are you?" How often is that said to most of us. I doubt if it was ever said to Tonks. Invariably, unmitigatedly, he *was* his singular self. Had six of his friends written character-sketches of him, their descriptions would, I'm sure, have tallied on every point. No one could fail to see his utter integrity, or that he was original, independent, vehement and uncompromising. As for his many endearing oddities and prejudices, they simply jutted out of him.

I have never known anyone so exclusively impelled by one single dominating purpose. Had he been Ulysses, he would have had no need to seal his ears against the song of the sirens. The preoccupation provided by pencil and paper would have been ample protection. Only one thing had power to distract his mind, or to deflect him from his determination to draw or paint. That was a friend in distress.

It must be admitted that Tonks who did not suffer fools gladly, could be as terse as his monosyllabic name. Added to this, his almost fierce defence of his privacy, his occasional sardonic outspokenness—he didn't always temper his words to the timid—his very countenance, undeniably severe except when transfigured by a delighted and delighting smile, made many people mistake him for a harsh, almost a ruthless man. In reality he was one of the kindest of human beings and the fondest of friends. His devotion to Steer whom he considered the greatest painter of his time was most touching. For nearly forty years he looked after this wise, simple and lovable friend with the utmost devotion. Every cold in the head—a malady most incident to Steer—was watched over with intense concern. As for Tonks's anguish when tragedy swooped and Steer's precious sight began to fail, it was unforgettable.

"There is no drawing without tears", was one of Tonks's axioms, and he could be harshly outspoken to any pupil whom he suspected of dilettantism. He is alleged to have reduced girl students to tears by the crushing question, "Can't you sew, cook, or knit?"

To him, teaching was an office only to be undertaken with the utmost seriousness and he was not going to waste his time or valuable space at the Slade teaching the frivolous or wholly untalented. That he should have been elected to teach drawing at the Slade filled him with deep humility. At times, indeed, he was almost overwhelmed by the sense of his responsibility. "Teaching is a terribly dangerous game", I remember his saying, wagging an admonitory forefinger and speaking with great trepidation. "It appals me to think how strong an influence over a beautiful natural gift a much less gifted man may exercise."

This responsibility was endured for nearly forty years, during which Tonks inspired an almost reverent devotion in hundreds of students. His delight at the discovery of any great talent was always eagerly expressed. The two pupils of whom I remember his speaking with the most excited enthusiasm were Rex Whistler and Daphne Baring. He invariably deplored the marriage of any student whom he considered promising. In his opinion it gravely jeopardised even a young man's career. For a woman artist he thought it fatal! I shall never forget the tragi-comic vehemence with which he bemoaned the marriage —"apostasy" he called it—of the brilliantly gifted Daphne Baring.

Had I not known it, I fancy I should have guessed that Tonks had been a surgeon before he became an artist. His appearance suggested an operating-theatre much more than a studio, and I used to think he looked like the portrait of a great surgeon, painted by a great artist. He loved to tell how as a medical student he had spent all his spare (and much of his unspare) time in drawing the human body—dead or alive—hence the origin of his remarkable knowledge of anatomy. He never lost his interest in medicine and surgery, and it was an immense satisfaction to him that he was able to utilise both trainings in his war-work. Attached to the Cambridge Hospital, he became the official chronicler of facial wounds, and the hundreds of pastel drawings made by him of the injuries both before and after repair, record all the cases treated by the great plastic surgeon, Sir Harold Gillies. After he had worked for some months at this macabre job, I remember his telling me that he had begun to find the look of an *intact* face quite insipid.

Throughout the years of the First World War I used often to bicycle from Baker Street to Chelsea to dine with Tonks in his house in Vale Avenue. Though by choice he lived with a simplicity bordering on austerity, Tonks loved to give his friends good wine. Usually a saddle of mutton was provided for dinner—in his opinion the proper enjoyment of claret demanded the plainest food—followed by biscuits and cheese. A wooden bowl filled with apples always stood in the centre of the table.

After dinner we used to go up to the chaotic studio—dozens of canvases all with their faces turned to the wall, plaster-casts, odds and ends of raiment and drapery, and one rapidly decomposing, jointed lay-figure. The whole of the large room was given up to work except for a small civilised area round the fire—a log fire that Tonks loved to poke into blaze. At this pleasant fireside we would often be joined by Steer and George Moore.

The gentle, unargumentative Steer—sweetness itself—as little angular in character as in physical build, was as unlike his greatest friend, Tonks, as could be imagined. After delivering himself of a few quietly sagacious remarks, he would usually fold his artist's hands across his comfortably rounded stomach and fall gently and quite inaudibly asleep. Tonks never failed to be delighted by his friend's enviable capacity to "drop off", however loud the controversy, and then just as suddenly to awake from his sleep to make some very mild but often quite conclusive contribution to the argument. Steer's remarks were nearly always received with deference, but at the more extravagant of George Moore's conversational gambits the host would snort, wink and shrug his shoulders in mingled irritation, mockery and delight—a pantomime expressive of Tonks's general attitude to the friend whom he described as being "in many ways a child of four". Occasionally, indeed frequently, he would be maddened by this "child of four" and the demands it made on his time, but he had an immense respect for George Moore's verbal artistry, and the Irishman had another great recommendation. To a caricaturist he could never pall as a model. Many of Tonks's best drawings are of George Moore "getting into bed trailing Cupids and roses" (I quote from Mary Hutchinson's lovely foreword to Hone's admirable biography of Tonks).

On the subject of wine, probably after Art the most sacred thing to Tonks, George Moore was considered an utter Philistine. There was a memorable scene when E. H. Coles

H   95

(always called "Coley") the friend to whom Tonks bequeathed his cellar, was dining in Vale Avenue. Host and guest, each wondering what the vintners could buy one half so precious as the stuff they sell, were considering with intense seriousness the relative merits of the two kinds of sherry between the choice of which Tonks was hovering.

There came a ring at the bell.

With a scared face, Tonks exclaimed, "Surely that can't be George Moore!" The company held its breath. A murmur of voices was heard. Tonks became almost frenzied. "It *is* him!" he wailed, "My God! My God! My God! The evening is ruined! We shan't be able to talk about wine!"

Enter George Moore. . . .

Scarcely glancing at him, Tonks said in a cold even voice, "Good evening, Moore." Then very curtly he introduced Coley and pointed the intruder to a hard unsympathetic chair. "Now, Moore, you must admit that I never asked *you* to come here to-night?"

George Moore admitted this indisputable fact.

"Very well, then," said Tonks, wagging, as was his wont when put out, his craggy forefinger. "Then you can't blame me if you have to listen to wine talk."

George Moore feebly waved his white, curiously boneless hands, and subsided on to the sofa. He looked like a dejected slug. Ignoring him, Tonks proceeded exhaustively to discuss sherry and claret with Coley.

But Coley's uncontrollable courtesy soon compelled him to try to bridge the gulf. Somehow—I can't remember how—he contrived to mention Wagner. Thrown this lifeline and finding in Coley an enlightened and deferential listener, George Moore revived and became eloquent and interesting.

Before long, Tonks, who at first had sat erect on the sofa, looking very sulky and frustrated, joined in the talk, livened up, and soon all was going well. When at last George Moore rose to go, his host cordially saw him off and came back saying, "Never have I seen George Moore in such splendid form. I had quite made up my mind not to see any more of him, but now I've promised to dine with him to-morrow."

This exemplifies the see-saw of Tonks's feelings towards George Moore, as well as his unwavering contempt for his palate, but however much Tonks's personal regard for George Moore might vary, he did always pay him the compliment of considering him qualified to hold and even to express opinions on painting, a subject in discussing which most people found themselves on the horns of a perpetual dilemma.

"What do you think of the New English this year?" he would ask. If, shamefacedly, I had to admit that I had not yet found time to visit this exhibition, he would blaze out, "Not been to the New English yet! But what more important than that can *you* possibly have to do?"

If, on the other hand, I ventured on some tentative criticism, he would be almost equally violent. "But how can *you* possibly know? No one," he asserted, almost waggling the top-joint off his forefinger in his vehemence, "no one who has not painted for years can possibly judge a picture!"

After he retired from the Slade and had more time for reading, Tonks discovered Shakespeare and became a passionate devotee. Because of his engaging love of piloting friends into the realms of gold, he would be quite taken aback, not to say hurt, to find you already knew some famous purple passage the beauty of which had only just swum into his ken. One day he began to quote "Our revels now are ended". Tactlessly I finished the passage—always an irritating thing to do. Never shall I forget how his face fell. His chin seemed to drop on to his chest. "Oh, *you* know those lines!" he said, as crestfallen as a child who finds his supposedly secret treasure cave is common knowledge. It was the same with his discovery of contemporary writers of whose existence he always hoped to find you ignorant. "I wonder if you have heard of T. S. Eliot as a poet?" he once jubilantly asked, and was evidently deeply displeased to hear that I had.

Decidedly it was not always easy to know how to please Tonks in conversation. Though he so much liked those whom he liked to share his opinions, he also loved argument for argument's sake—enjoyed the exercise. Forgetting his deferential nephew was only fourteen, he once shouted at the wretched boy, "My God! My God! Don't agree with me! ARGUE with me!"

Sitting to Tonks was very reposeful, for whenever he was at work the drawbridge would always be definitely up and all visitors were regarded as intruders. If anyone did break in, they were never asked to criticise. As for unsolicited comment, it infuriated him. But though Tonks always found it so hard to tolerate criticism, he was without a vestige of complacency, and always touchingly and avowedly aware that Steer was a greater artist than himself.

Like most over-zealous workers, Tonks seldom knew when to leave well alone. Once while he was doing a pastel of me, Steer very gently said, "Has it not occurred to you, Tonks, that that picture is finished?"

At which, to my surprise—for I had just been told to return for another sitting—the chalks were promptly and meekly laid down.

I remember how often in the wonderfully inviolate atmosphere of his studio Tonks would congratulate himself on not possessing, or as he put it, not being possessed by either a car or a telephone. In his opinion, practically every scientific invention only further complicated instead of simplifying life. As for the shrinkage of distance brought about by motor-cars, it terrified him.

"He who makes many acquaintances doeth it to his own destruction." Do *you* agree with this Hebrew proverb? Evidently not. You certainly don't act upon it. Tonks did.

How he used to deplore McEvoy's extreme accessibility! "All artists", he once said to me in his most emphatic manner, "should eat disgustingly or else have some equally effective social disqualification that will prevent them being asked out. See too many people, become an amiable member of Society, and the mind goes out of your art. . . . It isn't that I don't like people. I do. But they interfere with my WORK. . . . I delight in the company of many people, but with those who are merely social, I cannot feel at home. I suppose it is because as an artist I have a religion, and they have none."

However jealously Tonks guarded his time, he was never, as

are some reluctant lions, uncivil in his refusal of an invitation. Once—only once—I had the effrontery to ask him to come to a party during his working hours! His firm but courteous refusal was characteristic.

"I can only suppose", he wrote, "that your intense love of the comic has got the better of you and that, hearing the Prince of Wales is about to present to the Zoo an exceptionally strange antediluvian animal, you said to yourself, I too will exhibit my antediluvian animal. So you have asked me to Michael's coming-of-age party. There can be no doubt that my presence *would* cause much merriment and you know that I love to help you in all things. Nevertheless I must ask you to excuse me."

On the very rare occasions when for the sake of some friend in trouble Tonks did consent to break through his sacred routine, he naturally liked the outing to go according to plan and deeply resented any other claim on the attention of the person so signally honoured. Once when I had beeen very ill—officially I was still forbidden visitors—he was good enough to come all the way to Regents Park to see me. This was the occasion of a comic collision between him and another visitor, who was likewise under the impression that *he* was to be the only one.

Tonks arrived punctually at the appointed hour—a working hour!—of five-thirty. Unluckily Barrie, who I did not expect before six-fifteen, arrived at five-forty-five.

At Barrie's entrance into the sick-room, Tonks, looking very tall and cadaverous, indignantly rose to his full height and reassuming his discarded doctor's mantle, firmly asserted himself.

"Lady Cynthia should not have two visitors at the same time", he declared with the utmost professional authority, and obviously quite confident that Barrie would flee and await his turn below.

But he had met his match. The intruder was undeflectable. Barrie, his Scots accent thickening, as it always did in answer to a challenge, retaliated as if *he* were the physician-in-charge. "No, she certainly should not", he agreed. "But it won't matter your staying another two minutes", he added handsomely, consulting his watch as he spoke.

After this concession the invalid closed her eyes while completely ignoring her, the painter and the dramatist, each obstinately standing, talked at wholly cross purposes across her bed.

After the longest half hour I can remember, the hospital nurse came in to find her bronchial patient choking in dense clouds of tobacco smoke. Outraged, she drove my two self-appointed medical advisers from the room. . . .

Tonks was always expatiating on the brilliance and poetic quality of his sometime pupil, McEvoy. "That's the man to paint you!" he would tell me.

One day—I think it must have been in 1916—someone took me to see this artist of whom I had heard so much. I have seldom taken a more instant liking to anyone. Alertly alive, tautly overstrung, hair-trigger responsive to talk to, he was one of those people with whom you go through no probationary phase of acquaintanceship but immediately recognise as a friend. It's like beginning a book in the second volume.

Two days later I had a letter from McEvoy asking me to sit to him, and the following day I bicycled to his house on the Chelsea Embankment for the first, I should think, of a hundred sittings—all equally enjoyable, all equally exhausting.

McEvoy's studio in 107 Grosvenor Road was very small. Stacks of half-finished portraits made it almost impossible for one to move about. One day, in trying to thread my way to my chair, I brushed up against a canvas on which the paint was not yet dry. Imagine my horror when I saw that most of the Spanish Ambassadress's profile had come off on my white skirt! Appalled, I stammered out apologies for the damage I had done. Incredibly, McEvoy seemed far more concerned with the state of my new dress. Yet he had no idea how much it mattered. I had not told him I should not have been wearing what had been specially designed and made for the next day when, at Winston Churchill's invitation, I was, thrilling experience, to launch a ship—the last to be launched while he was First Lord of the Admiralty.

The artist's feverish first aid efforts with turpentine made matters much worse, but Mrs. McEvoy came to the rescue with benzine.

Even so, when I launched the lovely ship (alas, so soon to be sunk) I had to remember on which side to carry my handbag, so that it should cover the still only partially obliterated transfer of Her Excellency's face.

To console me for the harm I had done to his picture, McEvoy assured me that the Ambassadress's face was in any case just about to be painted over. This may well have been true, for despite his being so individual an artist, McEvoy's pliability of mind made him so open to suggestion that at a word he would scrap lovely all but finished paintings; and unfortunately he always invited criticism even from those quite unqualified to give it. From this—the defect of his qualities—his output suffered sadly. Though on and off I sat to him for years during which innumerable oil portraits were begun, all that survived at the end were the two watercolours I showed you.

To my amusement Tonks told me how austere and aloof McEvoy had been in his prentice days. Insisting that an artist must be a recluse, he used impassionedly to warn Tonks, of all people in the world, against "going into Society".

"You start going to lunch with Lady Cunard, Tonks, and you are done!"

You can imagine how Tonks chuckled over this story.

By the time I knew McEvoy it was, indeed, difficult to believe this tale of one so utterly without defences as he had become. He was already far embarked on what, to one who though so intensely vital was never robust, was the disastrous double overstrain of over-much work and over-much social activity. Too amiable, too easily amused to refuse any invitations, he had allowed his life to become as overcrowded as his studio.

Success—both professional and social—swamped him, for, since his vocabulary simply did not include the word "No", he could never refuse a commission to paint a portrait any more than he could refuse an invitation to dinner. Had he been a landscape-painter, his livelihood would inevitably occasionally have taken him into solitude, but as a portrait-painter it was so fatally easy for him simultaneously to combine excess of people with excess of work.

He always pressed me to ask people to come to the studio while I sat. Ostensibly to inspect my portrait, but really just to talk, talk, talk, friends and acquaintances crowded into that stuffy little studio, until the scene was more like a debating society than a sitting.

As I write I see the mercurial McEvoy, eyes starting out of his head with animation, suspended paintbrush shifted into his left hand to leave his right free to gesticulate while with all his eager being he talks to some member of the heterogeneous company that used to drop in to that seething studio. Who were they? I could not give an exhaustive list, but at the moment those most vivid in my memory are Charles Whibley, D. H. Lawrence, Evan Charteris, Desmond MacCarthy, Basil Blackwood, Robert Nicholls, General Bridges, Alex Thynne, Sir Ian Hamilton—except for the first two, they were all of them, even, anomalously enough, the artist himself, then in uniform.

Great fun these symposiums were, but disastrous to the portrait's progress, for like a doctor called in to a case, each visitor felt obliged to give some opinion, however perfunctory, and unfortunately McEvoy took them all quite seriously with fatal Penelope-web consequences. I could have wept to see so many lovely beginnings abandoned.

In so individual an artist, this influencibility of McEvoy's was astonishing. He really seemed to respect anyone else's judgment more than his own. "Do you think it will come?" he would feverishly ask in a quiver of suspense, and then, to my annoyance, be visibly set up or cast down according to the often quite valueless verdict.

Besides his disastrous deference to other people's opinions, he was also much too easily deflected from his chosen course by some chance new impression of his model. To see one differently dressed—say in tweeds instead of in a tea-gown—was enough to give him so different a conception of one's personality, that he would insist on a fresh start. If only he had embarked on a new canvas! Alas, he nearly always painted *over* his previous work. Thus, on a sudden whim, the result of weeks of work would in an instant be destroyed.

Neither were the idiosyncrasies of his technique conducive to finished work. "Now I must put you under the tap!" he would startlingly exclaim in the middle of a watercolour, and run out of the room to reappear with a blurred, opalescent— often lovely but, inevitably, quite different picture. Or he would be seized by a sudden impulse to paint by artificial instead of by natural light; the curtains would be drawn, the electric light turned on.

Never can any artist have had more need of an impresario; above all of someone to tell him when a picture was finished.

The moment I saw that he was about to begin to spoil the two lovely watercolours he did of my son Simon, his godchild, I secured them by firmly carrying them off before the paint was dry. Simon was very young—only three, I think, when the first of these was done. Hearing he was to be "painted", he thought he was to undergo the operation to which the front-door had just been subjected. He burst into floods of tears. Simon's other godfather, Barrie, convinced that he, and he only, could keep the child still, insisted on attending this sitting which was in our nursery. His demoralising method was to strike the contents of at least twenty match-boxes. Why such a fascinating display of fireworks should have been expected to keep a child still, I can't imagine, but it certainly prevented Simon, whose natural reaction was of course to puff out each match as soon as it was lit, from being bored.

When I described this fantastic sitting to Tonks, he said he must paint a Conversation Piece of the scene—the two god-fathers; the excitable artist, painting with one hand and gesticulating with the other; the silent dramatist doggedly playing with fire; the red-headed leprechaun puffing out match after match; the anxious mother hovering in the background.

To my delight McEvoy promised to paint Simon every year of his childhood.

Alas, the day I took Simon to his studio to be painted a second time is my last memory of McEvoy. Soon afterwards the news of his death saddened all who knew him and thousands who did not.

Mrs. McEvoy was one of the nicest women I have ever known. They had met one another at the Slade, where she had been one of the most promising of Tonks's pupils with a very individual style of her own. As Mrs. McEvoy she sank the artist in the wife. Relinquishing her own work to become in the most literal sense of the word a helpmate, she devoted herself to endless jobs. A restful, gentle, tuning-in presence, she perpetually hovered in the background; cleaned her husband's paintbrushes, mended his clothes, opened the front door which was never shut for more than five minutes on end, entered and—far her most difficult job—made him keep all engagements, both professional and social.

After the early death of her adored husband, Mrs. McEvoy took up her own paintbrush again for the remainder of her short life. She asked me to come and sit to her. Never shall I forget the poignancy of that sad, silent studio. Though she still painted very well, the artist in her had been too long repressed. The individuality had left her brush; her painting become the pale ghost of her husband's work.

It must have been in 1916 or 1917 that I first met Augustus John when we sat beside one another at a luncheon party given by my friend, Lady Howard de Walden. He asked me to come and sit to him the next day; if I had a previous engagement, it was unscrupulously broken. I bicycled to his house, 18 Mallard Street, Chelsea, and a portrait was begun.

I kept a copious diary—an outlet as well as a record—throughout the war. Unfortunately for my present purposes, two volumes of this have mysteriously disappeared, precisely those of the years in which I sat to John.

However, I need no record to remind me of my first meeting with anyone so striking. I remember my certainty that, even had I never heard of him, I should at once have recognised his magnitude. "Who is that?" I should have asked in any crowd.

He always gives me an impression of vast size, which is really deceptive (or is it perhaps symbolic?), because he is not actually in any way abnormally large. Others have told me that he had the same effect on them—like the shock of the first sight of a mountain to eyes accustomed to mere hills.

When I first saw Augustus John, who was then a major in the army, he was in uniform, so there was nothing whatever in his apparel to attract attention. Even had this not been so, he had already long since abandoned the earrings that had once been one of the notorious outward and visible signs of his non-conformity, and, indeed, no such externalities can ever have been needed to reinforce the strength of his personality or to make one aware of his extreme otherness.

Besides this otherness, one is also conscious of an immense, brooding vitality—often slumbering, but liable at any moment to burst into sudden blaze. Despite all—far too much—that has been said and written about John's "gipsy streak", I feel that at heart he entertains a great love of the Grand Manner in everything. Like Leonardo and Velasquez he should have been a magnificent figure at some resplendent Court. Beneath all superficial "Bohemianism" (to use a word he detests!), I divine a strong underlying reverence for standards, tradition—even ceremony. Several times I have heard him exclaim, "What beautiful manners So and So has!" and as though no higher praise could be conferred, the tone of his voice was almost devout.

On and off I sat to John for a long time, but, though several portraits were begun, alas, only one was finished. This, now in the Toronto Gallery, is I think a beautiful picture, specially remarkable—to use a cliché so overworked by the amateur critic—for its "rhythm". Some at first thought that by exaggerating the slightly Chinese upward slant of my eyelids, he had given me a sinister look, but most people came to like it. I remember how one artist who had refused to admit it to be a good likeness, suddenly exclaimed while drawing me, "I see that after all, you *are* exactly like your John portrait!"

For some time John worked on a portrait of me with my bicycle. This looked dazzlingly promising, but like so many others, was painted over.

But for the loss of those diaries, I could have told you of

many talks in John's studio. Of one visitor, an uninvited one, I need no record to remind me.

D. H. Lawrence's irruption into John's studio is one of the incidents most deeply etched on my memory. I had been lunching with him at Queen's Restaurant in Sloane Square. Hearing I was about to sit nearby, he took it into his head to come and see my portrait.

The collision between the two Red Beards was enthralling. D. H. was in a queer, challenging mood. Why the atmosphere of a studio and the impact of a brother artist should thus have affected him, I have no idea, but whatever spiritual revolt he felt made him—strange symptom—speak in Latin, a quite uncharacteristic vagary.

With his wide-brimmed black hat in his hand, he walked into the studio like some nervous, lightfooted woodland animal on the look-out for something to shy at.

There was some minutes silence during which he prowled about the studio, gloomily, mutely surveying the finished and unfinished works of art. Then, like a clock rustily clearing its throat to strike, he muttered, "Mortuus est. Mortuus est", several times. Gathering volume, his voice became a tolling bell. Suddenly, raising his head, he summed up the situation with the sepulchral utterance, "Let the DEAD PAINT THE DEAD!"

Pacing up and down, he knelled this lugubrious refrain several times.

John showed wonderful tolerance of this curious behaviour. That he had been pronounced to be dead did not seem to distress him. To one so plentifully endowed with vitality, the cap, I suppose, was too obvious a misfit to matter.

Whatever his unspoken feelings, the artist expressed great admiration for the writer's "head", and asked him to sit for a drawing. Lawrence consented, but unfortunately this plan never came off. . . .

Strange coincidence! Just as I had written the above paragraph the front door-bell rang, and when I opened the door whom should I see but Augustus John himself! It was as though, Prospero-like, I had summoned him up from the dark backward and abysm of time. After straining my eyes to focus them on him in the remote past, it was delightful to see him in the immediate present. Except for a mere sprinkling of snow on its crest, the mountain—still volcanic—was unchanged. Mountains don't mellow, do they? But I confess that word rushed into my mind.

Carelessly, I mixed him a drink—very carelessly, for to my shame be it said, it was equal parts Angostura and Gin! Equally carelessly he tossed it down . . . Lord Chesterfield could have set no finer example of manners.

We discussed our forthcoming books. Would we write of one another? If so, which would get their book published first and thus give the other the strategical advantage—the chance to return Tit for Tat?

We compared notes on the agonies of authorship—the travail, the never ceasing after-pains; above all the sheer disbelief as well as consternation with which one sometimes rereads one's own writing.

"The other day I read what I had written some months ago", wailed John, "and beads of sweat started out on my brow. Why, *why*, should I write like a minor Hebrew prophet?!!" . . .

In your last letter you again urge me when possible to draw for the sake of vividness on records written at the time instead of in retrospect. Though nearly all I wrote of sitting to Tonks, McEvoy and Augustus John was in those missing volumes, I have found a few passages about their studios. Here they are, for what they're worth.

1918. Bicycled through very heavy rain to sit to Tonks. He began another pastel. He raved about the potentialities and extreme delicacy of this particular medium—one he claims to have mastered in all the practice he has had at the hospital. Very much pleased with his beginning, he said with a sardonic chuckle that he hoped it would "anoy McEvoy".

How restful he is to sit to after the impressionable, catholic McEvoy! So concentrated. Painting so few pictures, liking so few persons. His craggy, cadaverous countenance expresses such unflinching purpose, surety of taste, inflexibility of standards and values. Talking of painters, he declared Michelangelo to be the greatest

"Swell", and expatiated on what he called his "divine sanity". He again maintained (how often have I heard him insist on this!) that a painter must always be a *poet*—"If he isn't, he should be put in the stocks", he declared and explained that whenever he spoke of Great Art—whether in painting, sculpture or architecture, what he always meant was that it had in it the element of "poetry". "But don't ask me to define", he went on, fairly flapping that inevitable forefinger, "what I mean by 'Poetry'. Very vaguely, I suppose I mean the mystery, and the spiritual side of life, though that brings me hardly any nearer to understanding it."*

Pronouncing John to be the finest draughtsman England had ever produced, he expressed unbounded admiration of his best work. "But you'll never persuade me to like his portrait of you", he added truculently.

When I spoke of the difficulty of reconciling a liking for solitude with the wish to see a great deal of a great many people, he said, "That doesn't trouble me. I am now quite deliberately 'Full Up' like a hotel. I don't want any more people in my life any more than I want any more furniture in my room."

He commented on the funny way in which I "brought my mouth to attention". Could I, please, allow it to stand at ease just for two consecutive seconds?

Unauthorised by me, Alex Thynne dropped in. Tonks very far from welcoming. "You mustn't look until I leave off working", he barked. How different from McEvoy's feverish canvassing of opinion—his avid, "Do you think it will come?" . . .

1918. Bicycled to dinner with Tonks. Overtaken by an air-raid. The suddenness with which the streets emptied was uncanny. In a second the houses swallowed up the whole population of Chelsea. Anti-aircraft guns grunted and coughed. Looking up, I saw two or three shells explode like bursting stars, and soon puffs of undispersed smoke clung like a wreath about the moon. In the darkness my bump of locality completely melted. I had no idea where Vale Avenue was. Propping my bicycle against a door I rang and rang until a head appeared at one of the windows. Fortunately that of someone able to direct me to Vale Avenue and I pedalled my way through the deserted streets. I was very glad to see a crack of a door open and Tonks peering out for me. Just as I arrived two little boys on bicycles whizzed by tootling the All Clear.

* Years later I heard him say that Housman's lecture on poetry was as good as man could hope to give.

We had dinner in the kitchen (wartime economy to save the dining-room fire), fried sole, a bottle of La Fitte 1870 (what a Philistine I felt!) and for me Cox's Orange Pippins in the dear old wooden bowl. Cheese for Tonks. He had fried the fish and the potatoes himself, and very good they were. When we adjourned to the studio, he gave me the pastel he had finished last time I came. He showed me what he hopes is to be his Magnum Opus—a painting of a Field Dressing Station—immensely impressive. Afraid that George Moore might come, he turned its face to the wall (he can't bear him to see anything unfinished).

"How right I was", he growled when the bell rang. But to my relief it was not G.M. but Steer. We had a delightful evening. I always find Steer equally lovable, awake or asleep, and he gave us samples of both states.

The two painters talked entrancingly of their craft. How sorry they are for all us poor wretches who can't paint!

They were very amusing about the risks of Holy Matrimony that they suspect Sargent to be running. Tonks reminded me of the time I had "pulled his leg"—surprising colloquialism from those austere lips!—by telling him that Steer was becoming engaged. Steer bridled at the mere recollection of the badinage he had so much enjoyed.

Tonks showed us some masterly caricatures—several of them of George Moore, against whom he had one of his attacks of resentment. He inveighed against the demands he made on his time. "Sometimes I can hardly bear it", he moaned. "Hang it all" (obviously this mild expletive was self-Bowdlerisation), "whatever it may be to the world, my work is just as important to ME as his is to him! I wouldn't stand such exactions even from Shakespeare!"

Now for some snippets about McEvoy.

1918. Bicycled to sit to McEvoy. Unfortunately the asphyxiating heat of the studio made me throw off the tweed coat that had inspired his bicycling conception of me, and, struck by my primrose blouse, he insisted on painting out the coat. Has any canvas been through so many metamorphoses? It started with the Mercury-hatted, Greek coin effect, then passed via two tea-gowns into tweed. Now everything is scrapped again!

At one moment the new picture was lovely—better than ever before—translucent and strange with moonlight background. If only I could have snatched it away at the right moment! Alas, before the sitting ended, destruction was far advanced. Mr. H. looked in and disturbed McEvoy with criticism. He told him he was "painting me too much *à la soubrette*". "I see her much more epically", he said.

"I don't agree at all", said Robert Nicholls. "I see her like a mermaid drifting."

For once McEvoy seemed disinclined for comment, or indeed, for company. I felt him to be depleted—edgy, and remembered Tonks (how he would love the job of watch-dog in this seething studio!) saying with many headshakings, "You mark my words, if McEvoy goes on going out so much, the mind will go out of his art."

Poor McEvoy yawned like a hyena, and his voice was shriller than ever. It seems to have gone up a whole octave. He admitted to nervous exhaustion, and said he had decided to go and live in the country. I wonder.

He bewailed the difficulty of painting me. "How can I get the preposterous fairness of your skin?" he squeaked. (My usual luck—tan complexions are now the fashion!) "You're impossible to finish!" he went on almost angrily. "Everything one says starts some new hare of an expression in your face. . . ."

Went to sit to McEvoy in my latest war economy—a black velvet dress with a removable dickey, so that it is convertible into an evening dress!

Under so many layers of superimposed paint, the canvas begins to look pipe-clayed, and after all these months and months, he decided to start on a fresh canvas.

Whibley came in. Great fun, but of course his volubility hopelessly slowed down McEvoy's brush. They get on too well. They compared notes on the inanity of nearly all literary and art criticism. W. was delighted with review of his new book. "Mr. Whibley has frivolity without humour and cleverness without intelligence." The critic also alleges that the author invariably writes with a quill pen—a new one every day. I said I would tell *The London Mail* (it's been so busy with McEvoy lately) that he invariably paints with a toothbrush, and asks his sitters to bring their own. They talked politics, not very seriously—and not at all disputatiously. Whibley gave a brilliant exhibition of self-parody. *Only* peers, he said, should have votes!

Augustus John, O.M.

Professor Tonks.

At one time the face seemed almost perfect, but alas, McEvoy did not stay his hand. "Why didn't you stop me?" he wailed. . . .

Nearly all my sittings to Augustus John came into the lost diaries. All I can find is:

Oct., 1918. Sat to John. He went on with the very fine head from which that fleeting Pre-Raphaelite look has now quite gone. I loved his portrait of W. H. Davies. The poet looks just like a bird— a bird listening to the song of another bird. Bernard Shaw appears to have his eyes shut. Symbolism? The effect is curious. . . .

Nov. 3rd, 1918. . . . I could have wept when John painted out the result of about thirty sittings and put me into quite a different pose. It's heart-rending to think of all those buried pictures. He took me to see his huge war cartoon. Thrilling to watch him at work on it. He rushed up and down a ladder. I've never seen anyone look quite so intensely alive."

You told me how sorry you were never to have met Rex Whistler, so before leaving the subject of painters, I'll try to tell you something about him. Of his work as an artist I am far less qualified to speak than you. A purely personal impression is all I shall attempt.

It is seldom that circumstances conspire to leave one with such vividly distinct memories of both the very first and the very last time one saw a friend, as I have of my first and last sights of Rex. I'll tell you of both.

Even had there been nothing memorably attractive in his personality, I should probably have remembered, because I had so much looked forward to it, my first meeting with an artist of whose genius and charm I had heard so much. (Never had I known Tonks so lyrical in anyone else's praise.)

As though it were yesterday, I remember my first delighted impression of gentle pensive good looks, quiet charm of manner, and that delicate blend of gaiety, sadness, irony, wisdom and wit. Yet what I suppose struck me more than anything else about Rex was his extraordinary sensitiveness—his intense *awareness*. Then, as to the end of his life, he had the easy, effortless charm of one who has always been much loved and to whom success has come early and without strain.

I   III

He was still very young but already conspicuous for that blessed capacity to bridge any gulf, however wide, of intervening years. At once I realised a new luxury had come into life—a companion with whom I could talk easily and truthfully, one who would make me both laugh and think, above all help me to SEE; for Rex could lend his artist's eyes even to the purblind. . . .

The last time I saw Rex was when, shortly before D-Day he came to spend the evening and stayed the night with my husband and me in our home on the West Sussex Downs. I had not seen him since before the beginning of the war. After so long and so momentous an interval, it was natural that my mind should revert to the first time I saw him. Remembering the fragile youth, so unmistakably an artist, I wondered what could then have struck me as more utterly incongruous than khaki and a command in the Tanks? Yet, now that the wheel had come full circle, and I saw Rex as a soldier, uniform seemed strangely natural to him. He did not "wear it with a difference".

He had all his old look of naturalness and unconcern. Added to it one of quiet resolve.

No one could have loathed war more than Rex did. That such a thing could still happen shocked him in every nerve and to the very core. He could not consider our present civilisation as anything but very far from perfect; nor was he simple enough to be able to console himself with any illusion that wholesale slaughter and destruction were auspices likely to usher in a happier Age. Nevertheless he did not question that what civilisation, such as it was, did hold of value *was* something worth dying for; consequently, untroubled by doubt, he had at once taken up the challenge, and spurning compromise, refused all offers of army work as an artist, remaining with his regiment all through the long slow years of waiting.

Thence that peaceful look of acceptance that comes only from the absence of any inner conflict.

How had the war years affected him? In place of his usual extreme pallor, there was a new appearance of sun-bronzed health. I was also struck by a noticeably carefree look—a look that goes with that complete "acceptance". His smile was as intensely amused as ever; his wit had the same quality of unexpectedness.

With him came a brother officer, Robert Cleveland Stevens who, though young enough to be our son, was also a great friend of our own. Robert was as much younger as we were older than Rex, but evidently years past made no more gulf than years to come, and through all their jesting intercourse, one could feel how strongly bound in fellowship the two soldiers had become.

For all its poignancy, the evening they spent with us will always live in my memory as one of the happiest I have known. Though the world was holding its breath and the two soldiers knew themselves to be on the brink of experiences unimaginable, it was even a memorably *gay* occasion.

They were both so full of laughter that they made us laugh, and almost forget the unforgettable. I wish I could quote Rex, but, alas, I can remember only how deliciously funny he was in his own special way and how much whenever—which was seldom—he was serious, we wanted to know his opinion. He spoke a little, not much, of the past; still less of the war, only once and then with characteristic lightness of touch referring to his own impending initiation. "I don't know that I exactly look forward to it, but at least it will be going ABROAD."

What he evidently preferred to dwell upon was the prospect immediately before his eyes. By a happy chance it was the most lovely evening of a summer that had so far stinted us of sunshine —an evening like a benediction. Bare except where grazing sheep dotted their silvery green, the Downs, bathed in golden light, seemed to breathe peace. Well as I thought I knew my own landscape, Rex's all-seeing eyes showed me hitherto never fully perceived loveliness of line and colour. And because of his delight in its summer beauty, I caught myself wishing that, just as one turns the pages of a favourite book, so I could in quick succession bring before his sight the same view in all the other seasons of the year.

That magical evening was far too lovely to allow us to go indoors until the gold with which the setting sun had rimmed the trees and the grazing sheep had faded and dusk began to thicken.

113

Late that night Rex suggested some reading aloud, and at his own choice I read *The Scholar Gipsy* and the *Lotus-Eaters*. Again I noticed how his extraordinary awareness made one more fully savour even beauty so familiar.

Apparently wholly intent, he listened to the poetry, but meanwhile, all the time, carelessly, almost unconsciously (so it seemed), his hand moved rapidly, and when the *Lotus-Eaters* ended, behold two pages of my visitors' book closely covered with exquisite "Rex Whistlers"; sheaves of corn, fluted columns, garlands of flowers:

> "With buds and bells, and stars without a name.
> With all the gardener Fancy e'er could feign
> Who, breeding flowers, will never breed the same."

Early the next morning Rex and his comrade-in-arms rejoined their regiment, and very soon they did go "abroad".

Rex had been so natural, seemed so unself-concerned, that at first it had not occurred to me to wonder whether his premonition, if he had one, was that he would not return. But suddenly, as he was looking at the cloud-shadowed Downs, and I noticed the peculiar intentness of his gaze, it struck me with a pang that deliberately, consciously, he was memorising what he saw. "Eyes, look your last", came into my mind and then, with an agonising stab, the thought, "Suppose *he* should be blinded . . .!"

I remembered that stab when I read the last sentence in this passage from his letter written from the Front.

"May I come back to your lovely Sullington when the wonderful days return and we struggle back from the blood bath. Meanwhile please write and tell me how everything *looks*."

The day after I got that letter came the news that he had been instantaneously killed. .

FIRST MEMORIES

Now, you condemn me to go right back to the very beginning, to comb out my mind for its earliest memories. I'll try, but I'm afraid the first discernible breaks in the darkness of unremembrance will light up moments of experience common to all childhood rather than peculiar to any one particular epoch; and what you want is a Costume Piece, isn't it? Nevertheless, probably the best way to try to recapture what it was like to open one's eyes on the world from inside the shelter of a late Victorian nursery—to convey the vast difference between Then and Now, when to all but a handful of children the very word "Nursery" is unknown, is to peer back through the golden haze of later childhood and search the mists of infancy for those very first tiny breaks in the surrounding darkness: here a scarcely perceptible glimmer: there a gleam; occasionally an isolated flash.

I'll try to confine myself to actual memories. For instance I won't describe those who surrounded me, nor the house in which I lived as I now know them to have been, but only such aspects of them as first fragmentarily impressed themselves upon my dawning consciousness.

No easy undertaking. Now that I have spent several hours and in the process literally strained my eyesight staring into that long, long ago, I see how difficult it is to disentangle actual from fancied memories. For instance, I have often thought I could remember the night when I and my two elder brothers were rescued from the flames that destroyed Clouds, the home of my mother's parents; but, as I had been born in that house only just one year before the fire, this of course must be an illusion. So vividly, however, had the oft-told story of the adventure impressed my imagination that it came to seem an authentic memory.

One very early venture, probably the most presumptuous of my life, I am quite certain I do remember—learning to walk, my first tottering steps, swaying from one pair of outstretched, encouraging arms into another, my sense of daring, elation and applause. Undoubtedly, too, I remember the consciousness of extreme smallness, what it felt like to be so very close to the ground, the tickle in my face of tall grasses, the warm scent of sunned earth, and, on those special occasions, when I was not teed-up for a meal in my own high chair, how the food on the table would be practically on a level with my mouth. I remember too the uncomfortable sensation of being towered over by grown-up people; my terror when suddenly a great pair of arms would swoop, snatch me from off the ground and draw me up, up, up through the whistling air until, dizzy, dismayed, I at last found myself perched on the hard, high shoulder of some giant stranger. This was a dreadful experience. It made my heart drum; yet already there was a troubled sense that I ought to try to look pleased, to appear grateful for the "treat". Yes, I distinctly remember forcing my fat cheeks into a narrow, placating little smile.

Another recurrent drawing-room horror was being kissed— pecked at by strangers, especially if they had prickles on their faces or made a bad shot at my cheek and poked a cold nose right into the inside of my ear. In blessed contrast to these physical ordeals was the bliss, the lovely reassurance of nestling back into my mother's cradling arms.

These are all memories of reiterated experiences. Now for one or two flashes that light up particular occasions.

First I see myself throughout the long, long day of some railway journey. Getting up by candle-light; having my boots buttoned up; feeling very stalwart at being about to face some huge adventure—my boots might have been armour so brave did I feel!—indeed, some physical fortitude was needed, for the briskly wielded button-hook seldom failed to catch up a little piece of my leg as well as a button; and no child of to-day can imagine the torment of a hat tethered to your head by elastic so tight that a deep red rut was left under your chin. Next I remember the railway carriage; rain-drops racing one another down the windows past which streamed fields, trees, cows and sheep; a kind man in uniform allowing me to punch my own ticket. . . . Nightfall and the endless drowsy drive, clop-clopping through the darkness, the lamps of our carriage silvering tree-trunks and fleeing rabbits. . . . Sleepily blinking up at the light when at long last the front door creaked open to let in the "Great Travellers"; and crowningly—that tribute to a journey—the special "Egg-to-Your-Tea" with fingers of toast to dip in brown and take out yellow.

Next—this memory is very vivid—an early birthday. The magnolia on the sugar-coated cake, the glimmer of the five green candles and the horrid smell when they were blown out; my unavowed dread of crackers, the tickling glory of the "Birthday Girl's" crown—for these occasions my mother always made us wreaths of flowers—and some mighty grown-up hand guiding my own to cut the cake. "All for ME!" I remember thinking. For in the little creature moving about in worlds unrealised, the sense of Me-ness had already awoken. How I used to puzzle over the dawning of this vague sense of identity! That which looked back at me from the looking-glass, and that others called "Cincie", was Me . . . "Me"? . . . What *was* Me? . . . Was everyone a Me?

Another very clear memory is of my first ride—an immensely solemn affair. Long-tailed, thick eye-lashed, a Shetland pony, round as a barrel, scarcely higher than a dog, and wedged into a high basket saddle, the absurd small proud bundle that was Myself uneasily perched on that broad, swaying back. Not only was the minute pony's head led by the coachman, but I was also tightly held on or rather into the saddle by both my mother and some other person. From that day I saved up lumps of sugar for daily visits to the stables, and I remember being taught how to make a plate of the palm of my out-stretched hand. I can still hear the whinny of welcome at my approach, feel the delicious softness of those warm, nuzzling lips.

My next memory is of a sudden enraptured sense of awe. We

had been out to tea—one of those occasions when a drop of "real tea" was put into your cup of milk. With a gingerbread-nut popped into my mouth to "keep out the cold", a leather strap buckled round my middle to secure me to the back seat of the four-wheeled dog-cart, and my legs packed into a fur-lined bag, I was driving home with my brothers through the frosted night. Perhaps it was the first time I had ever been out in the dark; anyhow excitement was making me bounce up and down in my fur-bag, when suddenly looking up, I saw that above my head the vast over-arching blackness of the night-sky was bright with myriads of glittering golden stars. Hitherto I had thought of the sky merely as the ceiling of the earth. If I had ever seen the stars before I cannot have realised them. I have never forgotten the thrilled shock of that sight, and my sudden sense of oneness with something immense, beautiful, mysterious—everlasting. After that revelation, "Please, may I go out in the dark?" was my most constant plea.

This is my best outdoor memory of something new swimming into my ken. A good second was my first sight of the world turned white with snow. Glee of silver-cold air; dazzle of blue-shadowed whiteness; crisp crunch underfoot; the gratification of looking back to see the tracks my own feet had made in the hitherto unbroken whiteness. But stars and snow, I hear you complain, are memories common to all children; nothing whatever to do with period or place. And boring at that! Sorry. I'll try to be more specific; I'll tell you of my first shadowy recollections of the particular house in which my own brief nursery days were passed. Knowing and loving, as I now do, every inch of Stanway, I can nevertheless remember how, like promontories of a distant land slowly taking shape in the spreading dawn, certain parts of the house first jutted into my perception. I remember the sense of chill vastness, the faint smell of washed stone in that No Man's Land I so much liked to hear called, "The Great Hall". Its roaring fire of logs that scorched me if I came near, but failed even to take the chill off outlying regions. On the walls, moth-eaten heads of antlered stags; ceiling-high, the glimmer of the stone-mullioned Oriel window with its hundreds of latticed panes. The oak shuffle-board table, twenty-three feet in length, along the polished surface of which I, with my hands clasped under my knees, used to be shot like a toboggan from one end to the other.

My own quarters—the day and the night nursery? I remember the faint all-pervasive smell of the then sovereign remedy, Pommadavine; but, except for the one picture of the Infant Samuel saying his prayers and the enlarged photograph of my mother in court-dress and feathers, I can visualise curiously few details of these rooms. It is more the name "Nursery" that comes back, and the sense of its enclosed apartness from all the rest of the house. A world of its own, presided over by that almighty, vigilantly protective, but by no means always kind, being called Nannie. I see her sitting bolt upright in bed, grey hair screwed up in curlers, sipping the early-morning tea borne in on a black japanned tray by someone neither grown-up nor child called the "Nursery-maid". I remember the way in which Nannie crooked the first joint of the little finger of the hand that held her tea-cup (this practice—to "quirk", I believe it was called, was then considered "genteel") and how she would try to bend my own stubbornly resisting little finger into the same unnatural position. When in a good temper she would give me and Colin, the little silver-fair brother in the other cot, a taste of the sweet dark brown brew, and a nibble of the Marie biscuit she always dipped in her cup of tea. Morning after morning this treat would be spoilt by the gloat and gloom of the tone in which she would say, "I hope you are properly grateful, children, for there are many poor hungry little boys and girls who would be very glad of what you are having." I remember the uncomfortable sense of guilt, not unmixed with injury, the implied reproach of these words gave me.

It was sitting on Nannie's rather knobbly knee that, at a very early age, I learned to read from a chubby brown book called *Reading Without Tears*. I remember the fascination of the alphabet pictures, the incantation-like charm of sentences such as "I met ten pigs in a gig. I met ten figs in a gig. I met ten wigs in a gig."

Then there was the evening bath—the house boasted of only one bath-room and for baby legs this was a good five minutes'

walk from the nursery—a low circular tin affair, placed on a
flannel spread out before the fire. I see the brown-lidded hot-
water can; feel the comfort of the enfolding bath-towel warmed
on the high fender around which there seemed always to
linger a delicious smell of hot buttered-toast; I remember
staring into the fireplace to watch the winking sparks—"little
people going to church" Nannie said they were—apparently
walking up the blackness of the chimney until one by one they
flickered out into nothingness. Then the warm sweetness of
"breadandmilk" (I thought the three words were one) and the
fun of chasing six—don't tell present-day children of this
nightly orgy—SIX lumps of white sugar round the cup with
my spoon. The "bread-and-milk" was enjoyed after we had
been tucked up in the two little cots that, divided by Nannie's
bed, were close enough together for whispered conversations
carried on long after we had been consigned to sleep by that
most curdling of all lullabies, "When the bough breaks the
cradle will fall". Left to ourselves, I remember the glimmer of
the night-light and the cosy happy sense of being alone with
Colin, that gentle nestling little creature, so near to me that he
was part of myself and yet was delicious "company", someone
to cuddle and with whom I loved to talk and to giggle. Through
him too dawned my first sense of responsibility, for being a year
and a half younger, he was my "Little Brother", so I must "take
care" of him.

Two very vivid incidents, both autobiographical, flash out
from the twilight of nursery memories. The first—a jumble
of panic, discomfort and self-importance—was when, having
thrust my disproportionately large head through two of the
wooden bars of my cot, I found I could not draw it back again.
The carpenter had to be fetched to extricate me, and he had no
choice but to saw right through one of the bars!

The other memory is one of exultation. It was after "Dinner",
as our mid-day meal was called. Wildly fidgeting, Colin and I
were supposed to be "resting" when my errant fingers chanced
on a small hole in the red eiderdown on Nannie's bed. Burrow-
ing into it, I pulled out a white feather. "Fun!" I thought,
and, widening the hole, I scrabbled out several more feathers.

I puffed at these provocative things and they spurted up towards the ceiling in a most attractive way. Ambition seized me. Summoning Colin to help with the job which I was determined should be thorough, we set to work, and our little Pickers and Stealers did not rest until every single feather of the stuffing had been taken out of that eiderdown. Then with a lovely sense of achievement we lay flat on our backs, giggling and blowing up at the great floating drift of feathers. Enter Nannie. Being the elder, I, of course, was the culprit. "But I had never been told I mustn't do it", I pleaded in self-defence, a soft answer that did not turn away wrath. Much as I minded being scolded, in so far as I could not wish the deed undone, I was not on this occasion brought to any real repentance. An incipient hedonist I must have been, for I remember deciding that what had been such huge fun and had hurt no one could not really be a "Sin", and my mind had already disentangled mere naughtiness from Sin. Yes, in spite of the scolding, the charge of leading my little brother astray, and the punishment of sugar-less bread-and-milk, the affair of the eiderdown—the first of an unending succession of pranks—is a *good* memory. Not so, my first recorded lie. The ineptitude of this, I think you will agree, points to a naturally truthful nature. Born of a recurrent horror, that first lie was. No child of to-day, when it is recognised that abhorred food is little better than poison, can guess at the torture of being compelled to swallow something at which your gorge rises. Forcible feeding was the bane of my nursery days, and milk puddings, in my infancy considered as unshunnable as fate, my special abomination. Oh! those sickening glutinous lumps of sago, and the dread threat, "Now then, Cincie, if you don't eat your nice pudding up at once, you shall have it cold for breakfast."

This was how my first lie was forced upon me. One day my refusal—or rather absolute inability—to swallow the second course of the dinner, for which I had just asked God to "make me truly thankful", was punished by my being locked up in an empty room. Solitary confinement confronted by that loathsome yellowing sago-pudding! Until I had "made a nice clean plate", I shouldn't be let out, pronounced Nannie, and saying she would return once an hour to see if I had become a good girl, she shut the door on me.

I heard the key turn in the lock and her footsteps die away into the distance. . . . After what seemed hours I could no longer endure the loneliness or the sight and thought of the now quite congealed mess on the plate. Scraping the nauseous globules off my pinafore I tried to spoon them all into the fire-place, and a very messy job I made of it!

"If you've eaten your pudding, then what is that mess on your pinafore?" demanded Nannie.

"I think that must be some *other* pudding", I mumbled. (A remarkably feeble effort, wasn't it?) Then I was smacked and plunged into the darkness of a built-in clothes cupboard—darkness so dense that it seemed quite solid. Surely I wouldn't be able to breathe? There, drumming with frantic fists against the door, I was left for what seemed an eternity of suffocating terror. A nightmare memory but no, thank you, it did not give me claustrophobia.

But what pangs of conscience I suffered! I knew a lie was a sin, and I had told a lie. When in my prayers that night I came to "Forgive us our trespasses", I writhed in a positive agony of supplication.

It was not Nannie's fault—for indeed her powers of descrip-tion were considerable—that I was not afraid of going to the Hell of her faith, a place of perpetual fiery torment, but I cannot remember ever being so. I don't think I ever believed in it; but I was terribly afraid of *not* going to Heaven. That, indeed, was my conception of Hell.

Besides Colin, there were two elder brothers, Ego and Guy, in my earliest recollections of them half in and half out of the nursery. I remember seeing Guy being pulled like a cracker between Nannie and the newly arrived governess, each deter-mined to claim him for her own special territory.

I wanted to be like "The Big Boys", as they were always called, as tall, strong, swift and rough. Above all I wanted like them to be trousered. As the only girl, I was ashamed of the sin-gularity of my attire. Besides, petticoats got terribly in my way.

Lovingly, admiringly, wistfully, I was aware of "The Big

Boys' " otherness from myself. They came and went, had larger concerns of their own and one another to fight with. Between me and Colin there seemed no real divisibility. So much so, that, though I cannot remember a time when I did not hunger for praise, it never occurred to me to mind that whenever we went downstairs to be shown to "Visitors", or very shyly arrived at one of those rare things called "Parties", to which, with hair-brush and bronze shoes in a holland bag, we drove in a brougham, the whispered words I overheard were always "What a lovely little *boy*!"

Neither did I mind Nannie declaring Colin's to be the sweetest nature of any child she had ever brought up.

Apart from his beauty—delicate as that of flowers and shells —which even had I not continually heard it exclaimed at, I am sure I should have perceived, Colin was a singularly loving quicksilver child, with an unforgettable gentleness and some quality that, for want of a better phrase, I suppose I should now call fineness of grain. . . .

The nursery window, against the cold panes of which Colin and I used to flatten our noses, directly overlooked the church-yard with its dark yew-trees and clustered graves—either mere mounds of grass or grey moss-covered stones, some lying flat, others erect or slanting at all angles. The heavy church bell donged out the slow hours of infancy. I remember how that familiar mournful clang would smite the silence and go on vibrating in my ears. Charged, as it now is with all the burden of the past, to which, swinging you back through each succeed-ing phase, it seems to consign you; the dong of that bell is now of all sounds in the world the most evocative to me.

Now and again the nursery party would be disturbed by the familiar note of that bell unwontedly breaking the silence in between hours; not on these occasions striking to tell the time, but heavily tolling for a death. Three dongs for a man. Two for a woman. One for a child.

I remember Nannie sharply pulling down the blinds when she found her charges hanging out of the window to watch what my elder brothers called the "Deader" being borne through the churchyard towards the open grave.

Later on a favourite escapade of Guy's and mine was to steal into the belfry, and straining at the great rope that dragged us right off our feet, struggle till we were purple in the face to ring the church bell. As our utmost exertions never produced more than the most dismal toll, villagers would assemble to ask who had "kicked the bucket". The vicar did not appreciate our efforts.

Two other sounds are inextricably interwoven with nursery days. One, at intervals startlingly cutting the air, the sharp, eerie cry of the saw-mill in the timber-yard; the other—one of hot days—when the lawn, its daisies flying into the air, was shaved in long narrow strips, the pleasant "whirr, whirr, whirr" of the mowing-machine drawn by the old white pony in his brown leathern boots.

Outside Nannie's special territory, the Nursery, I mistily remember how to my perceptions the remainder of the house gradually resolved itself into separate regions. The most enchanted of all was what the fat butler always called—the very name thrilled me—"Her Ladyship's Bood-war"—the special sphere of a lovely and loving being called "Mamma". (We, having been brought up to use the Victorian "Papa" and "Mamma", try as we would, could never call our parents anything else.) Mamma, though frequently irradiating the Nursery with her visiting presence, was, however, definitely not *of* it. The sense of her radiance permeated the whole house, but this mysteriously named "Bood-war" was so specially redolent of her that it seemed her very shrine. It was to this entrancing room that for the blissful part of the day called "After Tea" we rapturously repaired.

I remember the look of the sofa (were not some of my own "After Tea" frocks made of the same Morris chintz—a blue and white bird design—with which it was covered?). On this well-worn sofa, sentinelled by growling Chows, Mamma lay, and, as we chalked or cut waste paper into strips, she would read us fairy stories or, what I loved even more, Scotch ballads. In this cherishing room there was a whispering snapping wood-fire, mignonette in small silver vases, book-shelves, a crowd of very easy chairs, a Lear's *Nonsense Book*, in which we were allowed to colour the pictures, and a large cupboard full of very special toys. All too soon Nannie would reappear, holding up our Shetland shawls. "Bed-time" she knelled from the threshold. Once again—a little daily death—the Nursery reclaimed us.

Does this special "After Tea" visit to another sphere suggest the perfunctory "Children's Hour"?—that mere ration of parental time that must sound so strange and, no doubt, contemptible to the whole-time mothers of to-day, whose homes are either without any nursery at all or else without any room that is not nursery. If so, the impression is misleading. No drawbridge of inaccessibility was ever pulled up, but the fact that in entering Mamma's own precincts there was definitely a perceptible sense of, as it were, crossing a frontier did, however, add an appreciable thrill to the time spent with her. Also our realisation that Mamma, however fond of us and however available, was yet all the while busily engaged with concerns quite outside our own existence and as yet unguessed at, added much to her glamour. It also heightened the horizon of our own vague expectancy.

The long, beshawled journey through countless draughts was in itself a thrill. First, pattering along the corridor, then—my hand tightly held for the descent and each foot in turn planted on each step—stumping down the dark oak staircase that smelt of varnish and was so grandly solid to the tread; next traversing the long, high-ceilinged drawing-room; up another short flight of steps on to the landing, against the window of which jasmine tapped and where the few inches of hot-water pipes—the only attempt in the whole house to try to mitigate the mottling cold, then by rich and poor accepted as their inevitable winter lot— would give one of their sudden startling gurgles; finally, with a last little rush up to the door that let us into the fragrance and welcome of the fire-lit room.

Besides Mamma's boudoir, there was her bedroom with its silver brushes, rose-water in cut-glass bottles and always, so it now seems to me, the scent of sweet geranium or verbena. To this room we went each day to say good morning and, according to the perhaps peculiar practice of the day, to kneel by Mamma's bedside and in chorus though not in time loudly gabble through our prayers. (*To* her—herself—at first I used to think that we were praying. Why not "Our *Mother* which art in Heaven"?)

Very often she would be toying with that strange privilege of hers, "Breakfast in Bed", and most mornings the post would be brought in on a silver salver. Her pile of letters quickened my sense of mysterious, exciting concerns far beyond our nursery ken.

As well as indoor delights, there were manifold "going-out-with-Mamma" treats. Tip-toed, heart-beating explorations of the mysterious dark wood of yew-trees that skirted the magnolia-treed lawn and was said to be the headquarters of a dragon. Tea, or reading aloud under the great shimmering green parasol of the tulip-tree; inspection of the round pond in the kitchen-garden to see whether the gold fish were still orange-coloured or, as all too soon they always did, already patchily turning that nasty dull silver. We called it "going bad". Totteringly, we scaled the slippery grass banks and terraces up to the "Pyramid"—a stone building full of dead flies, perched high, high up above the house. Behind the Pyramid the great cedar stretched out huge branches. That this tree was said to be the largest cedar in Britain swelled my infant heart with unreasoning pride. To engirdle its trunk would, so I was told, take the extended arms of six men and one boy. I badly wanted —a wish never fulfilled—to see the requisite number embrace that noble tree.

Gradually, as legs grew firmer there would be longer walks— not merely within "the grounds", but out into the beech woods and up the blue, remembered hills. Then Mamma would tell us stories about "Mother Earth" and certain trees. One, a stunted and twisted fir—still to my imagination un-exorcised— "The Witch Tree" we called it—I am to this day scarcely able to pass without dropping it a propitiating curtsey.

Now and again when engaged on some irksome mystery known as "Calling", Mamma would take us for long drives in the low four-wheeled pony-carriage, with a dickey at the back, drawn by the two Shetlands Hog and Mog. Once, most exciting of all, just after she had taken to riding a tricycle, my

The author with her brother Guy Charteris.

Mary Wemyss with her sons and daughters.

mailcart, with me inside it, was precariously attached by odds and ends of string to her machine—to which part of it I can't imagine—and, strenuously treadling, she towed me for some miles along the road. As this enterprise was never repeated, I imagine some person more grown-up-minded than herself must have condemned it as dangerous.

But probably the most vivid of all my nursery memories of Mamma is of how I would lie in my cot listening for the sound of that light tip-toeing step coming along the passage; praying with beating heart that the approaching sound might draw nearer and nearer, till the door would open and Mamma glide into the room in all the shimmer and rustle of a low-necked evening gown. (One of softest yellow velvet—"The Canary Dress" I called it—I thought the loveliest thing in all the world.)

Beneath the Nursery floor stretched those seemingly vast, and for a long time quite uncharted regions collectively called "Downstairs". There was the dining-room into which we would be taken on the way out for our afternoon walk, when with luck a date, a raisin or some such delicacy would be popped into our mouths. Seated round the table, often—far too often I thought—there would be visitors to stare at me; remark how much I'd "grown", and ask my age, whom I loved best, and other outrageous questions. Some visitors at once made me feel at ease; others induced such a suffocation of shyness that the prescribed "How-do-you-do?" "Please", "Thank you", "Goodbye" simply could not get uttered.

"Where's your manners?" Nannie would ask. Shamed by this prompting, my cheeks would crimson, my eyes spurt with tears.

Apart from the alchemy of those who could wave the wand of charm, I think the common denominator between visitors who gave me an immediate sense of well-being was that they, unlike others, did not keep a special cajoling voice in which to talk to children, nor did they ask questions they would not ask their contemporaries. Above all, they did not run their fingers through my hair, pat my cheeks or indeed take any liberties with my face.

In those days, as in all succeeding days, my mother was fantastically unpunctual. The sound of the gong would act merely as a signal to remind her it was time to take the dogs out for a walk. Often on being taken into the dining-room, we would find to our dismay her chair empty, and unpresided-over visitors who had been told "not to wait", silently munching. Evidently, though they could eat, they could not talk much without their inspiriting hostess.

Besides my own delight in her company, I very early recognised, though of course without being able to put a name to it, the charm my mother had for others and the great difference that her presence made. If there was constraint in the air—and like all children, barometers that they are, I was acutely sensitive to atmosphere—it instantaneously lightened the moment she entered the room. Shyness lifted; faces smiled. All at once everyone seemed not only brighter but much nicer; the world a pleasanter place. Moreover, I very early realised that at children's parties strangers would look at me with special interest just because I was her child. "That's Cynthia Charteris—Mary Elcho's little girl", I would hear whispered. Later on this consciousness increased my natural diffidence; my mind's ear would add the unvoiced words, "Not at all like her mother, is she?" To me that comment was condemnation and, since I yearned to be a boy, to be described as the "only girl" was further disparagement.

"Downstairs" included a room with a very special climate of its own—a book-lined, ash-trayed room in which, usually behind a high white wall of upheld newspaper, sat a remote Being, utterly different from all others, intermittent and unaccountable but hugely important, called "Papa". Either in his moustached mouth or in between two of his long tapering fingers there was always a thing called a cigar, the scent of which would get into my nostrils to become so strongly associated with his presence that to this day I cannot breathe cigar-laden air without being wafted back to infancy and my very first impressions of "Papa".

As early as I can remember, my father, but for just the merest valance of hair about his ears, was quite bald. ("Unlike So and So's, *my* hair preferred death to dishonour", he said, comparing the bareness of his own with a cousin's head—a die-hard head sparsely trellised over with strands of eked-out hair.) Besides the impressiveness of that high bare polished dome, the sceptre-like cigar, and an obscure sense that, though seldom met with outside this particular room, he yet somehow pervaded the entire house, Papa's effect on me was wholly different from anyone else's. He was as unpredictable as the weather; I never knew what kind of experience a visit to him might prove. One day, perhaps, something I said or did would provoke loud chortles of explosive laughter—delightfully contagious laughter. Then I would feel happy and pleased with myself. Next day, though I had acted in precisely the same way, he might be completely unnoticing. His receiver would be off. Worse still, a previously applauded joke or prank, repeated because of its apparent success only the day before, might be received with unmistakable disfavour.

But whatever my reception, or however seldom I saw him, I was always acutely aware of Papa, consciously anxious to please —above all to *amuse* him. Through him I realised, long before I had been told of their existence, the full force of "moods" and their immensely disturbing effect on myself. On others, too! Some days on being propelled into the dining-room, I would notice that it was Papa, who, talking very fast, with his bald head darting from side to side, his face all alight, was setting the whole table in a roar. Next day, perhaps, he would be sitting either utterly aloof or obviously glum, imposing his own silence —a silence so palpable that it smote on one's ears more than any gabble of talk—on the entire company.

Here then, looming large in one's universe, was someone of immense importance, but not, like Mamma, someone to be *counted* on. On the contrary uncertain, often disconcerting, at times positively alarming. Trying to please him, to make him smile, was like bowling on a tricky, though possibly very rewarding wicket. In me, the too early strain of this conscious need for special bowling fostered what I was never to lose, an over-anxiety to please and, born of the need for reassurance, an excessive craving for praise.

Long afterwards I realised that the explanation of the extreme variability of my father's "weather"—he could seldom be said to be "Set" either "Fair" or "Foul"—lay largely in his being, perhaps, the only completely natural person I have known. If he happened to be preoccupied, bored or depressed, no matter what the occasion, he could not pretend to be anything else.

Though all through my childhood there were frequent times when Papa's company would be intoxicating fun, and we would be encouraged to belabour him with a pillow, or could, with confident impunity, prepare booby traps—even poise a wet sponge on the top of a door from whence it must topple on to his bald head; it was not until years later (how could it be?) that I came to anything like full appreciation of his charm, darting quickness of mind, brilliant wit and, quite distinct as it is from wit, of that supreme "funniness" which, inextricably bound up with manner, appearance—the very baldness contributed —and, above all, *timing*, can alas never be conveyed by quotation. Much later still, with the retrospective insight of great fondness, I came to realise how very, despite his social gifts, *shy* a man he was; and therefore greatly to regret that as a child I too had been so shy, too timid to "gate-crash" into a close relationship—intermittently into the familiarity of chaff and bear-fighting, yes, but never into spiritual intimacy. With him the bridge to span the gulf of years needed always to be built by the young. Any child bold enough to cheek him held the key to his heart. Deference was what he could not abide. In later years any young man sufficiently well-mannered to address him as "Sir" was for ever damned. I can still remember his expression of bitterly affronted gloom when, the first time he ever ventured into an omnibus, some well-meaning younger man gave up his seat to him!

To return to first impressions. On days when Papa, though in residence at Stanway, was not to be seen smoking a cigar behind the rampart of his upheld newspaper, he was often, so I would be told, inexplicably engaged in most puzzling pursuits. Perhaps "Sitting on the Bench". (Knowing nothing of magistrates, I could not imagine on what sort of a bench he sat, nor why.) Or the butler would say that "His Lordship" was "Taking the Chair" again. I remember thinking this habit of his sounded rather snatching. Was he—disquieting thought— selfish?

Then came a time when, somewhat to my relief, I heard my father was now "standing"—standing for Ipswich. But he did not continue long in this uncharacteristic position. No, very soon he was again "sitting". He had "taken his seat" in the "House of Commons". . . . What sort of a house might that be? . . .

Besides those sacred to Papa and Mamma, "Downstairs" held other thrilling regions. The large high-raftered realm with sanded floor, blazing fire, revolving spit and gleaming coppers, was the kingdom of a very great personage called the Cook who looked alarmingly like the Red Queen in *Alice in Wonderland*, but was nearly always gracious enough to allow us to beat up an egg, roll out dough, or, best of all, toss a pancake. Close at hand was a nightmare place known as the larder. This was full of horrors—red-slitted dead things hanging from hooks in the ceiling! A small particularly inviting room was called the pantry. This belonged to pleasant men in baize aprons, with cigarettes in their mouths, who, however busy they might be washing up at the sink or spitting on the silver, were yet always ready to leave off to show us a card-trick or answer any number of riddles, and quite often generous enough to open a gushing bottle of ginger-beer or fizzy lemonade for our benefit. Then there was the "still-room"—I liked that name—with floured scones and trays all neatly "set" for the morning.

Somewhere far above in a room full of reels of cotton, bits and pieces of material, and a most mysterious object compounded of wire and sateen, somehow inexplicably connected with Mamma, called a Dressmaker's Dummy, sat a very agreeable person who seemed almost perpetually to play with a fascinating mechanical sewing-machine. Right at the top of the house were the "attics". They were bare, cold and very full of bats.

Up there were the bedrooms of other delightful friends who seemed never too busy to be glad to see one, gave one a specially comfortable sense of one's "Me-ness", and were far and away the best audience for whom to "dress-up"—even though a corked moustache and the doffing of your skirt were your only disguise.

Tea in "The Room" with the heads of the "Staff" (I remember wondering why just this particular one of all others should be called THE room) was by far the least shy of all social occasions.

Last of all regions to be fully explored by us (though later on all unfortunate child guests would immediately be plunged into their damp darkness) were the mysterious cellars that under-ran one entire wing of the house. In these, dimly discernible, loomed barred dungeon-like places full of cobweb-festooned barrels, casks, crates and bottles. Alive with scurrying black beetles, the dread but irresistibly beckoning cellars did not seem to belong to any one person in particular, but Fletcher the "Odd Man" (perpetually "odd", for sixty years ago he had been an "Odd Boy") whose job was to tend all the many lamps that feebly lightened the darkness of the house—no electricity was installed until 1913—and whose only known recreation was to bowl us "Daisy Cutters" on the lawn, was often dimly to be seen trimming wicks or rubbing up brass.

Outside the house; hoeing and digging in the walled kitchen-garden; lighting bonfires, scything the lawns or rhythmically sweeping leaves off the paths; were four out-of-door friends with gnarled, weather-beaten faces, hands caked with earth and bodies bent and twisted like pollarded willows.

Apart from the retainers busied either in or outside the house, the almost equally familiar occupants of the cottages, and our own near relations, the most vivid personality in my infancy—a much loved what is called "Character" in the best sense of the word—who was to warm and enhance every phase of all our lives, was Eliza Wedgwood, our very near neighbour and my mother's great friend. In my earliest recollections, Eliza wears a composite halo derived from my first introduction to the White Rabbit in *Alice in Wonderland*, gingerbread-nuts, pan-cakes, and her way of talking to me quite seriously exactly as if I were a contemporary.

Whenever Stanway overflowed with a "Shooting-party", as periodically it did, we would be packed off to stay with her and her very picturesque old mother in that perhaps loveliest of all Cotswold villages, Stanton. In the attic of the beautiful gabled house was a great chest filled with eighteenth-century brocade costumes, and we were allowed to dress-up to our hearts' content.

Through the garden ran a little stream that because of its entrancing way of every here and there disappearing under the ground to bubble up to the surface again in some unexpected place, made an ideal course for boat-races. Immense deliberation was given to the choice of our boats which were either ready found pieces of wood or fragments of bark or of cork roughly fashioned into shape. The excitement of running stick in hand (if a boat got held up against a bank we were allowed to prod it) alongside of one's own champion, grew almost unendurably thrilling as the strange flotilla neared the winning-post. Quite often one or more boats would fail to re-emerge from a tunnel. Then, culminating excitement, a dam would be constructed so that the swollen current might dislodge the stranded craft. No later race either watched or taken part in has ever come up to the excitement of those garden regattas.

Oddly enough—for what contrast to the muffled green of Stanway could have been greater than the grime and traffic noise of Cadogan Square—I have practically no nursery memories of our London house.

More than enough now, I'm sure you'll agree, of these "first affections, these shadowy recollections". Once open the sluice gates, such a throng of memories surge in that to try to compress them into conceivable reading limits is like trying to spoon the ocean into a thimble. . . .

That first phase of existence during which, though my being was still fast-rooted in the nursery, salients from the outside world were gradually impingeing on my consciousness, was shortly after my fifth birthday to come to an abrupt and anguished end.

Christmas, that dazzling climax up to which the entire slowly revolving year seemed to lead, was at last there again! All agog, we had come to spend it with my mother's parents at Clouds, the house where I had been born and shortly afterwards so very nearly burned to death.

Brilliantly vivid, the morning of my last nursery Christmas returns to me. Waking at a preposterously early hour, I shook Colin out of his sleep to share the thrill of the first tentative probings of the bulges in our heavily weighted stockings, before, full of wild surmise, we dragged out the rustling parcels, and fumbled with knotted string and crackling paper until our cots were heaped high with the litter of unpacking. . . .

I can still see Colin sitting upright in his cot, his eyes ablaze, his cheeks flushed, and then tearing all over the house prattling of his new playthings and wishing everyone a happy Christmas.

Of the transition from rapture to misery I have no recollection, but in my memory the radiance of that morning is succeeded by a timeless blur of bewildered suffering. Burning heat, raging thirst, tossing and turning in sheets that seemed on fire. Disconnectedly, misty glimpses return.

On the little table by my bedside I see a covered-over jug of barley-water, a bunch of white grapes; a black-bearded stranger bends over me, lays some strange cold object on my bared chest, and tells me to say "ninety-nine"; a glass tube is slipped under my tongue. Not far from my cot is a screen, from the other side of which there seems to come a perpetual whispering; at times the sound of the washing of hands.

Whisper . . . whisper . . . whisper. In incomprehensible snatches a few words reach my ears. "Scarlet Fever . . . Scarlet Fever . . . Complications. . . ."

"Say ninety-nine . . . Say ninety-nine . . . Say ninety-nine." Again and again the black-bearded stranger repeats his inexplicable command. Each time I obey the soreness of my throat sharpens into an agonising stab. . . . Utterly dazed, conscious now only of thirst, pain, heat, I no longer hear the doctor's bidding. The barley-water and the grapes fade out of sight. The whispering behind the screen is miles and miles— thousands of miles—away from my own burning distress. . . . Quite suddenly, so it seems, comes the cessation of that raging heat. No more pain. . . . Coolness and the sense of having come back from some remote, remote distance.

With sudden returned awareness of my surroundings, I lift my head.

The sound of weeping?

Nannie weeping!

Then, looking round the room, I see the other little cot is empty.

Where is Colin? . . .

How what had happened was first broken to me I have no recollection whatever, but I remember Mamma coming into the room with a new face and folding me in her arms, and then the black-bearded man saying, "She'll be all right now. Let her cry herself to sleep." And, as vividly as though it were yesterday, I remember Nannie—it must have been a few days later—sobbingly telling me that because he was so good—such a little angel, God had taken Colin to be with him in Heaven.

"But then why have they put him in the cold earth?" I asked, for the nursery-maid had already told me what had happened in the churchyard—all about the little white coffin, the white flowers, the mourning village. How was I to reconcile two such wholly different stories?

Apart from my own panic-stricken loneliness, there was the sight of my mother's grief—my first sense of helplessness in someone else's suffering. I could tell that the resolute almost jaunty brightness with which she now came into the Nursery was merely put on like a garment; and one day when anxiously, wistfully I followed her out of the room, I found her sitting on the stairs weeping as if her heart must break. Then for the first time I felt all the torture of ingrowing love—the curse of that tongue-tiedness for so many years to be my affliction; and stealthily—unseen, unheard—I tip-toed back into the Nursery only to find Nannie weeping for her favourite nursling.

Apart from the anguish of loss, my confidence was for ever shattered by that first sorrow. Gone for ever the sense of security that children, who happen to be fortunately circumstanced, usually take for granted. . . . So, after all, that sheltering love, in which one had felt oneself safely enfortressed, was no real protection? No child had ever been more loved than Colin, yet it had not kept him safe. . . . Then no one was safe? Even Mamma herself might "die"! Never after that winter of weeping, could I watch her set off on even the shortest journey without the thought that I might never see her face, never hear her voice again. Thus every parting, however brief, became a foretaste of death. Since that early realisation of the precariousness of life, my first symptom of an incipient new fondness is always the onset of acute apprehension; and when I first came on Juliet's anguished cry as Romeo descends to disappear from her sight:

> "Oh, God, I have an ill-divining soul!
> Methinks I see thee, now thou art so low,
> As one dead at the bottom of a tomb!"

it was with a shock of recognition.

With the death of Colin, the Nursery—for the three younger children were not born until some years later—came to an abrupt end. This too was a shock—the shock of complete uprooting.

Nannie, who had never tried to conceal her preference for Colin, had not been very kind to me. One day shortly after his death, just because I could not eat my pudding, she actually said, "God has taken the good one and left me the bad". The words seared my very soul. Nevertheless, like most children, I was limpet-like and attached myself to anyone who was there. In any case I had always thought of Nannie as something quite as permanent in life as the sky or Stanway its very self, and to find that she was not so, added to my sense of general bewilderment. Without that familiar, all pervading presence, I felt as if my whole known world were dissolving around me—my very sense of Me-ness crumbling back into nothingness. . . .

Sunshine was decreed necessary, so I and my two brothers—both of whom, one desperately, had been ill with that fatal scarlet fever—went with a new governess to spend the rest of the winter in the South of France. Expecting me to be enraptured, the governess and another stranger, the French maid, hoisted me up into one of the top bunks of our sleeping carriage. Though I think I did realise what fun this should have been, it did not stop me crying. Even the rich steaming sweetness of the hot chocolate brought to me in the morning was salt with my tears.

The roaring, rocketing train seemed to be hurtling me away from everything I knew. Indeed, I was leaving my infancy behind. For yet one more traveller 'twixt Life and Death the first stage of the journey was over.

136

EARLY LONDON MEMORIES

How large a part, you ask, did London play in my childhood?
Most years we spent what—I wondered why—was called the
"Season", May, June and July, in a large grimy house in
Cadogan Square, but except for certain dazzling treats these
months seemed only an interlude in my real life. I remember
how amazed I was when some child spoke of her father's
London house as her HOME! It had not occurred to me that
the mere drop-curtain that periodically fell between me and the
country could be the permanent "Set Scene" of anybody's life.
Perhaps, indeed, it was beyond my childish imagination to
conceive of existence not lived against the golden background
of Stanway.

I hated the London pavements; I hated having to wear
gloves; I hated going for sedate walks. Naturally I quite un-
noticingly took for granted the every-day affair of the dazzling
pageant of Hyde Park—attempted reproduction of which film-
goers now flock to see. But what a wonderful sight it was! That
unending flow of gleaming carriages and pairs; high-stepping,
foam-flecked thoroughbreds tossing rosetted heads; proud
coachmen caped and cockaded, at the side of each a footman
rectangularly erect with arms tightly folded across his chest.
And Rotten Row with all its lovely ladies in long flowing habits,
squired by top-hatted gallants. Cavorting and bucketing, the
gay cavalcade swept on its way, but here and there champing
horses would be reined-in to paw the ground while, talking
with friends, their riders propitiatingly patted their arched
necks.

Transported back in time to that vanished London, what
child of to-day would not stare open-mouthed? But just as he
takes for granted all the motor-cars—at sight, sound and smell

of which we would have stood transfixed—so did we all that glitter of colour, elegance and grace.

I think what I most disliked about London was Mamma's being so much taken up with "People". She was dreadfully often either out, or resting because she was going out, and when she was in, her drawing-room was much too apt to be infested with visitors. Too often—for this meant she was out to dinner—the hair-dresser, bag in hand, came to "do" her hair. Sometimes I was allowed to watch him ply his tongs. From association I still dislike the smell of singed hair because I thought his art subtly disguised Mamma.

Other things besides her estrangingly waved head conspired to prevent Mamma from ever seeming quite herself—her real Stanway self in London. In fact I remember thinking that nobody I knew elsewhere appeared quite natural in London, but became a sort of society wraith of their true self. One exception was Arthur Balfour, who, seemingly as unpreoccupied as ever, moved with precisely the same leisurely effortless grace; beamed with the same shining courtesy and lent to any converser—contemporary or child—the same flatteringly intent ear.

Another exception was Gan Gan who, in her large house in Belgrave Square, was just as radiantly loving and welcoming as at Clouds. There, my governess and myself could always propose ourselves to luncheon, for—hospitality now difficult to credit—she kept open house for this meal to which numerous people had a standing invitation and could come any day without giving any notice whatever. It was a pleasantly informal meal. Nobody waited at table and the delicious food to which you helped yourself was, as at a country-house breakfast, kept warm in lidded silver dishes set out on long hot-plates.

Because I didn't understand certain accepted social conventions, I strongly disapproved of them, and ignorant of the formula "Not at Home", I once embarrassingly intervened. I can still see the drowning look that came into the discomfited butler's eyes. "Her ladyship is not at home", I heard him inform an untimely caller. "But she *is*", I butted in. "She's on the sofa in the drawing-room." With an air of triumph—half defiant, half uneasy—the caller, a lady to whom the words "Not at Home" were only too familiar, rustled upstairs in the butler's wake. After I had ruined her afternoon's rest, Mamma tried with much patience but little success to make me understand exactly why a "white" lie was not an untruth.

Even more noticeably than Mamma, Papa had a very pronounced London self. Nothing, I assure you, in any way artificial or what, with a shudder, I vaguely condemned as "fashionable" or Societyish. On the contrary, he was only too apt to be even more unaffectedly natural than ever. Inclined to be glum and preoccupied, he was seldom in his chortling, never in his pillow-fighting mood at Cadogan Square. Quite often too, he would be in, when Mamma was out, to luncheon. This meant that the whole meal might well be as uncomfortable as whatever fraction of it her unpunctuality made her miss at Stanway. Some days my father's palpable boredom would make the atmosphere so oppressive that I could scarcely breathe, let alone digest my food in the thick silence broken only by the champ of his jaws, the loud breathing of the butler and Fräulein's strained conversational efforts—mostly interrogative chirrupings about the weather or the Royal family—efforts usually received with the merest bark of a "What?". Sometimes Fräulein, riding for a certain fall, would try to make me display the improvement she claimed to have made in my French. "Répétez votre pièce, Cincie, 'Maître corbeau sur un arbre perché.' "

So much did I dread the atmospheric discomfort of those meals and the sense of personal failure they gave me that I used at intervals throughout the morning to slip downstairs to peep into the hall in the hope of seeing that the top hat and its attendant pair of grey gloves had gone out. Extraordinary that I should ever have preferred the absence to the presence of a father whose company I afterwards found so supremely amusing!

For me the gloom I associated with London began as we neared Paddington station, and the long lines of soot-begrimed houses on either side of the train seemed to stretch out black arms to enfold me. Could such sordidly mean dwellings really be *homes* in which human beings lived and died? Each one so deadlily like the next, except that some of the tiny windows were uncurtained, and some had wisps of dirty-white Nottingham lace. Tin baths hung from hooks, grey flutterings of washing dried in the soot-laden air. Here and there—pitiful aspiration—was some fragment of wilting vegetation, perhaps a dying geranium in a window-box, or a maidenhair fern.

Except for the workhouse—and the melodramatic horror of that place gave it almost the unreality of nightmare—there was little near Stanway to impress the inequality of human circumstances painfully on a child's mind. Hard, straitened and meagre though life in country cottages might be, at least it was not dingy, but from those town tenements there seeped a sense of sordid poverty that poisoned the very air. The East and the West Ends of London were too closely juxtaposed, the contrast between them too violent to fail to penetrate even the trance of happy childhood, deep though that was. However fast "asleep in lap of legends old" you might be, a sharp disquietude aggravated by a vague feeling of guilt troubled your golden drowse.

Each morning, only a few minutes' walk from our own house, we would pass haunting beggars—some distressingly crippled, others with faces pitted with smallpox, and sealed eyes. Bloodless supplicating lips quivered into tremulous thanks when with a "tonk" my halfpenny fell into a tin mug. Thinly shawled, pinched, peaky babies were perched in baskets on barrel-organs. Or in their place wretched shivering monkeys in scarlet jackets and military caps, their poignantly human hands clutchingly outheld and all the sorrow of the world in their captive eyes.

Nothing more effectually swings me back to London childhood than the now so conspicuously rare sound of a barrel-organ. Even when it was constantly heard and therefore not, as it now is, so wistfully redolent of the past, its music—either resignedly, openly sad, or else jadedly, doggedly grinding out a resolutely cheerful tune—smote mournfully upon my ears.

Which do you find most evocative of the past, noises or scents?

A brass band is another sound that infallibly wafts me back into the London bedroom where I slept as a child. Every Monday at six o'clock a German one marched into our Square and for a whole hour blared out stridently patriotic or yearningly sentimental tunes. Yet another sound, now in most parts of London rare enough to make a child turn his head in his perambulator, is the clop, clop, clop of a horse pulling a heavy van. Whenever I hear that patient, plodding sound, the long long ago surges back.

In the London of the nineties there was plenty to distress readers of *Black Beauty*, both amongst the bearing-rein-tortured thoroughbreds of the rich and the over-worked, underfed cart-horses with their bearded fetlocks and sticking-out ribs. Sometimes, heartrending sight, you saw one who, fallen between the shafts of some heavy van, lay feebly kicking on the ground, while his master mercilessly lashed him to make him struggle on to his feet again.

"Sweet Luv-ven-der" and countless other street cries, now no longer to be heard, still ring in my memory's ear. Muffin-bells too, and the hoarse echoing shouts of running newspaper boys—"Orrible Mur-dah! Orrible Mur-dah!"

"Sixty-two", as we always called it, was a large corner-house in Cadogan Square; to my mind—I don't like purely residential quarters—one of the dreariest, least interesting addresses in London. Built of inflamed red brick in the period of most elaborate ugliness, "Sixty-two", though I grew fond enough of it to be sad when it had to be sold, was I think a singularly depressing abode. Five stories high, with a basement; the surface it presented to wretched maids to try—their failure was signal—to keep clean, was dauntingly large; yet the accommodation the house provided was inadequate, for it abounded in those waste spaces by house-agents grandiloquently called "entresols".

I think "Sixty-two" must have been in one of the dirtiest corners in all London—"zulus" we used to call the huge smuts that congregated on the small leaded window-panes.

The immensely high dining-room overlooked a small square

yard, in which the sole feature was a saucer for the cat with the backbone of a fish in it.

The embossed walls of this room—olive-green in colour— were studded with some eighty engravings of historical personages. The combined effect of these was about as en- livening as a sheet of postage stamps.

My father's room, halfway up between the dining-room and the first floor, was of an angry red.

The yellow-papered drawing-room was pleasant with some- thing of Mamma's Stanway self in its atmosphere. Here, with green taffeta cushions at the back of her head she would recline on a long sofa, or seated in front of a large silver blotting book at a round table littered with invitation cards, cover page after page with her lovely flowing hand-writing. The broad window-ledge held quantitites of vases filled with flowers that came up every week from Stanway.

I had a great liking for the "practicable" balcony on which I would stand on the lookout for the "Enemy" (callers) or, if Mamma was out, to watch for her return. From this point of vantage I also threw pennies at organ-grinders, and when the mood took us, Guy and I would pelt passers-by with spat-out cherry-stones or drip water on to their elaborate hats.

The back drawing-room—the schoolroom of my governessed days, my "Bed-Sitter" after I came out—was most unfortun- ately situated between the back and the front stairs. Through this, the main artery of the house, flowed all day long a con- tinuous stream of life—Nannies carrying down babies from the alpine heights of the nurseries; housemaids with dustpans; footmen staggering with heavy trays or dragged by chows straining at the leash and trying to choke themselves in their collars.

Unlike Stanway, "Sixty-two" had two "big baths", both encased in heavy mahogany frames.

The small, square, quite impersonal bedroom of my school- room days opened on to the gated landing of the fourth floor. I remember how strange I found it the first morning after our migration from Stanway to awaken to the rumble of traffic instead of to the twitter of birds, and to look out on to chimney-pots instead of on trees. The only feature of any interest in the outlook from my bedroom was the Great Wheel. At this I would gaze every night, and try to convince myself that, slowly though the weeks might crawl, Eton's Long Leave *would* come and then we should go to Earl's Court again!

I remember my envy of those lucky people who, happening to be in the Great Wheel when it got stuck, had to spend the whole night in it! As though such an adventure were not in itself sufficient bliss, sailors swarmed up to the Wheel with baskets of buns, and each passenger was given £5 *compensation*!

"Sixty-two" had one permanent housemaid whose hair was perpetually in steel curlers—in preparation for what occasion we never knew, for just as some people boast of having no vices, she would self-righteously affirm that she had no friends—"I keeps myself to myself". I wonder she did not wholly lose the faculty of speech during the nine months when but for her and the mangy cat the house was unoccupied. All the other "servants"—for so we then quite unselfconsciously called those who so benevolently ordered our lives—"came up" for the season from Stanway. But even these well-tried friends seemed different in London. There was no cricket on the lawn to keep us in close touch, and apparently the footmen were too busy to invite me to play Nap in the pantry. Even the naturally bright dispositions of Eliza and Leah, the delightful first and second housemaids, were somewhat darkened by their losing battle against the army of unalterable smuts. There was never any pancake-tossing or toffee-making for me in the London kitchen. The cook's temper was chronically inflamed. With her cheeks several shades a more fiery red than at Stanway, she looked as though she had overcooked herself. Indeed, on a hot summer's day the heat of that blazing fire was ferocious, and in the groans of the revolving spit and the view on to the back yard and the cat's fish-bone there was nothing to sweeten her imagination.

I remember the tense, tight-lipped bustle that preceded a dinner-party—the hot blasts of cooking that came up from the basement. Sometimes Mamma took me with her when she went to Harrod's Stores to choose the dessert for these special occasions. That was about all the housewifely shopping Mammas, as I remember them, ever seemed to do, and for this no shopping-basket was needed. All goods were promptly delivered at the shortest notice. First directed to the requisite counter by several bowing-from-the-waist floorwalkers, Mammas, instead of having to stand in queues, were assiduously served by assistants who no doubt owed their jobs to the excellence of their manners, and who apparently had unlimited time to discuss with proper deliberation the relative merits of various varieties of peaches.

A purchase finally made, the salesman would fervently thank the buyer for the "favour of her custom".

Besides fruit, Mamma used to buy dinner-party sweets—"fondants" and "bon-bons" in little paper boats. Some of these I usually managed to snatch during their transit from basement to dining-room.

One day I was told a real live Princess was coming to luncheon. Thrilled, I watched the roll of red baize being unfurled across the pavement from our doorstep. Nurtured on fairy stories, I of course expected to see alight from a crystal coach a lovely apparition in gorgeous raiment, with a crown of stars on her golden head and glass slippers on her feet. It was an unforgettable shock when a perfectly ordinary one-horse brougham drew up at the door and from it there stepped an aquiline Elderly Person—not only strictly plain but hatted, tweeded and sensibly shod! No wonder I bungled my curtsy. That was my first sight of Royalty. My second—a distant one— was of a small black bundle, pink-faced and bonneted; but even at such long range that black bundle had dignity, authority— even majesty, as well as poignancy. Moreover there were the famous eight cream-coloured horses. Also the sound of cheering. My eyes filled with tears as Queen Victoria passed on one of her last drives.

When Mamma was not in residence, "Sixty-Two" was wonderfully gloomy with sheeted furniture, newspapered pictures and uncarpeted, reverberating stairs, but I never came to London between the end of July and the following May unless for an odd night or two to have my teeth seen to, then an excruciating ordeal that punctuated the year of every well-looked-after child. In those days, I think a dentist must have been esteemed in direct ratio to the amount of pain he inflicted. Mine had a great reputation. I have but to see a bound volume of *Punch* to be back in an agony of anticipation in his waiting-room.

What was my everyday life throughout the Season? Lessons alone with Squidge from nine till twelve, followed by exercise in Hyde Park. Like all children and many grown-ups I enlivened London walks by imposing arbitrary legislation on my feet. Either every crack in the pavement must be stepped on or not one single one. The penalties for infringement of these self-imposed laws were severe. Another pastime was to attract compassionate glances by counterfeiting a heavy limp. "Poor little girl. I wonder how that happened", ladies would whisper and I enjoyed Squidge's blushes. I also thought it very funny to ring front-door bells and make my escape the moment the butler appeared.

On our way to the Park we always conversed with amiable crossing-sweepers and boot-blacks; and we had two other great friends—an old man to whose crippled hands was tethered a tugging bunch of balloons, and a dear old lady with her stock-in-trade of whirring paper windmills.

Some days there would be the excitement of meeting soldiers. A sudden jingle and clatter, and all heads would turn as horse-guards in gleaming breastplates, with black muffs on their heads and fur under their saddles, trotted by; or infantry in scarlet tunics and pillbox caps marched past, their feet swung forwards by the stirring music of their drums and fifes:

> "Oh, listen to the Band,
> Oh don't you think it grand?"

My governess loved walks in the Park, especially on Sunday mornings between Church and luncheon when a dazzling parade of fashion was always to be seen. Furbelowed ladies in shimmer and sheen of flounced taffetas, watered silk and satin with hour-glass figures, leg-of-mutton sleeves, and ostrich-feather boas, slowly sauntering beneath fringed parasols and eyeing one another's vast hats, bright with flowers, feathers and fruit. It was like a herbaceous border come alive!

I thought the Park tedious. What I loved was romping in the communal garden to which every householder in Cadogan Square had a key. Unless some special engagement forbade, I enjoyed this every evening after tea, and it was the one great redeeming feature of my London routine. From this exceedingly rough fun I returned evening after evening in tatters (oh, the rows over my ruined clothes!) my face black with soot, my kneecaps scalped by tumbles on the gravel paths. Sometimes we would be as many as thirty children. Flags, or as it was then called (what would it be called to-day?) "French and English", was my favourite game. I also loved "Gymnasium"—hotly contested high and long jump championships and two garden benches put together for parallel bars. Thanks to the length and strength of my limbs and my *then* admittedly highly competitive spirit, I was for some years the queen of Cadogan Square. Since this was the only sphere in which I ever achieved recognised ascendancy, I suppose it was only natural that I should not want to be encumbered by a baby sister clinging to my petticoats. Nevertheless to this day my cheeks burn with shame at the memory of Mary's gently reproachful appeal, "Please, Cincie, do *try* to remember that I'm your sister."

Once great vicarious prestige came my way. Before motor horns had made futile the muffling of other traffic noises, serious illness was dignified by the laying down of straw outside the sufferer's house. One year my father fell desperately ill with double pneumonia, and to deaden all noise a lovely thick bed of straw was spread for many yards to each side of our house. Never before or since have I felt such self-importance. "That's for my father", I announced, trying to keep my voice casual. I then organised relay races in which, to the detriment of our clothes, I and my Cadogan Square cronies luxuriously rolled in the delectable but far from clean straw. When some lady with a face like a hen asked me how, with my father "lying at Death's

Door", I could be "such a callous little girl", I was hurt to the quick.

Swarming with the pets as well as with the daughters of its residents, Cadogan Square was the arena of fierce dog fights. My huge Chow, well named Siegfried, a mighty warrior armoured in impenetrable fluff and an adept at freeing himself from the then legally enforced muzzle, was all conquering. When the Roll of Honour of Siegfried's victims reached a certain length, the Square called a committee meeting, and to my gnashing rage unanimously carried a resolution in favour of his excommunication! Thereafter poor Siegfried's exercise was limited to tearing round and round outside the railings of his Paradise Lost, with myself, like the feeble tail to a huge kite, at the end of the steel chain on his collar.

Occasionally I went out "calling" with Mamma. Not so much to leave visiting cards (this I think was done at the end of the season by a footman) but when she visited some friend by appointment. This was not always an enjoyable treat, for my fate, whether or not I was welcome, was to be precipitated into the nursery or the schoolroom of the children of the house and left to their mercies while our respective mothers conversed.

I was given a startling reception on one of these occasions. Scarcely had the door closed on my timid entry before the six-years-old son of the house, my host on compulsion (a future Cabinet Minister) snatched up a whip and slashed me thrice with its leather thong. When both our mothers asked why three crimson weals decorated my face there was some embarrassment. I have often wondered what motive prompted that embryo statesman. Possibly, by treating me exactly like a sister, to make me feel quite at home.

The more formal kind of calling—the leaving or returning of visiting cards—I associate with my country rather than with my London mother, and perhaps more with the breach than with the observance of this now rapidly dying custom. Towards the end of her life I remember her setting out to return a call that had been paid her over forty years before! Her neglect to return it more punctually had been a pure oversight, and she had been much distressed to hear that she had given offence.

Never was there a more triumphant instance of "Better late than never".

Mamma did not have her own carriage and horses in London. Occasionally she would hire a vehicle called a "coupé", but usually we relied on the ordinary hackney carriages. Four-wheelers—"growlers", as they were called—I did not like. They crawled, and smelt strongly of ammonia and straw. Hansom cabs—the gondolas of London, as someone called those gayest of conveyances—I have never ceased to regret. I loved their jauntiness, the jingle of the bells on the horse's head, and the way the doors closed across my legs like a wooden apron. When the butler was in a good humour he would allow me to call a cab with the tin whistle kept for the purpose—two blasts for a four-wheeler, one for a hansom.

I loved going on the tops of omnibuses when they were still horse-drawn, and I can just remember the bliss of once sitting on the box beside the driver, an unforgettably witty Cockney, and being allowed to hold the reins.

Shopping was a fairly frequent outing. Hours were spent and innumerable cardboard boxes taken from their shelves in the attempt to fit my "difficult" feet. The black-satined saleswomen did not say "Ta", address you as "Dear" or "Ducks", or tell you "the other young lady" would serve you, but their patience and courtesy was inexhaustible. It was a family joke that my mother could never transact the smallest purchase without taking whoever was serving her into full confidence and telling her the whole story of all our lives. Being herself so intensely interested in others, she naturally assumed a reciprocal interest, and I must say she was very seldom disappointed.

London Sundays were gloved and gloomy; the houses as well as the shops seeming to have their eyes shut. I was always taken to Church, either to the children's service in St. Peter's, Eaton Square, where my parents had been married, or to Holy Trinity, Sloane Street, where I was myself to be married. Compared with the little country churches, the large London ones struck me as cold and without atmosphere—rather like dining-rooms between meals.

Occasionally Sunday was irradiated by a visit to the Zoo.

As soon as we had clanked our way through the turnstile, Mamma ensconced herself in a bath-chair, and gave the offer of her lap to any child not too proud to perch. Much as I loved the Zoo, it was not an unmitigated treat. The lions troubled me—that proud slow padding of their narrow confines, and the majestic melancholy of the tawny unblinking eyes that stared right through me. I hated to see the keeper shovel hunks of raw meat—surely no meal to set before kings?—into their cages. "But when are they going to eat the *Man*?" asked one little girl. Perhaps some such thought strayed into my own mind.

Neither did I ever wholeheartedly enjoy what many children considered the crowning treat at the Zoo—a ride on the elephant. But since my moral then outstripped my physical cowardice—they're neck to neck now!—nothing would have induced me to confess my reluctance to join the cargo of children on that immense, crinkled grey back. When my turn came, I pretended not to mind being perched up so dizzyingly high with the iron railing of the saddle, into which I was strapped, biting into my backbone.

I also flinched from the ordeal, considered such a privilege, of holding a bun out to the elephant. Oh, that dread questing trunk—relentlessly narrowing its swing until, horribly twitching, it pointed right at me!

I had a very special tenderness for the wart-hog, the poignancy of whose extreme ugliness seemed almost to reach sublimity. Poor bleary-eyed monster in his coat of furrowed leather with its wisps of bristling hair! He was exactly my imagination's picture of the spellbound hero of my favourite fairy story *Beauty and the Beast*.

What I thought *the* star turn at the Zoo was the feeding of the Sea Lions. But enough! There's nothing "Period" about Zoo memories. Except that neither the Mappin Terraces nor the Ape Hill existed, nor yet that triumph of architecture, the Penguins' House, I fancy going to the Zoo was very much the same to a child of the nineteenth century as it is to-day. For the same reason I won't tell you of my emotions at the Dead Zoo, as we called the Natural History Museum; the Bloody

Tower; the Military Tournament; Madame Tussaud's (Chamber of Horrors strictly out of bounds) and the British Museum—in my childhood associated only with Egyptian mummies. All these things children can still sample for themselves, but there was one superlative treat that alas I cannot give my grandchildren, for Earl's Court no longer exists! For years that "Amusement Park"—for thus I suppose it would now unworthily be called—was exactly my idea of paradise.

On the night of the Eton and Harrow cricket match the whole vast place seethed with boys and girls; echoed with their yells of delight. The switchback was good enough (its climax of the double dip made even the phlegmatic shriek) but the water-chute! That really was ecstasy. I suppose it *was* only a physical experience, but heaven knows it seemed spiritual enough. The rapturous suspense of the slow stammering ascent, the at first stealthy downward glide instantaneously accelerating into a breathtaking swish through the air. Down, down, down, shot the boat, until with a gigantic slap it struck the surface of the water and bounded off it high into the air; again and again like a pebble in Ducks and Drakes, the boat rose until—its subsidiary bounces gradually diminishing—at long last it settled itself on the churned and foaming waters.

Besides the switchback and the water-chute, Earl's Court had many other attractions, less delirious but very enjoyable. There we first enjoyed the germ of the cinematograph—penny-in-the-slot machines in which, by turning a handle, you saw simple and sometimes very mildly "risky" stories told by photographs. And each year in an immense tent some dramatic performance—half play, half pageant with a terrific din of gunfire and Zulu yells and a stench of gunpowder, commemorated some triumph of our Island Story. My Jingoistic little soul used to swell with pride at these glorifications of British triumphs over "Lesser Breeds Without the Law". I remember being especially moved when a noble conquering Britisher, standing over the corpse of his fallen adversary—a Fuzzy-Wuzzy—generously exclaimed, "A BRAVE MAN is a BRAVE MAN no matter what the colour of his skin may be." How we all cheered!

Despite the bliss of Earl's Court, the real glory of the London of my early memories is of course as the place in which I first knew those pinnacles of all childhood experiences—FIRST THEATRES!

I was nine when I was taken to my first play, *The Two Little Vagabonds*, a curdling melodrama in which even the hero, an undersized and wholly innocent child of exactly my own age, was stabbed to death. On my return almost unconscious from the theatre, I was catastrophically sick in the hall and so ill afterwards from over-excitement that I had to stay in bed for a fortnight.

The following year I went—perhaps the greatest milestone in my life—to *Julius Caesar*. Read aloud, the play had profoundly moved me, and I was in an absolute fever to know how various things would be "done". The thunder and lightning? And Caesar's blood? Above all what would the GHOST be like?

All through the long-drawn-out dinner I was in a torture of suspense lest we should start too late to reach the theatre before the curtain rose. I shovelled down my food, but what was the good when my parents ate so slowly? They would talk too. Not about the play, but of wholly unimportant things. It had never occurred to me that the ice I'd golloped down was not the last course, but to my horror I saw the hovering butler advance with a savoury—little bits of liver wrapped in rolled-up slices of bacon mounted on toast. In no mood to be amused by being told these were called Angels on Horseback, I groaned and fidgeted while Papa carefully salted, peppered and mustarded his dismounted "Angel", and then very slowly, appraisingly chumped it up. He then asked for another!

"Oughtn't we to go now?" I mumbled.

"Go now?" chortled Papa. "We'd be twenty minutes too early!"

Mamma assured me we should not be late. Meantime the minutes ticked by. To my despair the butler appeared with yet another tray. Coffee! What was this crazy meal? Breakfast, luncheon and dinner all in one? I just managed to endure Papa's slow sipping of his coffee, but when having drawn a cigar from his case he deliberately snipped off its nose and lolled back in his chair, I could restrain myself no longer. My tears —they were very well laid-on (a constant supply of salt water) —gushed out.

Taking pity on me, Mamma, to Papa's visible relief, said she would take me on ahead. The butler whistled twice for a hansom. Before it had quite pulled up, my foot was on its high springy step. The drive seemed endless. Half way through it Mamma nearly stopped my heart by saying she had left the tickets behind. (I don't remember ever going to a theatre with her without a recurrence of this panic.) However, when an astounding variety of objects had been spilled out of her velvet bag on to her lap, the alarm was found to be false.

At last the cabman pulled at his long reins, and with a scrape of hooves the horse drew up outside Her Majesty's Theatre. I saw the words "Julius Caesar" in electric letters. Crowds were streaming through the open doors. Ushering them into heaven, two magnificent men with powdered heads—commissionaires in gold braided uniform and silk stockings—shouted in voices of thunder, "Stalls this way, please. Dress circle upstairs." With cold shivers running down my spine, I followed Mamma down the carpeted slope to the stalls. To this day I never descend that incline without a faint stirring of those first tremors, and if I am with children, the ricochet I get from their excitement reawakens nearly all the original thrill.

Awestruck I gaped at that epitome of all mystery, the heavy, solemn curtain. We were in very good time. The air was alive with thrilling twangs, pluckings and scrapes. The great orchestra was still only tuning up. Soon it was playing on my very heart strings. Ten minutes later the curtain twitched, looped itself up into crinkled folds and slowly swung apart on a dazzling scene—blue sky, white pillars, clamouring "citizens", haughty, togaed "Tribunes". I was in Rome!

A few minutes later I had fallen fathoms deep in love—it lasted for years—with Brutus. I suppose Lewis Waller did have something to do with it, but I swear I never thought of him by that name or, indeed, imagined him as anything other than the "noblest Roman of them all". Was it his melancholy aquiline face, or that deep, mournful, husky voice? Mostly his voice, I think.

Enthralled, my own identity quite forgotten, I became dazedly but indignantly aware of some wretched late-comer trampling over my feet. Blocking my view of Brutus, a bulky body shoved its way in front of me and plumped itself down in the empty seat at my side. My ear was pinched. The late-comer was my own father! Mamma turned her head to whisper to him. Appalled lest she should miss a second of the play, I seized hold of her chin and twisted her head towards the stage. Papa gave an only half stifled snort of amusement. "Stage-struck, I see", he said. How *dared* he talk? Brutus was actually speaking!

The curtain fell with a swoop; the theatre burst into a blaze of light and the audience into loud chatter. Far, far away, everything seemed—utterly unreal. I couldn't speak.

Thunder muttered and rumbled; the curtain rose on flashes of lightning and hissing rain. Through all the din of that "tempest dropping fire", I could hear Casca with commendable calm describe the startling walk he had just had during which, so he said, he had met "a slave whose hand did flame and burn like twenty torches joined; a lion that glared upon him and went sadly by without annoying him, and a hundred women transformed by their fear!"

In the moonlit orchard of the next scene, Brutus looked terribly careworn, and deepened my love for him by complaining that he could not sleep. When Caesar was assassinated I wept, but not, oh not for him, but because Brutus looked so sad at having to kill him. The supply of blood was generously lavish—sufficient to make two long crimson sleeves for each conspirator. . . .

The curtain rose on the seething, yelling mob in the forum. Even to the most hardened play-goers this was a memorable stage effect. The crowd, four hundred in number, had been produced by Reinhardt.

In the quarrel scene in the tent, the poignancy of one lock of Brutus's raven hair having gone white from grief and anxiety was yet another turn of the screw in my heart.

The ghost, merely a phosphorescent head, was a disappointment, but the Battle of Philippi was superb—plumed helmets, clash of swords on shields, "alarums", and "excursions".

My tears gushed out afresh when Brutus said goodbye to his friend.

> "For ever and for ever, farewell Cassius.
> If we do meet again, why we shall smile;
> If not, this parting was well made."

A few minutes later his beautiful voice—now the merest husk of a whisper—gasped out his last words:

> "Caesar, now be still.
> I killed not thee with half so good a will."

Before the curtain fell, those around me began with unbelievable callousness to grope for their hats and umbrellas in a practical, disengaged way. This jarred on me terribly. But when the curtain rose and—inexplicable resurrection—the newly dead came forward and took calls, my feelings were still more outraged. Utterly dazed—I was still in Rome—I was led from the theatre. Hazily I heard the clop, clop, clop of hooves; the click of the latch-key. Soon a sandwich was in my mouth, but it seemed someone else's mouth. Vibrating with emotion I fell asleep with snatches of Brutus's words still ringing in my ears. . . .

The memory of Julius Caesar hung like a thick curtain between me and reality. Nothing could distract me.

Somehow—no doubt the fluency of my tears helped—I prevailed on Mamma to let me go to the play again and again. The sixth time I suffered hideous disillusionment. Some well-intentioned person thought I should like to go Behind the Scenes, and took me to see Mark Anthony in his dressing-room. Flushed, panting, his forehead beaded from the exertion of his great oration, Beerbohm Tree graciously received us. My love for Brutus had of course made me hostile to Mark Antony, however, I was touched to see that the tears he had shed over Caesar's corpse still glistened on his cheeks. Imagine my

feelings when—most amiably, wishing to please me—the great
actor-manager tore off his tears in two strips. They'd only
been stuck on! "Good dodge, isn't it?" he said. "My own
idea. Well placed gelatine. Looks well from the front,
doesn't it?"

Enthusiasm fired Mary Vesey and me to learn the quarrel
scene between Brutus and Cassius. In this, our stock
dramatic piece, revived unnumbered times for the
"entertainment" of visitors, we wore bath-towels for togas,
and our legs were cross-gartered with hair-ribbons. I became
more than a little bored by the sarcastic remarks on my
suitability to the part of a Roman because of the shape
of my nose—a feature I was sensitive about, for no one
had yet had the elementary courtesy to call it tip-tilted,
instead of "turned up".

Despite my unswerving loyalty to Brutus via Lewis Waller,
I was deeply moved by Sidney Carton via Martin Harvey.
Never has drunkenness been so delicately depicted. So romantic
a figure did he make of the poor wastrel that you felt there must
be something radically amiss with anyone who did not waste his
life. Lucy Manette! Simpering golden-haired doll! Fancy
loving that drearily respectable Charles Darnay instead of that
glamorous rake!

Our enthusiasm for *The Only Way* stirred Mary Vesey and
me to vaulting ambition. We decided we must act the whole
play, and *I* decided that Sidney Carton must be played by
Cynthia Charteris. As many of the housemaids and kitchen-
maids in the neighbourhood as we could cajole were enlisted
to act the revolutionary mob and coached to murmur "Rhubarb,
Rhubarb, Rhubarb".

We planned to do things on a really grand scale and charge
very high prices for the seats. I shall never forget our agony
of disappointment when we were kindly but firmly told our
project must be indefinitely postponed. . . .

For years I continued rapturously stage-struck (in fact, I've
never really got over it), and it was a very long time before I
ever thought of a play as a performance—something to be

criticised. To me it was not entertainment, but *experience*, far more real and intense than any of my own yesterdays and to-morrows. Identifying myself with the characters, I suffered all their vicissitudes. Had the curtain been about to rise on my own future, I could not possibly have been more concerned.

Instead of "Would you like to go to *The Only Way* again?" the question should have been, "Would you like to *be* Sidney Carton again?"

The spell has broken once a child begins to enjoy the more sophisticated pleasures of play-going—criticising the actors, detecting their make-up, overhearing the prompter, glimpsing scene-shifters in the wings.

I remember how much it jarred on me even to hear actors and actresses talked of by their real names.

As for my contempt for grown-up people with souls so dead that they would arrive at the theatre after the curtain had gone up and begin to rootle under the seats for their umbrellas before its final fall!

The shock of return to the everyday world of omnibuses and schoolroom-tea after a matinée was too painful. This was one of my many reasons for preferring an evening performance. Instead of going home to the anticlimax of the tail-end of the day, I came out into the spangled darkness and tumbled into bed with the sound of clapping still in my ears, the insubstantial pageant fading only into my dreams.

Thanks to my early initiation into Shakespeare, he became (and remained) my favourite dramatist. Apart from the glorious pomp of the words, I revelled in the sheer size of the casts in his plays. There was then no minimum wage, and many otherwise employed were glad to earn a few shillings a night by "walking-on" parts.

My heart leapt up when I saw on the programme the promise of "Lords, Heralds, Messengers, Attendants, Citizens, Courtiers, Serving Men" and so forth. *Macbeth*, of course, was easily first for categories. First, Second, and Third Witch, and First, Second, and Third Murderer!

Disliking to see my favourite fairy-stories travestied, I did not

approve of pantomimes, nor, though I remember wallowing
in *The Country Girl* :

> "There would I rest,
> Close to his breast,
> Under the Deodar."

did I greatly care for Musical Comedy.

Irving, alas, I saw only in *The Bells*—an unforgettable
experience—and as Coriolanus; Ellen Terry—but it was
enough to make me feel all I'd been told of her lovely witchery
—only as Queen Katherine in *Henry VIII* and as Mrs. Quickly
in *The Merry Wives of Windsor*.

The first comedy I remember with delight was *The
Messenger from Mars,* in which the ineffable Charles Hawtrey
(to this day I never go to a comedy without a pang because he
cannot be in it) was at his incomparable best. The moral and
action of this play closely resembled those of *The Christmas
Carol*. For the good of his sleeping soul, Hawtrey was made
to take a midnight walk through the slums of London in deep
snow. The best moment was when that stern missionary, the
Messenger from Mars, arraigned him with the words, "Your
heart is as cold as a stone." "It isn't my heart", deliciously
amended Hawtrey, with chattering teeth, "it's my *feet*."

Never have I heard a line so perfectly spoken!

My mother, whom I can reproach for so little, *was* guilty
of two sins of omission. Why, oh why, was I not taken to see
either Dan Leno, or Eleanora Duse?

BROTHERS

Since both Mary and Bibs were so much younger than me, the companions of my childhood were brothers, not sisters. I was very sorry not to be a boy myself and, longing to excel at whatever activities were then considered most unfeminine, I quarrelled fiercely with my petticoats and hankered after bruises and scars. Deploring the fairness of my skin, I sought to remedy this girlish defect by holding up my face, still wet with salt water after bathing, to the sun in the hope that it would blister and peel. Another wish was to have very large feet. For this blessing I literally prayed. In this respect, I was given no cause to doubt the efficacy of prayer.

Needless to say these ambitions were short-lived. Before long I was assiduously cold-creaming my face and wincing at my father's horrid habit of discomfiting his daughter by telling well-grown young men who came to Stanway unequipped for lawn tennis that they could borrow her shoes!

One disadvantage of being brought up with boys instead of with girls was that I had nobody to quarrel with. I imagine all brothers who are much of an age do quarrel. Certainly Ego and Guy sometimes fought like two dogs—I used to find them in a panting tangle on the floor—but naturally their younger sister was left out of these rough and tumbles. Had I had a contemporary sister, I should, no doubt, have waged some sort of warfare, but with brothers, no.

Ego, three years older than myself, was invariably the ideal protective elder brother—a shield and a guide.

Guy, only a year and a half my senior, of course teased me at times as was only right and proper, but I can't remember our ever having anything approaching a quarrel. Perhaps that is partly why I am to this day still such a poor hand at a quarrel.

Yvo Charteris.

Drawing of author's brother, Ego, by Violet Rutland.

Such things, no doubt, like others, require early practice. At times my incapacity for quarrelling worries me. With Hamlet I ask: "Can it be that I am pigeon-livered, and lack gall to make oppression bitter?"; but rake my memory as I will, I honestly can't remember ever missing any real cue for a quarrel with either brother. I really don't think there was any "oppression".

The only way in which Ego and Guy tortured me in my early infancy was by periodically asking which of them I loved most. For this question—far too delicate to be answered in words—a dumb-show reply was devised. Two horses were taken from a box of tin cavalry soldiers—one brown, the other black. If the answer was Ego, I must silently replace the black horse in the box; if Guy, the brown.

The worst of brothers was that they went away to school leaving me to solitary schoolroom routine in a house gone deadly quiet.

After you grow up, life seldom allows you to concentrate on any one particular thing—not even on one grief. But in childhood, so completely are you in the grip of the present that no faintest gleams can be discerned through black tunnels of immediate misery. Then, partings are dramatised out of all proportion to the length of impending separations. No later leave-takings ever quite came up to the agony of those thrice-yearly seeings-off—eternal farewells they might as well have been—when Ego and Guy went back to school, and my anguish at the railway station was complicated by the terror of disgracing my brothers in front of their schoolfellows. Whatever emotions Ego and Guy themselves might feel could be hidden behind some upheld newspaper—*Tit-Bits, Punch* or the *Strand Magazine* for choice—but for myself vainly trying to restrain my welling tears, no such convenient shelter was possible. Instead of being publicly pilloried on the departure platform, I would really—though of course I never admitted this—much have preferred to stay at home, where locked into the bathroom I could have wept myself into stupefaction. In the childish hopes that tears were exhaustible, I used by copious weeping overnight to try to empty my salt-water reservoir only

M   159

to learn that with tears, as with other commodities, the supply directly depends on the demand, and that no worse preparation for the morrow's ordeal could possibly have been made. There was nothing for it but to pray for self-control. When this failed, I turned my back on the train and simulated the most unnatural absorption in the penny-in-the-slot machines. Once, unable to see what I was about because of a blinding veil of tears, I put my very last penny in the wrong slot, and instead of a solacing slab of coconut-cream, the wretched machine spat out an arid packet of cigarettes!

When the agonising day of Ego's first departure for school came, he confided into my keeping the so-called battleaxe— really a wooden truncheon—that had played so large a part in our "Let's Pretend" games in the dark, mysterious little yew-tree wood. When we were not Red Indians, most of these games were inspired by Morte d'Arthur, and you can imagine how tired the girl who wanted to be a boy became of her rôle of the Damsel-in-Distress.

Deeply moved that Ego should have entrusted me with his sacred weapon, I hid it in the hollow of a tree. To my horror it disappeared and was never seen again!

I can't tell you how much I dreaded having to confess that I had failed in my trust. But what happened was far, far worse than any imaginable reproach. When Ego, partly a stranger brother—for the boy who goes away to school never quite returns—came home for the holidays, he never so much as asked after his truncheon. Evidently he had forgotten all about it. Initiation into school—for his first term at Cheam was not happy—had been too obliterating an experience. With other fond trivial records, that once cherished weapon of childish make-believe had been wiped from the table of his memory.

In early boyhood, Ego and Guy, though good friends, were very unlike. Guy at that stage was very noticeably the least shy of the three of us and therefore able to cheek his father—this approach was always the best passport to that shy paternal heart—so with him at first he was the favourite. Most of us in turn had our day.

I remember how amused Papa was when he gave Guy, who

had been caught smoking with the footmen in the pantry, a very strong cigar—the idea being that such a violent homœopathic overdose would put any small boy off smoking; instead of which, Guy puffed away with the utmost enjoyment until the cigar was quite finished and then asked for another! Papa was also delighted by Guy's remarkably early prowess with a gun, and as pleased as Punch—for to a fault he liked praise of his children—when a report of his success at a shoot at the age of nine appeared in the newspaper.

One marked difference between the two boys was that whereas Ego at every age was enthusiastically keen on all orthodox games, Guy, though he became a loyal and very useful member of the cricket club that played so large a part in Stanway life, always had a great predilection for Natural History. Indeed, he had so strong a bent for this that it distresses my mercenary mind that he has never turned so much knowledge and talent to worldly gain.

In the cricket field, he had a tendency to watch the flight of a bird rather than that of the ball; and in the bird-nesting season to play truant from team-games, as well as to absent himself from all dining-room meals. In my most vivid pictures of Guy as a boy, he is climbing a tree, blowing an egg, or skinning some dead animal.

As he may read what I write and is very far from devoid of a critical faculty, nothing would induce me to attempt a description of Guy. I shall let him off by gratefully recording that many of the most enjoyable, though perhaps not what grown-up people considered the most praiseworthy, hours of my childhood were spent in his company.

But I must try to tell you a little about Ego. For one thing I'd like you to have some idea of him, and for my own sake I shall be glad to summon up remembrance of things past.

First, I think I should explain the possibly misleading nickname universally adopted of Ego. You might suppose it to derive from the word egotism, and that would be very wide of the mark. It came merely from his own babyish attempt to pronounce his real name, Hugo.

There is no doubt that Ego did represent something special

to his own generation. What was it? Something most difficult, indeed impossible, to define. To say that he was unique is futile—the least of us is that! But some rare quality that left on those who knew him an impression they cannot forget inspired an instinctive respect as well as affection. A friend of his once said, "As a human being, Ego is like a classic in literature or in art. I mean to say that suppose I were unable to appreciate him, I wouldn't admit it. I'd be ashamed to own up to such a blind spot."

No doubt his appearance helped. There was something in the steady gaze of his dark eyes—intensely solemn, often melancholy eyes with a riddle in their depth—that set a sort of standard. I can't remember a single syllable of anything remotely like a sermon ever stiffening his lips. Yet I know that, though probably it was quite as unconscious as it was silent, his influence over me was great.

Somebody said that anyone contemplating a mean or dishonourable action would feel ashamed if they looked into Ego's eyes. Evidently this expression, whatever it may have been, was there at the very beginning of his life, for once when he was a baby and the conversation at Stanway touched on the horror of a child of your own turning out badly Arthur Balfour said to my parents, "Anyhow, you need have no fear about Ego. You have only to look into his eyes."

The intense seriousness of his gaze set off the radiance of the rare, sudden, rewarding smile—a smile that always began in his beautiful eyes.

It's so difficult to know how to begin a portrait of someone you remember so well both as a boy and as a man. I've no idea what the right proportions are. But if I look long at Ego, here, set down pell-mell, are some of the things that strike me. Despite so much humour that it might well have been expected to encroach on other senses, his conscience was always unusually alert and delicate. Sense of humour, sense of justice, sense of obligation—all three seemed equally but quite unclashingly developed. Never more than kindly, humorously critical of others, he was severely as well as derisively critical of himself. His being so sensitively alive to the claims of others—to the claims of family, friends, tenants and country—resulted in a perpetual conflict between his natural excessive diffidence and reserve and his ardent wish to serve. Though no one was ever more amusing—just sheer *fun* to talk to—yet I don't think it was possible to be with him and fail to realise the impelling strength of ideals quite tacitly and very probably unconsciously followed. His interests were wide; he had a remarkable faculty for seeing all round a subject and a capacity for sudden blazes of enthusiastic admiration that some found surprising in one whose fibre of mind was so fastidious.

Nothing is more futile than surmises as to what those who died young might have achieved. Ego and Yvo were of course only two of many thousands of their doomed generation for whom high hopes were entertained. Whenever someone dies young, it is like losing two people—all that he is, and all that he might have become.

But had Ego never become in any way a public figure, I cannot doubt that his influence would have been as strong as it was gentle. Anyhow I do know that for others outside his family, life without him seemed ever afterwards to lack something essential. Besides laughter, understanding and sympathy of a very special brand that no one else could supply, a touchstone had gone. Yet I can think of nobody who would have been more surprised to hear himself described as a touchstone!

I suppose it was some clear integrity of spirit—a kind of inevitable uprightness—that made him, albeit so unconsciously, an arbiter of right and wrong.

Though at times Ego's almost preposterous diffidence may well have disconcerted strangers—it must be admitted he could be dauntingly silent!—this weakness was turned to the immense gain of his friends, for he was the unchallenged master of that humorous self-depreciation to which many of his family are addicted. Maintaining that he was destined to be a buffoon and in his own inimitable way telling stories against himself in which he invariably figured as a "Rabbit"—his symbol of ineptitude—he would painstakingly and plausibly try to convince his friends what a failure he was.

It was about his social reverses, his lack of small talk that he was funniest. I remember how we would look forward to his going to a ball or—most unwillingly—to a country-house party, so that he should tell us what a failure he had been. Before going to his first big London dance, he said he thought he ought to "be all right" because fortunately he had a really spectacular bruise from a cricket ball on his shin which he would be able to show to his partners, and no doubt it would provide an admirable conversational opening.

Queen Alexandra was to be present, so Ego borrowed his father's knee-breeches, bought a very special pocket handkerchief and set forth full of faith, hope and charity.

He did, so he told us, unbuckle his knee-breeches to show his bruise to the Beauty of the Season, but her reception of this favour was so chilling that he never again gathered up courage to address a single word to anyone else until he went home in a hansom at five o'clock in the morning and had an "extremely good talk" with the driver just before he—the driver—was arrested for drunkenness.

Ego's nervous system was woefully apt to play him false on critical occasions, both in examinations and at the games at which his brilliant successes were interspersed with unexpected failures. I think the bitterest disappointment of my whole life— for as you know, I'm an ardent cricket fan—was when, after he had not "come off" playing in the Eton Eleven against Winchester, he did not, as we confidently expected, play at Lords. Alas, similar failure met him when he played for Gloucestershire at the Oval. Though he spoke little of them, these reverses were a great blow, not only in themselves, but because he regarded them as typical of what he called "Rabbitry", and they increased his self-distrust. But during the last years of his life this over-diffidence was fast falling from him like an outgrown garment. He was gaining control over his nerves, rapidly becoming the master of his fate. Though he never lost his extreme modesty, the hampering self-consciousness had left him.

As I write, many pictures of Ego in boyhood rise before me— far, far away, but in sharpest focus.

First I see him bowling on his beloved Stanway cricket field, running in long loping strides before his arm wheels over, and like a breaking wave he leaps into the air. I also see him sprinting after the golf ball he has just driven out of sight, or intent on some stubborn game of chess (he was a brilliant player, and he and my husband were so keen that they used to play even in the train); arriving at Stanway begoggled and white with dust on the shattering motor bicycle that terrified his family; dancing at the local hunt balls—for he never did things by halves—like a Dervish, with some wretched girl quite breathless and her face as scarlet as a hunting coat, being whirled round and round from the very first to the very last bar of an unending dance. Very clearly too—for his sense of humour was not under control—I see him rolling on the floor in hopeless inextinguishable laughter. As a family we were sadly subject to giggles at the most untoward moments.

Ego was such a keen cricketer that when we were children he used to practise bowling at me by the hour. One day when for some reason we were confined to our London house, I remember his bowling me out sixty times with an apple. A fire shovel was my bat; the coal scuttle our wicket. Needless to say the same apple did not survive. About three dozen were reduced to brown pulp. Later on I had to serve even stranger purposes. When Ego reached whatever eminence at Eton involves chastising your schoolfellows, he was terribly anxious as to how he would acquit himself in the discharge of this distasteful duty, so he practised "cutting in", or whatever it was called, on his devoted sister. In preparation for these rehearsals I was allowed to armour myself with two books. I chose *The Peerage* and *Who's Who*.

After Eton, Ego went to Trinity College, Oxford. Here at first he was shy and quiet. (I remember our amusement at hearing a fellow undergraduate, a Rhodes scholar, had said, "I can't make it out. I always understood that all 'Honour-ables' were fast, but Charteris seems quite a quiet sort of chap".) But he soon made plenty of devoted friends. Never shall I forget that topmost peak of shyness—going for the first time to lunch in his rooms to meet some of these friends—the terrible sense of being on approval, and my distress because a midge had bitten my face. It was then that my mother and I first met Ego's boon companion, Robert Smallbones—to our family always Bones—who became a lifelong friend of my own.

There were several Oxford Reading Parties at Stanway, at which Bones always made one. Though I do not think that either Stubbs's *Charters* or Hobbes's *Leviathan*—the two main *pièces de resistance*—were ever got through, deference to Clio did at least prevent her students from enjoying any lighter books.

Soon after he left Oxford, Ego went to Washington as Honorary Attaché to the British Embassy, where Bryce was then Ambassador. Writing home from America gave plenty of scope for humorous self-depreciation.

I can't tell whether the letters that I think funny would seem so to those who never knew Ego. As I read them, I, of course, see his expression and hear his voice, and I know that this is half the battle. I'll quote some passages and you can judge for yourself.

"I think I ought to say here how fully aware I am what a good start I enjoy by being your son. Hostesses beam upon me with pleasurable anticipation when first I darken their doors, and greet me with a sunny smile that gradually withers when actual performance renders impossible further illusions. I don't know how many people have not come up to me and said, 'Lady Elcho is the most charming woman I have ever met. . . .'

"My hostess took ten minutes introducing me, raising false hopes by giving a list of my titled relations and urging mothers to introduce their débutantes to me. Under her efforts the group gradually dispersed until I was left alone with her and her secretary. . . .

"I did succeed in raising a slight laugh at dinner by burning my mouth with a hot potato, but this was my only contribution to the mirth of the party. . . .

"I am thanking my stars that I went to Italy. Last night I found a woman—a member of the reigning house of Roosevelt—I could interest and impress by talking about Italian Art. We got on the subject at soup and talked about it without a second's pause slap through the meal! Scraps of our conversation must have vastly impressed the company. Botticelli, Giorgione, Fra Angelico, Lippi Fillipino and Fillipo and other magic names bubbled from my lips.

Of course I need not tell you that our talk consisted merely of a string of names. We never thought of discussing anything the artists had painted, or their technique. But every extra name I managed to remember was greeted with a squeal of delight. In fact she got so excited that when we contemptuously dismissed the Flemish School she roared out something about 'stupid German faces' with the attaché at the German Embassy sitting directly opposite us. . . ."

In the next he complains of his unsuitability to the life of a diplomat.

"I am wondering if it is possible to change my whole manner of life, for that, I see, is absolutely essential. Scrupulously tidy dress is necessary, and an equally revolutionary change in social conduct —always jumping up to offer chairs and tea, asking people to go for walks! and going right across the rooms to sit next to WOMEN! All this I must now do, giving up the policy of *laisser faire* I have always pursued. . . . The people whom I have seen go into diplomacy have always been diametrically opposed in temperament to me."

And here is an account of his being a "rabbit" in a tournament.

"By a characteristic failure to rise to the occasion I have narrowly escaped winning the Championship of the Middle Atlantic Golf Association (a three days tournament and the final was a thirty-two holes match). The first two days were the hottest I have ever known, and as my opponent in the final was exceedingly stout I prayed that the hot weather would continue, but unfortunately it cooled and he waddled round and just beat me. However I won an exceedingly handsome fruit-dish as runner-up. We were followed by a crowd, and there was great jubilation when the 'Englishman' was beaten. The crowd was seething with Yankee hostility, and dreadfully nervous lest I should win, not only because I was not one of God's own Americans, but also because I represent the antithesis of their idea of a 'Sport'. A little Scotch man who was frightfully keen that I should win kept saying *they* were 'no Sports'. The most humiliating thing about the whole affair was that the man who defeated me was notoriously intemperate, while I, as you know, am notoriously abstemious. He was blind drunk all three nights of the tournament and drunk most of the way round the course.

I watched him with desperate eyes, trusting to see him any moment fall to pieces, but he just held together. Hope leapt up when at the foot of a hill and at a critical stage of the game, he produced a flask. But he drank, climbed the hill and won the hole by ramming down a putt from the very edge of the green. In my person temperance and England sustained a joint defeat. However it was Providence that I did not win for I should never have had the foresight to buy champagne for the ensuing dinner and that would have put me in a ghastly position. As it was it was an awful ordeal. I did not prove myself a 'Sport'. I can't understand their humour. I never can make out when they are serious, and when trying to be funny."

Two more passages from Ego's letters from America show that he could occasionally be funny about other people besides himself. The first of these is about an amateur conjurer.

"The guileless and simple Mr. J. was the success of the party. He drew me aside before dinner and said he had a trick which had always been a huge success at other parties. Would I be his accomplice? 'Just in case someone were to suggest tricks after dinner. He did not want to suggest it himself.' The trick was that the onlookers were to think of some object in the room, and when he came in he was to ask questions apparently of himself. If the answer was 'Yes' I was to waggle my toe; if 'No' I was to remain still. Thus it should be possible to narrow down the possibilities and discover what had been thought of. As a bribe for my assistance he generously gave me permission to make any use of this trick I liked afterwards. In his opinion it would greatly add to my success in Washington. After dinner I saw Mr. J. whispering to his hostess in a corner. As a result she asked him publicly if he knew any tricks and he consented to oblige. Thanks to my intelligent complicity cloaked by well simulated surprise, the trick very much impressed the party. Encouraged by his success, Mr. J. proceeded to 'will' a poker to stand up (he had a piece of black thread attached to his trouser and apparently always comes down to dinner thus prepared.) This again greatly puzzled the company, and all the men retired into corners with pokers and vainly tried to make them stand up. Having thus thoroughly mystified everyone, Mr. J. began like a really confident conjuror to explain some of his tricks. One, he said, required some preparation. The conjuror must arrive already provided with (1) a long hair, (2) a penny, (3) a small piece of chewing gum. (Or, he explained, you *might* borrow a hair from one of the ladies in the room.) One end of the hair you insert in your button-hole. To the other you attach a tiny piece of chewing gum, which in its turn you stuck to the penny dropped into a glass of water. By means of the chewing gum and the hair you could make the penny mysteriously rise in the water! Mr. J. should come to Stanway. He would be appreciated there. In his Collins, apparently feeling he had been deceitful in claiming such occult powers, he explained the trick in which I had assisted him—generously adding that anyone who wished was welcome to use it."

The second tells of a trip to the South on which Ego accompanied Bryce.

"The journey was rather fatiguing at times, as the philanthropists were a little bit heavy. They talked tremendously and told anecdotes as a relaxation. Bryce was splendid with them, but in the end they overcame him and one completely floored him. He pinned him into a corner and told him anecdotes by the hour. The poor old man sat huddled up in an armchair civilly muttering, 'Indeed', and 'Really', shooting pathetic glances from under his shaggy eyebrows and looking in vain for an escape, which on a private train does not exist."

Ego had always loved anything to do with soldiering. As a boy, I remember him perpetually playing with soldiers or drawing—greatly to the glorification of his own country—pictures of battles between the English and the French. Later on he took an immense interest in strategy, and was for ever poring over Marlborough's and Wellington's campaigns. Then there was a remarkably uncomfortable phase when practically every inch of 62 Cadogan Square—staircase and all—was given up to a war game invented by H. G. Wells and played with toy mechanical guns and tin soldiers.

But Ego's love of soldiering in general and his devotion to his own beloved yeomanry—the "Gallant, Glittering Gloucesters", as he called them—did not cramp his style in ridiculing himself as an officer in the making. Here is an extract from a letter written from Salisbury Plain:

"I have just finished my training on Salisbury Plain. It was not a fortnight of unmixed glory and success.

"First day I turned up at stables at 6 instead of 5.45, and was well blown up. Second day, was beckoned to by Adjutant and thus addressed: 'I say, Charteris, you get your hair cut and singe your moustache and you will look a different fellow.' I immediately obeyed him, but *feel* the same fellow! Third day, horse which I had so carefully selected by my own unaided wits went dead lame. Fourth day, borrowed spirited grey from brother-officer. Spirited grey tossed back his head, banged me on the nose and drew at least two buckets of blood. I had to lie on my back before the whole squadron for fifteen minutes and then ride slowly home with the Quartermaster. Fifth night, was violently ill and had to spend next day in bed. . . . You have heard of 'ragging'? I *knew* I should be the victim of it if ever I ventured into a military atmosphere and visions of strawberry jam and feathers floated before my eyes. What really worries them is my moustache, and I had always thought it was rather in the Cavalry Officer's mode. . . . I liked my troopers very much. They gave three cheers for Mr. Charteris when they went away in the train, and none of the other officers standing there received the same flattering attention. I hope the mildness of my rule was not alone responsible for this. As a matter of fact, swearing is no use. My troop, led by kindness, was by far the smartest in the squadron. Of course my methods were not really founded on policy, but the result of constitutional inability to do anything else."

Ego's marriage in 1910 to Letty[1] delighted all his family. Fate was only to allow them four years together, but for those years their happiness was complete.

Enchanted with his two beautiful baby sons, who, alas, cannot remember him, he was eagerly looking forward to their being old enough to be given their first lessons in cricket.

During the years between his marriage and the war he was called to the Bar and was soon to stand for Parliament. He was a good speaker. . . .

"Far I hear the steady drummer
Drumming like a noise in dreams."

[1] Lady Violet Manners.

Many, I know, claim always to have foretold the war. I had no such premonition.

> "On the idle hill of summer
> Sleepy with the flow of streams."

I never heard that drummer drumming.

Nor even when war broke out did I for the first few days in my ignorance and preoccupation—my son Michael had just been born—realise that all my brothers would at once be involved. I suppose I thought wars were still carried on by professional soldiers and sailors. After all Yvo was still only a boy of seventeen at Eton, and Guy had never had anything to do with soldiering. But before the end of August, 1914, Guy had joined up; before long he went out with the Scots Guards, and by 1916 we had sufficiently readjusted our standard of what must now be considered good news to be glad to hear he was invalided back from the front with his third severe attack of Rheumatic Fever.

Ego embarked for Egypt with his Yeomanry in April, 1915. Just a year later he fought in the disastrous battle of Katia, in which the entire squadron was either killed or taken prisoner.

News came to us very slowly. Agonising suspense was cruelly protracted by false hopes. We heard the wounded had been left at El Arish, and as Ego's name had not been amongst the killed in the first report of the battle, we hoped and tried to assume that he was amongst them. In June there came a telegram from the Red Cross: "*Un Lord Elcho fait prisonier à Katia est à interné a Damascus.*" The relief was marvellous. It seemed too good to be true. It was too good to be true.

What the explanation of that telegram was we never knew—possibly "*aucun* Lord Elcho". A month later we had a telegram from the prisoners with the Turks, amongst whom was my brother-in-law, Mary's husband, Tom Strickland, who at first had been rumoured to have been killed, certifying that Ego, whose identification disc was never found, had been killed at Katia. Then the truth had to be finally accepted; the emptied future faced.

Long afterwards accounts of the battle came from survivors of Ego's troop. They described him as "twice wounded, once in the arm and once in the leg—but continuing wholly regardless of pain and fire to encourage his men". "Lord Elcho acted magnificently", wrote one of his sergeants on a postcard to his mother.

For those who loved Ego and knew how deeply, though he never spoke other than jestingly of them, those early disappointments—failures to "come off" on the day—had been taken to heart, it was something, indeed much, to know that at the last crisis in his life, even he—if he thought of himself at all —cannot have failed to know that he had fully risen to the occasion.

The following passage from a letter written by one of the sergeants under him, shows that long before the final ordeal of that fierce battle Ego had proved himself in every sense of the word a good soldier. "Lord Elcho loved his men and they loved him. Whenever in after life I think of this war, he will stand out as one, who by his kindness, lenience, and thoughtfulness helped us through all our troubles, made our hardships easy to bear and won the undying love of the men who were proud to serve under him."

His own letter to his mother shows both his complete acceptance of his fate and his love for his home:

"The only sound thing is to hope the best for one's country and to expect nothing for oneself in the future. To write down everyone one loves as dead—and then if any of us are left we shall be surprised. To think of one's country's future and one's own happy past. The first is capable of vast improvement; as for the second, when all is said and done we were a damned good family. I couldn't have had more joy out of anything than I have had from my family. . . . Tell Papa he must write his sons off, and concentrate on his grandsons who, thank God, exist."

Now I shall try to give you some idea of my youngest brother, Yvo whose humour, imagination, quicksilver understanding, and bright charm made him all through his brief existence such a delight to family and friends.

Because of a certain—for want of a better word—*shining* quality about him, the thought of Yvo always brings to my mind three tags of poetry that for me no amount of over-quoting can ever blunt:

> "Golden lads and girls all must,
> As chimney sweepers, come to dust."

> "They carry back bright to the coiner the mintage
> of man"

and

> "Brightness falls from the air".

I told you that Yvo was at first something of an Ugly Duckling, but this phase was brief. He very soon blossomed into shiningly—that word again!—fair, sensitive good looks. As his nine years Elder Sister I remember him first as a comic, top-heavy, over-excitable, oddly lovable little boy, always having the most terrible tumbles and perpetually plying one with alarmingly intelligent questions—precious few of which I could answer. I also remember—not without shame—how difficult it was to resist teasing him because of the swift flush that at a word crimsoned his extraordinarily fair skin, sweeping across his face and over his huge rounded forehead up to the very roots of his bright yellow hair. Except for brief gusts of passion Yvo was a very good-natured child and remarkable for the fact that something—instinctive tact, I suppose—prevented him ever for one second being a bore; not even in the conjuring trick and riddle phase in which he was irresistibly absurd, but never tedious.

There was less than a year between him and his elder sister, Mary. They were like twins. I can scarcely remember even seeing one of the pair come into the room without the other.

Another quotation that reminds me of Yvo is, "His life was gentle and the elements so mixed in him"—for both in nature and in mind he was so noticeably well blended—young in spirit, old in understanding; subtle and sound; ardent and balanced. Though no one could defend him from the charge of being clever—brilliantly so—he seemed entirely to miss out the aggressively "Clever Boy", supercilious stage, and was always able to tune-in to the most divergent minds.

I remember once seeing him again for the first time after a long interval—I suppose he was fifteen or sixteen—and being literally startled by his charm and the extraordinary rapidity with which he had developed. Without losing any of his dewy freshness—his new deep bass voice was such comic contrast to the flower-like fairness of his skin—the baby brother had mentally more than overtaken me; become a most enchanting talker; an admirable listener too, not only delightfully amusing and sympathetic, but able to bridge any gulf of age or circumstances.

Another blessed quality for others was his perceptivity. His remarkably sensitive antennae—"wireless", I suppose I should call it now—made him know a mile off if you had a headache or were troubled.

Though, no more than other members of his family, immune from violent fits of depression, Yvo seldom failed to be a delighting presence. He aroused expectancy. All the wine of life seemed at his lips. Indeed, a sort of bright eagerness and swiftness might well have made one think of that passage in Maeterlinck—do you remember it?—about those who are to die young. "Les Avertis" he calls them.

In August, 1914, Yvo, still only seventeen, was at Eton. Till then he had been very content there in college, but once the w ar had started he found it intolerable to stay on.

While training in the Grenadier Guards, he had some happy months going about with his beloved sister, Mary, flinging himself with zest into the strange new exciting social life of war-time London, and making many delightful friends who were enchanted by his wit, subtlety, originality and sympathy, and the contrast between his extreme youthfulness of appearance and his mature intelligence.

Despite his enjoyment, he was young enough to be in a fever to get to the Front. He had not long to wait.

In September, 1915, he was sent out at very short notice. He came all the way up to Scotland with his mother to say goodbye to his three sisters at Gosford.

Because of his excitement over the first Zeppelin raid on London, the two travellers had missed the night train and left King's Cross only at four in the morning. Yvo had to return the same night. Even so, those few hours made the longest day I can remember. For him, however, I think it was a happy day. He bathed in the sea, went for a walk with his sister Mary, inspected and kissed his sleeping nephews; and between early dinner and his going away we sat, happy and miserable, in a family huddle in my mother's sitting-room until—so young and fresh and fair—he went out into the night, and we never saw him again.

Needless to say there had been nothing in our talk in any way special to the occasion. Like countless other families in Britain, then in precisely the same plight, we spoke desultorily of quite ordinary things and exchanged old family jokes. No allusion whatever was made to what awaited him. Only to Mary—probably of all human beings the closest to him—he said with his quick, shy smile: "Of course, you know that I may not return."

His ordeal was brief. . . . Only a few weeks after he went out he was killed, just after his nineteenth birthday.

We were told that when he first took over his platoon he looked so young that the older men chaffed him by singing, "And a little child shall lead them". They were right. The "little child" did lead them. Shortly afterwards the same men showed signs of giving ground in a shallow enfiladed trench, and Yvo was sent up to rally them. This he succeeded in doing. Then, in leading a fresh attack, he was instantaneously killed.

Fortunately he was still young enough—perhaps too, the war was still young enough—for him to be able during his short time at the front to enjoy with an almost childlike appreciation all there was of glamour and sinister beauty. Loving the night marches, his impressionable imagination found "the noise of the whistling of the shells wonderful", and he could still laugh at himself cheering his men "with heavy wit about the Kaiser and little Willie".

Though it had begun to sadden him, the horror had not had

time to overwhelm him. The excitement and the fellowship still outweighed the fatigue, the strain, the sadness.

It was amazing how often and at what length he managed through those arduous weeks to write home, and his letters—some dramatic and picturesque, others humorous and ironic —seem to me full of vivid phrases. I would like to quote a few.

"All day I have heard the rumbling of guns like distant breakers reminding me of what awaits us. . . . I enjoyed those marches very much, one's legs swung onwards by a thousand singing men. . . ."

"Great lorries lumbering by—limbers jolting on the pavé road— all the sweat of war behind the line. As it grew darker the guns became louder and the flashes more distinct, and every now and then the skeleton of a house stood out against the sky. Sometimes a blood-red sun low on the horizon looked out from the clouds, to retire before the brighter flashes of the guns. The last street we passed through was very ruined on one side, the wounded laid out on the other. Here troops with rifles and fixed bayonets and hordes of German prisoners; beyond, horses and flickering fires, and always the jolting of limbers on that pavé road, and crowds of troops telling their stories of the battle. . . ."

"The German rockets are delightful and quite compensate for any discomfort attendant on watching them. Their noise is stimulating. The sound of a machine gun in the distance is the most sinister thing in the world. It is like the death-rattle of a giant; and a shell leaving a gun is an incomparably dreary sound—rather human—as though it loathed its mission."

"By a series of thrilling night marches, drawing ever nearer to the distant rumbling guns—sleeping, the men in barns and us huddled on the floor of some estaminet—sometimes sent miles out of our way by some horrid blunders—we arrived in this bleak mining country—the dreariest spot in France and the scene of all this fighting. The final march was very thrilling—setting off in the afternoon through ruined towns seething with wounded men, the skeletons of houses silhouetted against the setting sun, the roads lined on one side with stretchers and wounded men; on the other the gleam of bayonets surrounding German prisoners. We arrived at Vermelles by night. Oh God! Vermelles! Was ever Sodom or Gomorrah more desolate than the utter ruin of this town, a heap of crumbling brick-work, a desert slowly shot to ruin for more than a year; rank grass growing all over shattered walls and covering sorry graves—German, British and French? . . ."

"I think one of the effects of this war will be that people will give up their feeling for ruins, *qua* ruins. There will be no more parties to Wardour Castle from Clouds, and I expect the Parthenon will be restored as soon as peace is declared. . . ."

"I have had a letter from Mamma in which she says she is impressed by my being appointed a Platoon Commander. As this is the lowest rank an officer can hold, it is a doubtful compliment. . . ."

"A grim sight in our graveyard here. From one of the graves the tombstone has been laid open by a shell and the coffin-lid has been torn off, showing the skeleton of a man. A toad is sitting on his chest and little brown mice are playing on his bones. R.I.P. says the tombstone. . . ."

"People at home seem more real than this war, which seems weary of its own melodrama and does not know how to give it up. . . ."

Though such a poem of course applies equally well to how many thousands of other "golden boys", it was about Yvo that my husband wrote "The Fallen Subaltern" of which one verse is:

"And those who come this way in days hereafter,
Will know that here a boy for England fell,
Who looked at danger with the eyes of laughter,
And on the charge his days were ended well."

BREADWINNING

You asked when I began to write.

I decline to inflict on you the old, old, story, common to every child with any ambition, of early literary aspirations and first ludicrous attempts. What could be more boring?

But, since you ask, I will tell you how and why I first started to *publish*; who it was that first encouraged me to become a breadwinner, and in what way the first crumbs my pen ever earned led on to a loaf, and one loaf to another. Nothing, I assure you, in the tale to irritate the Dr. Johnson of the dictum: "No one but a blockhead ever wrote for anything but money."

In concession to your taste for early memories, I'll tell you how my childish literary ambition was discouraged. When I was fourteen I wrote some doggerel in praise of my hero, Sir Philip Sidney. Longing to know how my verses would strike another ear, I introduced them into the chapter on English Literature I was reading aloud to my governess, as something written by Byron at the age of only fourteen. My feeble fraud was punished by a douche of cold water. Instead of exclaiming at the astounding precocity of the boy, Byron, my governess merely remarked, "The poet Heine wrote a very much better poem when he was fourteen." She then read me "The Two Grenadiers". Alas, I did not feel I could dispute her verdict. After this unintended snub, my next attempt, a "poem" addressed—with startling originality—to "The Stars", was kept to myself.

Not until very many years later did it ever occur to me to try to make money with my pen. The discovery that a friend— obviously no more a "Born Writer" than myself—had started to write paid articles, was what ignited my breadwinning ambition. If she could do such a thing, why not I?

Having without anything to show for it passed the age at which Keats died, I now thought it time finally to bury any hope of myself becoming a poet. Since, alas! I was not intended to write poetry, why not try journalism? That I should make some extra money was most desirable. The war had put an end to my husband's career at the Bar, and as his army pay did not exceed his expenses, we seemed at that time mainly to depend on two sources—what he might make by his poems, and what I might win—*earn*, I called it!—at Poker; and alas, neither poetry nor Poker, however congenial as pastimes, can be regarded as reliable means of livelihood.

I happened just then to meet that kindest of instigators, most assiduous of literary midwives, Mrs. Belloc Lowndes, and she suggested that I should submit an anonymous attempt to the assistant editor of *The Times*, who was then running a daily article for women. *Could* I write an "article"? By a strange coincidence, whilst rummaging in my writing table next morning, I chanced on a wholly forgotten letter from my grandfather, Lord Wemyss. To my surprise I read, "Most enterprising of young women" (the letter had been written on the occasion of my, as he considered, very imprudent engagement), "I only hope the enterprise will turn out as successful as you feel confident it will. Don't forget 'Fire' " (this was a school-room essay of mine which—why, it is difficult to see— had been handed round the family), "I'm sure you could do much in the writing line and thus help to keep the pot boiling".

Was this a message from the grave? And from one accustomed to have his behests promptly obeyed? Various as were my compelling grandfather's gifts, no one could have accused him of being of a literary turn of mind; but, for this particular column "literature" was scarcely what *The Times* required. Anyhow, I now felt encouraged by both the Quick and the Dead. The next step was to lay in a large stock of foolscap paper. I then placed myself at my writing table. What should I write about? Practical advice but written in a "playful" style was what the editor demanded. Because I was at that time being painted both by Augustus John and McEvoy, "How to sit for your portrait" occurred to me as a possible theme. On this I set to work.

After some two hours of writhing application, I had gnawed off the end of my pen-holder, become as ink-stained as Caddie Jellaby, and reached that phase of despair—I've never yet undertaken any writing without passing through this phase— when one feels convinced the thing will never get written. Then at last comes that moment of intense relief when you realise the back of your task is broken. Suddenly, with a sigh of satisfaction, you find yourself on the other side of the hill.

Arrived at the end of my thousand or so words, exhausted but elated, I darted out of the house to post my "article"—if article it ever was to be. I can still hear the momentous little plop with which it fell into the pillar-box.

Two days later came one of the best moments of my life. Listlessly opening my morning paper—I did not think the time even to hope had yet arrived—the headline, "How to sit for your portrait", leapt at me from the page. Admittedly the page was not the most important of *The Times*; but still, there was the intoxicating sight of my own writing in PRINT! Cut of course, in fact barbarously mutilated—naturally the paragraph that had been the most difficult to write had been omitted—but yet *my* article!

Jubilant, I rushed out to buy several copies of *The Times* (did I expect to see divers versions?), and, boarding the first bus, read and re-read my article. I can't tell you how much I wanted to draw the attention of my fellow-passengers to that flaring column. With the utmost difficulty I restrained myself, and also from showing the nice burly policeman, who chided me for so nearly getting run over, the reason for my absent-mindedness. No sense of proportion? None whatever, thank Heaven! But surely any woman with sufficient sense of proportion not to be excited the first time she sees herself in print might just as well be dead?

Two days later came another very good milestone of a moment. I opened a type-written envelope and out fluttered a cheque for five pounds.

Breadwinning

So, after all, I could be a breadwinner! True, I had already just begun to earn a salary by becoming secretary to J. M. Barrie. Yes, but—crushing any incipient complacency—common sense told me this heaven-sent job must be regarded only as a lucky fluke. Not only was I unacquainted with the rudiments of shorthand, I couldn't even type. Fortunately Barrie, who detested the clatter of a machine, considered this technical inefficiency a recommendation. But for this convenient idiosyncrasy of his, I might long have sought another post in vain. Though by no means a sinecure, my secretaryship was a fancy job in so far that it did not prove my ability to have earned a salary, had so unusual a being as my employer not existed.

But this glorious cheque earned by my own pen was a wholly different matter. If I could get one article accepted, why not another? Why not *hundreds*? Then—intoxicating thought—I really should be earning my own living!

The epoch-making fiver was immediately spent on something wholly unnecessary—consciously, deliberately, gloatingly, "blown". I then started to pelt that discerning editor. My second article was advice to mothers on how to have their children photographed. This, too, was promptly printed. To my delight, with the ensuing fiver came a letter of approval and the injunction to "go on writing about children". Evidently I had struck a lucky vein. The result was a succession of articles of "playful" admonition for mothers—"Children and the Doctor"—"Your Child's First Theatre"—"Beware of Grandparents", etcetera, etcetera, each punctually followed by a cheque.

You can imagine how potentially rich I now felt. If I could write an article in two hours or so, how much money could I make in a year? . . . A few moments' calculation gave a highly misleading answer, and, needless to say, the fallacy of my potential wealth loosened my purse-strings so much that for the time being I was soon considerably more insolvent than before I started to make money.

For a long time, timidity prevented the idea of writing anything signed with my own name from so much as crossing my mind, but meantime a spate of anonymous articles was sent off to every kind of newspaper. By no means all were accepted. I soon knew the ugly look of an envelope addressed to myself in my own writing—a returned manuscript, a sight to make you feel chilly and grown old. After each rejection, it was difficult to crank myself up to the next attempt. Most of these very slight articles were, however, printed. The other day I unearthed a bundle of them—an absurd miscellaneous collection. In case it amuses you, here, chosen at random, are some of their titles —"Mothers-in-Law", "Dogs-in-Law", "The Plot Shop" (all authors catered for), "Advantages of a Violent Temper", "The Importance of Appearance in Food", "No More Middle-Age", "Why I Don't Wish to be Rich".

Under the heading "The Woman's View", my series for *The Times* continued for some months, during which, unknown to the Editor, one article written by neither woman nor amateur was slipped in. This, called "The Private Private Secretary", was written by Barrie, who made his secretary send it in as though written by herself. Besides being the kind of hoax that amused him—he had recently refused some vast sum for a *signed* article—it was perhaps a delicate way of letting his secretary, then new to her far from ordinary job, know precisely what it was he required of her. The article ended:

"The post is thus not merely confidential, it calls for an understanding of the man who is employing you, particularly an intimate understanding of his weaknesses, out of which you may well get some private entertainment. You must know by instinct that he does not want to lunch on Tuesday week with Lady A., but that, if the answer is left to him, he will weakly say Yes, and then when Tuesday comes scowl at you for not having improvised an ingenious No. You must also know that if it had been Mrs. B., and he had shouted at you (while in the grip of an inspiration) to tell her to go and drown herself, what he really means is that by Tuesday he will want to attend that luncheon. If you are really the right sort of person you will soon be worth more than your salary, and you will also have the satisfaction of knowing, as he knows, that you are using your brains intelligently."

I remember my pique on noticing that, unlike my own, *this* article had not had one single word cut out!

Once embarked on writing, I found myself on a slippery slope. Before long I was asked by a publisher to whom my identity with the writer of the articles for women had been disclosed, to write a *book* for mothers. He wanted it on the lines of my *Times* articles, and written, he stipulated, on the same note of "playful pedagogy".

Was that publisher a hypnotist?

Having entered his office uncertain whether I should undertake a book at all, and anyhow with a die-hard determination to cling to anonymity, I emerged with a signed contract to write a book under my own name!

After this, so it seemed to me, desperate step, I asked my friend Charles Whibley's advice. Should I back out of the undertaking? "All writing for publication is prostitution" was his gloomy reply, "but since from the first day I met you, I have always known that sooner or later you would write, you may just as well start to cash in on it now. Call on me", he continued, "if you need any help in un-splitting infinitives—really about all the help one author can ever give another, but always remember", he added (relevantly *he* seemed to think!) "that Shakespeare and Congreve are the two greatest masters of English prose." Though interested to hear this evaluation, I did not feel I had been given very much practical help.

I then confessed my undertaking to Barrie, on whose melancholy countenance compassion struggled with extreme distress. In his deep hoarse voice—Walter de la Mare told me it reminded him of a horse-chestnut—he tolled out the injunction, "Please try, unlike other women, to be very chary in your use of exclamation marks—those hairpins of literature." As I already fully shared this distaste for exclamation marks, I still thought I owed precious little to expert advice. Certainly, my book would run no risk of being called a collaboration.

Though well aware of the slowness with which I wrote, I had rashly committed myself to deliver this commissioned book in three months.

All my life I had been feverishly aware of the fleetingness of

time. Scarcely a moment in which I could not have cried with
Marvell:

> "But at my back I always hear
> Time's winged chariot hurrying near."

Pursued by a harassing sense of the shortness of life, not only
did I always run both up and down stairs, but, assimilating
neither, I consistently bolted both my food and my books. No
day ever seemed to give me sufficient time either to see my
friends or to be by myself. I had always felt the need for at
least four—one for reading alone—simultaneous separate
existences. With only one, each day became far too tight a
mosaic.

> "What is this life if full of care
> We have no time to stand and stare?"

Now came the discovery—sooner or later made by nearly
everyone—that with its mysterious inexplicable elasticity,
Time has no reality. Though, in addition to a regular job—
really in itself a help because it imposed routine—as well as a
home and children to look after, I was now writing several
hours a day; yet I seemed to have more rather than less leisure.
I believe this seeming paradox always results from having one
settled purpose, the compelling claims of which seem to stretch
rather than crowd the days. Is the explanation that a sort of
safety-curtain of preoccupation falls and makes all other claims,
however imperative they may previously have appeared, recede
into inessentiality? Or does the mental stimulus so much
accelerate your whole tempo that everything undertaken
throughout the day—from tooth-washing onwards—gets done
six times as quickly? Both factors, I think, are powerful.

Despite these influences, it was, however, no easy matter to
finish that book in three months, five weeks of which coin-
cided with the Christmas holidays, spent that year at Stanway
in a hurly-burly of children. I remember the absurdity of
finding myself annoyed because, while I was actually engaged
on a chapter called "Encourage Children to Dress Up", my
own children disturbed me by rushing into the room dressed up
as pirates!

Breadwinning

For the children of that most distracting house-party there was at least the blessed institution of bed-time, but their elders and worsers, a very mixed and un-self-sufficing lot whose after-dinner parlour-games needed a great deal of direction, seemed to think there was some virtue in sitting up late.

Lined with its musty volumes of eighteenth-century sermons, the "Old Library", as it was always called, was set apart for my use. This was the room in which Professor L. P. Jacks had twice "felt" (he said it made him "come over queer") the presence of a ghost. In this very far from inviolable sanctuary I started to write at seven o'clock each morning. I think the matter-of factness of my book must have "laid" that perturbed spirit once and for all. Never since then, to my knowledge, has Professor Jack's visitant made him or herself felt.

Back in my own London house, where my husband was also engrossed in writing a book, interruptions were perhaps fewer, but there were terrible days when I would find myself stuck fast in the Doldrums. Then, having given my parlourmaid strict injunctions that I was "Out" to telephone callers, I would at the first sound of the bell tear downstairs six steps at a time to grab the receiver—a proceeding undignified, and bewildering to the parlourmaid. Other mornings, my husband and I, neither of us in the mood to write, would absurdly meet on the landing, each armed with a hammer, and snatching at any pretext to postpone the effort to get started on our work, solemnly proceed to re-hang some irreproachably-placed picture or take up the stair-carpet.

Then, of course, each in turn must listen to the reading aloud of the other's book. Is there any job in which it is more difficult to give satisfaction? Do you remember Dr. Johnson's pronouncement, "He to whom an author reads his own work is put to the torture and is under no obligation to speak the truth"? Are you good at undergoing that particular torture? I should think you would be, but don't be alarmed, I promise never to put you to the test. You are certainly an unusually agreeable person to criticise. How seldom, after being pressed to give an opinion, is one forgiven the slightest breath of anything except approbation. I seem nearly always to hit on the author's favourite passage to criticise. I'm not sure that being given the whole manuscript to read to yourself isn't even worse than having it read aloud, particularly when the author, scanning your face for a yawn, sits in the room and *watches* you read! If you get through a newly-written book too quickly he is maddened by the thought that what took him so long to write can so quickly be read. (It's like seeing the flashing descent of a toboggan one has so slowly, painfully dragged to the top of the hill.) On the other hand, if you don't read the book all in one go, he is offended at your being able to put it down unfinished. A hopeless dilemma!

Such as it was, my book did get written by the decreed date, and soon afterwards, thrilled and exasperated, I was lying on the floor—it seemed the only way to tackle such incredibly awkward things—correcting the long, twirling strips of my first galley-proofs. Before long the book came "out"; so far as its unobtrusive outward appearance went, a volume to pass in a crowd of books, but surely with a fascinating smell all its own? For some days merely to handle it was a thrill. Trying to take myself off my guard and imagine myself a casual disinterested reader to whom the contents were unknown, I would pick it up and read now very slowly, now very quickly; then I would lay it down again, and soon, as though to take it unawares, reopen it at random.

I hung about book-shops and could have embraced one woman whom I saw in the very act of buying my book. Still more gladly would I have struck another, who—wretched vacillating creature—after picking up and laying down my book three times, bought a novel instead!

You can imagine the authorship of a book called *The Child at Home* exposed me to plenty of derision on the occasions— frequent enough—when I glaringly disgraced myself as a mother, notably when ignoring the notice, "No child under fourteen allowed on", I dragged my reluctant nine-year old son Michael on to the Giant Switchback at Wembley, thereby causing the destruction of two of his front teeth!

Neither was the preoccupation of writing a book on the theory of mothercraft conducive to its practice, a fact smiled at

in a pretence-letter written by Barrie, purporting to come from
my then three-year-old son, Simon.

". . . Mother is writing a book about children and she takes notes
of all the things we say and squeezes us to make us say literary things.
With the same objec she crawls about the nursery-stairs listening.
She and Daddie have fights which is to get the study to write in.
For a test Michael ran down and called out 'I have flung Simon out
of the window same as Punch does the baby' and all Mother said
was 'I'll see to that at one o'clock', and all Daddie said was 'All
right—I'll put that in'."

After this first book, though my skin was still painfully thin,
I did drop the compromise of anonymity; and feeling it to be
my duty to my children (and my creditors) to earn as much
money as I could, I accepted all commissions as they came,
including the writing of a large number of articles for an
American syndicate.

As I had written about children, why not try to write *for*
them? So once I had succeeded in getting a few stories into
magazines, I wrote two full-length children's books.

When writing for children it is a great help to have one
particular child in one's mind as a target. As soon as my own
children grew up, I left off writing what publishers (I wish
they wouldn't) call "Juveniles", but now I have grandchildren
to aim at.

The publication of these two books led to a delightful job.
I was asked to edit a Children's Annual for Christmas. The
terms offered were very good—the only stipulation being that
the book should include contributions by Thomas Hardy and
Barrie. Fortunately both were amenable. Hardy gave me a
poem about his beloved dog "Wessex", and Barrie agreed to my
suggestion that he should write something about Captain Hook
—the result being "Captain Hook of Eton".

In alphabetical order (tact!) other contributors included
Hilaire Belloc, David Cecil, G. K. Chesterton, Clemence Dane,
W. H. Davies, Walter de la Mare, Margaret Kennedy, Desmond
McCarthy, A. A. Milne, Henry Newbolt, and Walter Raleigh.
For this book, *The Flying Carpet*, published in 1925, I myself

wrote two long stories; but still much too shy to add my own name to so distinguished a list, I adopted the *nom-de-plume* of Sara Moon.

As *The Flying Carpet* was a success it was followed next year by *The Treasure Ship*. In all, I edited seven of these Christmas books, a very pleasant and profitable task with two delightful perquisites: a collection of letters (mostly acceptances) from practically every famous contemporary author, and the making of many delightful new friends. One of the most welcome visitors to my nursery was Hugh Lofting who had just written and illustrated the first of his enchanting Dr. Dolittle books about animals. Not only did he draw delightful pictures on the title-pages of his own books for my son Simon, but he also gave unforgettable proof of his affinity with animals by a sensational success with our exceedingly misanthropical Cairn terrier. No dog had ever had a longer biting list—it included his own master's nose!—but at the first whiff of Hugh Lofting, this "difficult" dog sped with widely-wagging tail into the room, leapt on to the visitor's lap and, unchided, larruped his face with a very wet tongue.

Another unforgettable visitor was Mary Webb. So far from being a dog-tamer, she refused so much as to enter the house until positively assured that all dogs—she had heard a bark—were chained up in the basement. She sent up a message to this effect and I found her trembling on the doorstep. I shall never forget the hunted-hare look in her large prominent eyes—the tortured over-sensibility of her face. She told me what bitter banishment she found it to have to live in London instead of in the country, and that what she most minded about being poor was the deprivation of not being able to buy flowers. To my delight, when I spoke of her to Barrie, he gave me a hundred pounds to send to her anonymously. I hope much of this windfall was spent on flowers to solace the very short span of life that still remained to her.

The year after my first Children's Annual came out I suggested to a publisher that I should edit a book, also a collection of specially written stories, but this time for grown-up readers instead of for children. This led to *The Ghost Book*. For this, which had a very large sale, D. H. Lawrence wrote an excruciating and, to my own and many more critical minds, unforgettable story, called "The Rocking Horse". Again in alphabetical order, other contributors included Algernon Blackwood, Enid Bagnold, Walter de la Mare, L. P. Hartley, Desmond McCarthy, Arthur Machen and Oliver Onions.

Slightly hardened though I had now become, I was not yet sufficiently brazen to add my own name to such a list, and my story, "The Corner Shop", sneaked into *The Ghost Book* under the pseudonym of Leonard Gray. Familiar *ad nauseam* as you are with my want of self-confidence, you can imagine my delight when in my editorial capacity, I received a letter applying for the French translation rights of *one* only of the stories in *The Ghost Book*, and that story was my own anonymous one!

The following year I edited a collection of murder instead of ghost stories, called *The Black Cap*. For this volume, to my publishers' great approval, Barrie gave me the first book rights of the recently produced first act of *Shall We Join the Ladies?* his never-to-be-finished play. Encouraged by my French "fan", my own contribution to this collection appeared under my own name.

The Black Cap was followed by several other yearly collections of the gruesome—*Shudders, When Churchyards Yawn*, and so on.

In the process of bringing out so many books, my skin, as an editor at least, if not yet as a writer, must have thickened, for in my diary I find I wrote to one of my most distinguished contributors—and most amiably accommodating he was—asking him to "take the humour" (facetiousness was what I meant) out of his ghost story! Possibly to give scope to this frustrated jester, my next year's collection of the macabre was accompanied by a volume of "humorous" stories called *The Funnybone....*

Besides all the loaves made by itself, this editorial branch of breadwinning had many lucrative by-products. As well as being reprinted in anthologies, my own stories were translated, and some of them went "on the Air".

New topmost terror—before long I myself gave some "Talks"; read stories of my own and took part in a play for which each performer wrote his or her own part. Never shall I forget my trepidation before my first—it was in Savoy Hill days —broadcast, and the pathetic futility with which I purchased an expensive new hat and, feverishly consulting my mirror, powdered my nose at the microphone. Still less having steeled myself to the actual ordeal, shall I forget the sickening shock of first hearing a recording of my own—could it really be my own?—voice.

The hardening process continued. I at last broke my own ice at a Foyles' luncheon by making a speech, a thing I had always sworn nothing on earth could induce me to do; but the truth is, if the date given were sufficiently far off I would accept an invitation to Belsen! After this début I found my amazed self travelling long distances—to Bolton, Newcastle, Hull, Leeds, the Isle of Man, etcetera, to address literary societies! My repertory included only two lectures—"Ghosts in Literature" and "Feminine Beauty in Literature". Usually they were given at the end of a large luncheon—you can imagine how much of these meals I was able to enjoy and digest—scarcely the right atmosphere for dilating on the supernatural. Before one lecture I remember being rather disconcerted by a question shot at me by the secretary of the Literary Society. "Do you think you could appeal to *men*, Lady Cynthia?" It turned out that she was concerned not with the sex-appeal of the lecturer, but merely with her suitability to address a stag dinner instead of a hen luncheon.

In my new rôle as a lecturer, an appalling practical joke was played on me by my mother. She asked me to give my "talk" on Ghosts at Stanway. Understanding that my audience would be merely the local branch of the Women's Institute, with possibly a vicar or two thrown in, I dutifully complied. Imagine my feelings when, as in a nightmare, I saw in the front row the brightly alert faces of Max Beerbohm, H. G. Wells, and Edith Wharton! Never had I felt nearer matricide!

Fortunately David Cecil, without whose brilliant support I should have collapsed, was in the "Chair".

Though as a breadwinner it brought in no more than a cottage loaf, a book whose production was sheer delight was

She Walks in Beauty, my anthology of descriptions of feminine loveliness. The light labour involved was blissfully enjoyable; and since I copied out all the excerpts in my own hand, I temporarily acquired the gratifying illusion that I was not merely the transcriber, but the *author* of all those lovely passages of poetry.

Another publication was a game-book of literary questions and answers called *Cans and Can'ts*, in which David Cecil and I nost enjoyably collaborated. Though *Cans and Can'ts* is still my own favourite form of quiz, we made but very few crumbs out of its publication.

In 1927 came the chance—so very nearly not taken—of breadwinning on, to me, a sensational scale. A letter from my agent and dear friend, Miss Pearn—"Pearnie" to all her grateful clients—followed me to Germany. She asked me to write for a serial publication in *The Woman's Journal*, a life of the then Duchess of York. Book rights would follow. The payment offered seemed to me quite fantastic (I thought the last nought in the figure must be a clerical error!) however, I all but decided to reject the offer then and there. You see, I had not at that time the honour of knowing our present Queen and did not feel in any way qualified to write her biography. No, it did not seem a possible undertaking.

In a letter to my husband I did, however, just mention the offer. To my amusement, not unmixed with dismay, I received from him the following telegram, "For Heaven's sake don't refuse that offer in a hurry."

I hadn't yet posted my reply, and that telegram made me think again. After all, had I not always considered lack of enterprise the eighth deadly sin? Who was I to refuse a good offer? Had the book been wanted at once, I am sure I should never have had the nerve to undertake it; but since no date was given, I could relegate the matter to a remote future; and to any challenge other than an immediate one my imagination is mercifully dormant. So I did accept the offer, and then almost simultaneously forgot all about it.

Some months later came the shock of a letter from the Editor of *The Woman's Journal*, demanding the first instalment in a few weeks' time. Panic now seized me, but after a sleepless night racking my brains as to how to get material, I started to clamour for interviews.

You know the comic and pathetic degree to which I always see myself in whatever happens to be my rôle at the moment? So you can imagine what a "scrubby little reporter" I now felt at the prospect of having to pester people to see me.

My first interview in this new impersonation of mine was with my heroine's mother. No one could have been kinder or more willing to help than Lady Strathmore, but I did wish that, like myself, she were a Child-Bore. No doubt had I had nine children, I also should have failed to keep any record of their sayings and doings. As it was, how easy—so far as the supply of material went—could I have made the task of any would-be biographer of a member of one of my own meagre family.

It was good news to hear that the Nannie of the Duchess of York's own babyhood was now in charge of Princess Elizabeth; also that there was an ex-governess—she was to prove invaluable—with whom I could be put in touch.

Before long I was allowed to visit our future Queen herself. Like everyone else, I immediately fell under the spell of her charm, gentle radiance, delicate dignity, and that heaven-sent gift for setting others at their ease. Though from that moment my task appeared magically lightened, at the same time I foresaw a new, unexpected difficulty. How, unless I deliberately went in for understatement, could I hope to escape the charge of sycophancy? Unrelieved praise makes monotonous reading. Would not readers accuse me of bad advocacy? Where—they would complain—is the light and shade indispensable to good portraiture? Yet for the sake of safeguarding my book from the charge of sameness and insipidity, I could scarcely be expected to *invent* faults.

During my first visit to 145 Piccadilly, Princess Elizabeth, then a radiant and courteous baby, tottered into the drawing-room and was graciously pleased to be amiable. Having relieved me of my handbag, she displayed a precocious sense of the proper use of all its contents; spectacles were promptly perched on tiny nose; pennies pocketed; the mirror opened and powder deftly applied.

Steeling herself to be a dogged bore, my "scrubby little reporter" Self, now importuned ladies-in-waiting, music mistresses, miniature painters, girlhood friends, ballroom partners—anyone who might provide material. All were kind; few very communicative.

Next, I went to stay with Lady Strathmore at Glamis Castle. There I cross-examined relations, neighbours, factors, and domestic staff; all alike lyrical in their praise, but how I wished them gifted either with memories more retentive or with imaginations more fertile!

Having collected as much material as possible, I now set to work. Quite time too, for the first instalment was all but due; and the fact that every word must go for approval not only to the Duchess herself but also to King George V, would greatly retard the delivery of my typescript. Before long the Editor was clamorous.

Very rapid writing was therefore necessary, and my immediate circumstances could hardly have been less propitious. I, my husband and children were staying at Stanway, which Barrie for many years in succession rented from my parents for the month of August. Besides doing my usual secretarial work, I was acting as housekeeper and hostess in a large house filled to overflowing with relays of often strangely-assorted guests. Unfortunately that year I was also responsible for the correction of the proofs of a new complete edition of Barrie's works for America. These had to be ready by September. Besides this, I had undertaken a number of articles for periodicals, the editors of which were pelting me with telegraphed injunctions, "Make them snappy", "More pep please". Never had I felt less "snappy" or more deficient in "pep".

When I declined to include in this possible book letters to myself, you said "then why not quote letters from yourself or passages out of your own diaries?" So here, chosen at random from the laconic diary kept at that time, is one typical day of that August "holiday".

"*Tuesday*: Except for giving the children French lesson, and bandaging poor Whibley's head, I worked at the biography all the morning from 7 onwards. The post had confirmed my fears. To-morrow's expected guests *do* outnumber by three the beds in the house. A housemaids' strike followed this news. Picnic luncheon. Appreciated by children but not by Barrie, a large posse of pigs joined our party. By my hospitality with ham sandwiches, I converted these uninvited extra guests to ardent cannibalism. Conscripted to play croquet 2 till 3 o'clock. Frazzlingly hot. Rehearsed children in *Romeo and Juliet*. Huge birthday tea on shuffle-board table followed by croquet tournament for staff and guests. Dinner-table had been particularly difficult to arrange; and just as the gong went C. sneaked in, and entirely to suit himself, shifted all the name-cards! Result, three men all in a row and those two dumb animals, Mr. and Mrs. So and So side by side! 'Intellectual' (?) games with the Galsworthys etcetera. Wrote arrears of own and Barrie's letters until 1.30. To bed weeping with fatigue."

Does this make your lip curl? Compared with your own daily routine of toil, mine, no doubt, seems a slack day? In output of actual work, yes, but remember your fully recognised activities are protected by metaphorical traffic-lights. While you actually write, isn't the light outside your door red?

Despite all distractions, the biography was delivered by the decreed date. After a brief interval I was asked to write a sequel to be called *The Family Life of the Duchess of York*. This book necessitated many fresh interviews, and as it also came out in instalments it had to be rushed. Most of the writing was done on cups of strong black coffee in the small hours of the night while I sat up with my husband who was then desperately ill. What do you write on? Something considerably stronger than coffee, I'm sure. Do you agree with this passage I've just found in *Sheridan le Fanu*?

"I believe that everyone who sets about writing in earnest does his work *on* something. I suppose in the exertion there is a material waste that must be hourly supplied, or we should grow abstracted, and the mind, as it were, pass out of the body, unless it were reminded often of the connection by actual sensation."

While battling with my second royal biography, I was still writing miscellaneous articles and reviewing children's books.

"Hack"? Yes, and proud of the title! But though I still considered it lazy or cowardly to decline any commissioned work, there were, I would have you know, offers that I did refuse—the queerest, I think, being that I should write the *auto-biography* of Lady Astor! With a proper sense of my own limitations, I also declined to undertake the lives of either Mary Webb or the artist McEvoy, for neither of which tasks could I consider myself in any way qualified.

Another rash commitment was to write both for serial and book publication a jubilee book on King George V. This had to be finished in six weeks. It, too, was written by night, and evidently I became more than a little addled in the process, for glancing through my manuscript before sending it off, I found its closing words, written at 3.30 the previous night, were "God Save the *Quing*"!

Another Silver Jubilee publication was the *Princess Elizabeth Gift Book*, edited by my friend Eileen Bigland and myself. This was a book for children, published by Hodder and Stoughton, who generously gave the entire proceeds to the Princess Elizabeth Hospital for Children. For this, I thought it would be fun to collect photographs of all the distinguished contributors, taken when they themselves were children. I was right. It was fun, but at the same time it very nearly held up the book. Why? Because the authors found it so difficult to choose between various versions of themselves when young. I never saw such agonies of indecision. One of our team simply could not make up his remarkable mind whether his small self had been more appealing in Little Lord Fauntleroy costume or in the manlier garb of a sailor suit. He sent three telegrams, each cancelling the last. Another crisis blew up when at the eleventh hour an author violently objected to some lines of his story being printed in italics. "Well", philosophically remarked the printer, "we must expect some trouble when we have such a Ga-*lax*-ly of talent. . . ." How right he was! The editor's troubles were indeed manifold. One of the "Ga-*lax*-ly held up printing for a fortnight by a series of telegrams telling us just why he could not possibly allow his story to come "after a Mouse". Since *we* considered the acquisition of a Mickey

Mouse cartoon the biggest feather in our editorial cap, this was very wounding. To obtain this feather had, indeed, been no easy matter. It had taken many weeks' pleading with Walter Disney's London manager, whose opening preamble was always: "You think I'm a tough guy, but I'm really only an unborn babe." Having lulled him into this embryonic state, we were terrified lest a change in Mickey's order of precedence should precipitate him back into maturity.

Another author warned us that if we billed him as the brother of his sister, we should hear from his solicitors.

A third had a redoubtable wife obsessed by her determination to protect her husband's literary rights. She nearly drove us distraught by telephonic enquiries as to whether every possible and impossible form of copyright had been safeguarded.

Worst of all, a renowned poet sent us verses much, much too bad to print!

As a thank-offering for our success in getting the book to the printers at all, we foolhardily decided to give a party for the contributors to meet one another and asked a great many of our own friends to meet them. This was tempting Providence. The temptation was not resisted.

To start the ball rolling, quite the most difficult of our whole pride of lions arrived an hour too early, and long before the cocktails. Thirsty and bored, this untimely guest watched his hostesses battling with caterers and shifting the furniture in attempts to make more room in my house—far too small for the occasion. My ordinary pre-party nerves had been greatly aggravated by the news that my son Simon had had a most regrettable brain-wave, and rung up Uncle Dick (Pip, Squeak and Wilfrid of the *Daily Mirror*) to ask him to bring his live penguin—the mercenary child's plan being to mulct the guests of sixpence each for the privilege of a private view of this famous bird together with J. M. Barrie!

My husband, diplomatically ill for the afternoon, was staying upstairs, and Barrie had announced his intention of devoting himself to his so-called invalid host instead of coming down to join the company, thus facilitating Simon's plan of turning him into a profitable peep-show.

Breadwinning

Simon's invitation to the bird who was to co-star with Barrie had been gratefully accepted. In my liking for a penguin in its proper place I yield to no one. But in my drawing-room, NO! I tried to improvise arrangements for the celebrated bird's entertainment. There was no fish in the house.

It was an immense relief when Uncle Dick telephoned to break the news that owing to an outbreak of artistic temperament on the penguin's part, it had been impossible to coax him into the taxi.

Even without the complication of a penguin, it was no easy party to manage. The lions were aggressively conscious of the relative heights of their own and each other's brows; when Uncle Dick came he proved, even without his bird, so great an attraction that all the lion-hunters clustered round him and his artist confrère, while neglected lions, resisting all the blandishments of their hostesses, glowered in separate corners of the room.

For glimpses of Barrie un-"supported" by the penguin, Simon reduced his charge to threepence—for which fee he opened the door of the study just a few inches to reveal the dramatist and his supposedly ill host playing draughts in thickening clouds of tobacco smoke. . . .

In 1936 I was asked to write a novel, a proposal that threw me into an absolute dither of indecision, self-distrust and panic.

As you urged me to draw on contemporary records, here for your mockery is an extract from an extremely egotistical letter to my mother:

"Why, oh why did you call me after the moon? 'Cynthia, she that never sleeps, but walks high heaven all the night.' Those lines always did have an unfortunate auto-suggestive effect on me, and once again they describe your insomniac daughter. No doubt my present 'condition' is partly to blame. To be 'expecting' a novel is no sedative. It was only after a hell of indecision that I committed myself to such an undertaking. For one thing it means condemning myself—even the slightest novel is such a long, long way to go—to months of strain and preoccupation, during which I shall often wish my best friends dead rather than that they should ask to see

197

me, and the sound of the telephone-bell will make me scream. Then, weakness though I know it to be, I am still morbidly sensitive to ridicule. I shall hate wondering how bad you all think it—not only not good but very likely in the dull, negative sense of the word 'vulgar'. Or will it be just a case of vapid vacuity?—'So *that's* all there is in Cynthia!' So long as I confined myself to writing about the Royal family, children and ghosts, I could retain much of my native evasiveness; whereas this venture will—or anyhow should— involve coming out into the open—a sort of spiritual strip-tease. And to what purpose?

"Apart from people thinking it bad (which even in the hundred to one chance of its being good, my own friends will) I shrink from that cap-fitting readers who do not themselves write always indulge in—'That's Herself'—'That's Him'—'Who is the other woman?' Should I succeed in drawing any character remotely resembling a real human being, this cap-misfitting will be inescapable. Financially I don't think it sound either. I probably earn far more money by articles than any novel by me is likely to bring in, and once launched on a book it will be so difficult to switch off to write other things. Even a short story hangs like an opaque curtain between me and life. As you know, I get so foolishly obsessed by any occupation. Do you remember when, finding total abstinence so much easier than moderation, I was obliged entirely to give up knitting?

"But why should I inflict all these Pros and Cons on you? To be honest, I know the determining Pro is that a large part of me eagerly *wants* to write the book. Anyhow, the thing to remember is the unimportance of the whole affair. How little it will matter to anyone but me—but what a big But!

"However bad you may think it, I hope I can trust you not to be 'put off' your own daughter—no more than if she had made a bad pudding. I write as though my novel were nearly finished, whereas I haven't yet even begun it, but it's banging about in my head and I take notes all day and most of the night. If and when it comes out, I have decided to spend most of my time at the Zoo. What a comfort it is that animals can't read! But last night I had an awful dream that our new puppy *was* reading my novel and shaking with ill-natured laughter!"

Once I had embarked on my book the preoccupation at first provided a complete safety-curtain. Clearly, whether or not it ever got read, the experience of writing it, sharpening every sense, was an end in itself, and one not to be missed, exhausting, isolating, indeed terribly lonely, but wonderfully kindling and vivifying.

Unfortunately, however, almost as soon as I began, everything conspired to wrench me out of this blissful, evocative absorption.

Those six months in which I wrote *The Spring House* chanced to be the least leisured and the most difficult of all my life. Everything was going elaborately wrong. Never had I been distracted by such shoals of red herrings, all acute anxieties and perplexities. Dogged by misfortune—its production again and again nerve-rackingly postponed—Barrie's play, *The Boy David*—his first after sixteen years' silence—was being rehearsed in an atmosphere of growing tension. Attendance at these enthralling rehearsals reduced my writing hours to very few, and alas—harrowing preoccupation—day by day the author's health was visibly worsening; making him more and more distressingly unfit for the immediate strain and the impending disappointment.

At the same time, several members of my own family were also disquietingly ill.

While in the double throes of my novel and of life, I was asked to plan a book about the two little Princesses, an undertaking that, of course, necessitated innumerable interviews in search of material. My novel was now tugging at me like a pulling horse, and I longed to be able to give it its head. Once I was driven to remain in bed—my only possible chance to concentrate. "Stayed in bed all day and wrote nine hours", reports my diary, but there was not more than that one day on which such escapism was possible.

However few the hours to which its actual writing had to be relegated, the preoccupation of my novel did, I think, nevertheless provide a certain immunity to other troubles. Though far from impervious, up to a point I became, like Ophelia, "incapable of my own distress".

Not until my task was done did I too feel utterly finished, overcome with nervous exhaustion, quite unable to cope with pressing problems and morbidly hypersensitive about my book.

Still no sense of proportion? Not the germ of one!

Mercifully for my frayed nerves *The Spring House* had good reviews; but my original fears—by then in abeyance, so careful had I been to give no real pretext for cap-fitting—were now more than realised. Flagrantly unlike myself though I thought my heroine, people accused me of writing a camouflaged autobiography!

Had I attempted an autobiography they would of course have pronounced it pure fiction. Yes, friends will always say you are indebted to your memory for a novel, and to your imagination for your memoirs. Worse still, I was accused of deliberately pillorying my nearest and dearest, by "putting them into a book"!

No doubt most of the characters of the greatest writers, Tolstoy, Dickens, and so on, are closely drawn from real life. Not so, I think, those of the lesser fry; invention being surely the smallest part of a novelist's outfit. To invent, indeed, being far easier than to depict.

Probably certain facets of actual people find their way into every book, but their introduction is often unconscious and nearly always unintentional. Most of the characters in novels are synthetic, partly made up of little pieces chipped off various acquaintances and partly imagined. To illustrate how determined readers are to find a likeness, one of the feminine characters in my novel was recognised by my London friends as a certain Londoner, and by my Gloucestershire friends as a certain country neighbour; yet of all the women I have ever known these two were the most utterly dissimilar!

The trouble is that readers who approach any book from the angle of personal acquaintance with its author, are too much on the lookout for recognisable likenesses. That is why no one who thinks of the author primarily as a person and only secondarily as a writer, can ever judge a book on its literary merits or demerits. "Who's Who" is too great a preoccupation. . . .

The moment my novel was finished I set to work on *The King's Daughters*, a delightful task brightened by several visits to the enchanting pair of sisters. Again I felt that if my pen did anything like justice to my subjects, I should be accused of over-statement.

By previous engagement, I happened to go to tea with the Princesses and their charming governess, Miss Crawford, the very day of the abdication. Cheering crowds seethed outside 145 Piccadilly; and as I drove up flashlight photographs were being taken of the Prime Minister alighting from his car.

Though outwardly she still displayed her habitual self-control, Princess Elizabeth's brilliant blue eyes were dark with suppressed excitement. From time to time when a specially loud cheer proclaimed the arrival of some other important personage, she would dart to the window, glance out, and excitedly whisper, "Thousands of people outside"! When I rose to go, she escorted me down the stairs. On the hall table lay one solitary letter which she picked up and fingered. She saw the envelope was inscribed to "Her Majesty the Queen" and her face went very solemn. "That's Mummy now", she said, with a tiny tremor in her awestruck voice. Beyond that one remark she made no allusion to the event that, changing the course of history, must so profoundly affect her childhood, and confront her with so formidable a future.

To all appearance her usual blithe self, Princess Margaret Rose insisted on a game of Demon Pounce and seemed to take a purely personal view of the crisis. "Isn't all this a bore?" she prattled. "We've got to leave our own house now!" A little later she exclaimed, "Just think, I had just learnt how to spell York—Y-o-r-k—and now I'm not to use it any more. I'm to sign myself just Margaret all alone." As though it involved some mysterious loss of her own identity, this disuse of her second name went on rankling in the little Princess's heart, and some weeks later she was heard to complain, "Since my Poppa turned King, *I* don't seem to be anyone at all."

For me the abdication meant the most copious inkshed. My publishers now demanded an entirely new book to be called *Queen Elizabeth*, but, since both the previous books were still selling, they wished these to remain in circulation, so, while engaged on the new book, I must, by adding to each some ten thousand words, bring both the earlier ones up to date. This triple task had to be finished in two months. You can imagine what this involved in the way of paraphrasing, padding, transposing—all the things one should never do; also how confused I became between the three versions, all of which in instalments were simultaneously being typed by different typists. For the first time in my life I was driven to attempt dictation, but I found the expectantly poised pencil and brightly blank smile of the robot much too paralysing. To complete the confusion, I was now harried by demands to deliver my book (scarcely begun) on the Princesses in good time for the Coronation. Those weeks of fever and fret have become a mere blur in my memory, so you had better have some more entries from my diary.

"*January 2nd*, 1937. Moment of intense relief when I felt I had broken the back of my task.

"*January 9th*. Assembled and corrected typescript of Queen Elizabeth. What a relief!

"*January 17th*. Frightful bombshell. Queen Elizabeth book pronounced twenty thousand words too short! How *can* I add so much to it?"

How indeed? Harassed into idiocy, I could think of no way except to replace all the adjectives I had quite rightly struck out, and then add several more to each sentence. This really was a nightmare. Pretending to be even iller than I really was, I now bolted ostensibly for a cure into a country clinic where in between bouts of violent physical tortures (I had to pretend I was there for treatment) I wrote eight hours a day and by puffing and padding, somehow elongated each sentence, A strange "cure", but not without a certain exhilaration. I always enjoy the sense of being thoroughly over-wound up. . . .

My next book—another novel—was produced under strangely different conditions. So far from being rushed, no one was in the slightest hurry for its delivery, and I wrote it in the paradoxically peaceful atmosphere of an Air Warden's Report-Post, where for shifts of three or four hours at a time, usually very early in the morning, I was agreeably marooned with no more exacting duties than the transmission of air raid warnings, and no fear of any disturbance more personal than a bomb.

My next effort, though whether it should have a place in a record of *breadwinning* is more than doubtful, for it was not a commissioned work, was a sudden impulse—in fact, a gate-crasher. This is how it came about. I had planned to write a book on the sufferings incurred (and inflicted) by the wives of great men. For this purpose I had read everything I could find about Countess Tolstoy. Suddenly I saw the last tragic phase of that ill-fated marriage as a drama, and in an absolute paroxysm of writing, I began and finished my first play in a fortnight. There most probably the matter will end. Doubtless I have joined that large company of frustrated play-writers perpetually tantalised by false hopes, but destined never to see their plays performed. Neither will my projected book, *Wives of the Great*, now ever get written. That unproduced play* "stops the way".

For a long time all ambition for any writing other than play-writing was suspended. Unless the wolf drew very close to the door, it looked as though my breadwinning days were ended. I thought I should have to take up knitting again, perhaps even, in defiance of you, crosswords! However, this mood lasted no longer than other moods.

---

* *No Heaven For Me,* produced at the Little Theatre, Bristol, 1947.

EDUCATION?

I AM, indeed, touched as well as amused that you should want to hear about *my* education; a word whose use, alas! confers a courtesy title on a most haphazard, happy-go-lucky affair—a thing indeed of shreds and patches. Of formal, sustained education in the sense of any systematic training of my mind, I had none.

To take the smooth with the rough, I suppose I was fortunate to escape with so little *mis*-education. For example I was not, like so many of my contemporaries, put off poetry by its being forced on me as a distasteful lesson. (I once asked a sultry little girl which kind of punishment she minded most. Being sent to bed? Having her pocket-money docked? Or what? "Poetry", was the furious answer.) To go on counting the blessings of my childhood, I had the opportunity of hearing plenty of stimulating talk; if I asked questions, the answer, "Wait until you are older, dear", was not often given; and, besides the advantage of being brought up in beautiful surroundings, I was early and often taken abroad. Best of all, Stanway had quite a good library in which, free as a butterfly in a herbaceous border, I was allowed to browse. I can't remember any book being put on the Index.

As I've already told you, my first lessons were from the even then old-fashioned primer, *Reading Without Tears—Tears Without Reading*, we called it. By the time I was five, I could, I think, read everything. Writing I found much more difficult. Considerable mortification darkens the memory of a long succession of copy-books, through which, breathing hard, with obtruded tongue, I slowly struggled; wielding at first a pencil, and later on—"going into ink" the promotion was called—a spluttering pen. The upward strokes had to be light, the downward thick. It was on the downward stroke that the point of my pencil always broke, or after I had "gone into ink" my copy-book got blotted. "Don't write with your tongue out, Cincie!" That reiterated injunction still rings in my ears, but so little command had I over my "Unruly Member"—as in schoolroom jargon it was always called—that so far from writing with my tongue in my cheek, I could never restrain it from waveringly describing in the air whichever letter my tightly clenched fingers were at that moment trying to form.

Copy-book calligraphy began with mysterious hieroglyphics called, if I remember rightly, "Pot-hooks and hangers"—what on earth can a hanger have been?—and culminated in sentences, such as "Make hay while the sun shines", "It's the early bird that catches the worm", and other exhortations.

Holding my pen properly was an art I never acquired. How I marvelled at the effortless flowing swiftness with which, apparently poised on her little finger only, my mother's letter-writing hand flew across the writing paper.

Precipitated from the nursery at the age of five, I came under the ægis of a newly arrived English governess.

Charlotte Jourdain, a sister of the Miss Jourdain of *Versailles Adventure* fame, was a remarkable woman. She had been one of the first of her sex to go to Oxford and was a fine classical scholar. Deeply religious—she subsequently became an Anglican Sister—her great strength of character, and complete freedom from any "sick fatigue" or "languid doubt", in every way qualified her to influence an impressionable child. Had she stayed on until I grew up, I should, I think, for better for worse, for richer for poorer, have turned into something quite different, but she left when I was only ten and after her departure there was no follow-through, no continuity, no discernible system of any kind in my so-called education.

With Miss Jourdain I at once started to learn Latin. This delighted me, not only because I enjoyed it, but because I thought it a boyish study, and to follow as closely as possible in the footsteps of my brothers was always my ambition. "Amo, Amas, Amat" had remained imprinted on my memory ever since some years before I had listened to Ego's first lesson in that key verb. In the declension of nouns, the vocative case held a peculiar fascination that gave me the habit of apostrophising inanimate objects. "Oh, Pudding!" I would cry reproachfully, "Oh, Peach!" dotingly.

Undoubtedly the brief "grounding"—queer word—Miss Jourdain gave me was the best teaching I was ever to know. Had it continued, I should have learnt not only Latin and Greek, but also my own language, which because a foreigner took her place alas, I never did.

I'm sure Miss Jourdain had a real gift for teaching—a rare capacity to ignite interest in any subject on which she touched. Though few children can ever have been born with less cosmic curiosity than myself, I have never forgotten how enthralled I was when she showed me—an orange was used for demonstration—the movement of the Earth—explaining how (with myself upon her) "She"—I liked the earth to be called "she"— spun round the sun, so that in turn each hemisphere was alternately lit and darkened.

Because, I suppose, of these first enjoyable memories of lessons—a word to so many children evocative only of yawns and clock-gazing—the mere sight of a schoolroom and all its paraphernalia—ink-stained tablecloth, globe, wooden ruler, margined copy-books, neat time-table—is to me always a nostalgic sight. Or is it, perhaps, a subconscious desire for the order and routine that my nature craves, but my character cannot contrive, that makes me hanker after the enforced rhythm and mild discipline of schoolroom life? Whatever the reasons, whenever I look into a schoolroom, I feel "the weight of too much liberty" and long to "do lessons" again. . . .

The Stanway schoolroom overlooked the pear-tree-clad backyard into which at all hours clattered the carts of the baker, the butcher, the grocer, and the milkman, and the time of day was loudly passed between them and various members of the household. In this small square room, eternally chawing the end of my pen-holder, day in, day out, I sat tightly folded up to compress my rapidly growing frame into the narrow limits of an infant's writing desk. Oh, that "Little Ease" of a desk, used for

Drawing of the author, aged fifteen, by Violet Rutland.

The Author.

so many years after it was outgrown! Its lid was the most ink-scored piece of wood I have ever seen.

Miss Jourdain's wide learning did not include proficiency in modern languages; her French accent was staunchly patriotic, and in futile attempts to fill this gap, a procession—to the eye of my memory blurred, so quickly did one follow another—of French or Swiss maids, all quite as eager to learn as we were willing to teach English, streamed through the house.

Neither had my classical governess any taste for fiction. Occasionally—either as self-imposed discipline or in an attempt to understand the minds of others—she would set her teeth at a Dickens or a Jane Austen, but I don't believe she ever read a novel for pleasure. No, her one idea of recreation was to dive straight back into Latin or Greek. This limitation did not cut her pupil off from the delights of fiction, for my mother very early introduced me to the laughter and shudders of Dickens; and my aunt and god-mother, Lady de Vesci, to the quieter but great enjoyment of the Waverley novels.

Outside the realms of fiction, Miss Jourdain's influence was supreme. Religion, hitherto more or less confined to morning and evening prayers, grace before and after meals, and Sunday church-going, now permeated the whole of life; and every night, instead of a bedtime story, an informal confession was held, after which I would fall asleep with a lovely spiritually cleansed feeling and would awake to a sense of beatitude.

So far as I can judge in retrospect, the main fallacy of Miss Jourdain's teaching lay in her over-emphasis on the imputed complete cleavage between—each spelt with a capital letter—the Body—the "vile" Body—and the Soul, an over-simplification from which I was slow to liberate myself.

In my most recurrent memory of Miss Jourdain, I see and hear her reading *Pilgrim's Progress* aloud. Under the influence of that oft-read book, so deeply did I become imbued with the allegorical conception of life that I always pictured myself as a pilgrim with a bundle, varying in size, of sins strapped on to my back, perpetually either breasting the Hill of Difficulty—every difficulty was a hill—or else struggling to drag my feet out of some Slough of Despond. Not without vain-glory was my awareness of that burden on my back. "I suppose everyone has a bundle of sins, but some don't *feel* it", I smugly remarked. "Christian felt his because he was so good. I admire Faithful and Hopeful, but Christian means it all. *I* am going to be like Christian."

I must, however, have possessed some rudimentary sense of values of my own, for when told once too often to wash my hands before meals, I protested, "I really can't keep all these niggling little Pharisee rules! If I do, I'm sure I shall break one of the big commandments some day!"

My most acute theological worry concerned Judas Iscariot, whom I saw as the fore-doomed, indispensable instrument of the Divine Will. "If", I pleaded, "in order to fulfil the scriptures, Our Lord had to die and was *willing* to die, why then was it so wrong of poor Judas to betray him?"

I don't know exactly on what grounds it was decided when I was ten years old that Miss Jourdain's influence had grown too strong to be wholly desirable. You know that inane phrase, "I like a dog in his place" (where, one wonders, is that place?). Possibly there were those about me who liked religion "in its place". Now I come to think of it, I did overhear a visitor exclaim in precisely the tone in which she would have deplored a child writing a novel likely to be banned, "I hear Cincie writes *prayers*!"

Perhaps it was feared a solemn prig was in the making. Or, quite likely, the decision was not made entirely for my sake. Though devoted to Miss Jourdain, my mother may well have found both the force of her personality and the strength of her devotion to herself too much for continuous proximity. Whatever the reasons, it was decided the time was come to put an end to a situation that had somehow become over-charged; but on no account must *I* be told what was impending. When— ostensibly only for a short holiday—Miss Jourdain went away from Stanway, the plan was that she should return in about a fortnight's time and later on in the year leave for good. No one had anticipated the extraordinary way in which her pupil would now behave. Indeed the effect on me of this supposedly merely brief absence was most peculiar. Was my dependence on my lode-star so great that even a parting of only two weeks was an unendurable prospect? Or did this temporary separation make me realise for the first time that my governess, though so absolutely essential to me, was yet not an inseparable part of my universe? Some premonition must have warned me that this terrifying separation would some day be permanent. I have no clear recollection of my state of mind. All I remember is the agony of grief, the absolute panic of loneliness that seized me.

"Bun", my hitherto adored German god-mother, came as a stop-gap, but loyalty to the absent made me violently hostile towards her. Poor Bun, what a terrible time I gave her! Neither she nor anyone else could check the flow of my tears, but to all questions as to the cause of my distress, I maintained a lock-jawed silence. Glazed-eyed, my mouth a thin hard line, I neither ate nor slept. Still less would I speak. Before long, I had cried myself into such a state of hysteria that my unfortunate mother had to be telegraphed for and doctors called in.

After this crisis, it was unanimously decided that on no consideration could such an experience as this first stage of separation had proved be faced again. Wisely, it was decreed that Miss Jourdain must not return. No, not even for one day. Again, my reaction was surprising. Instantaneously, I—so it was put—"recovered my sanity". Why? Had I already subconsciously accepted as a fact, what I supposed myself to envisage only as a dread possibility, and thus enabled the process of readjustment to get well under way?

Possibly that particular "Cincie" brought into being only by Miss Jourdain, could not long survive her departure. Unguarded, the flame, if flame it were, flickered and went out.

Whatever the cause, no sooner was I officially told that the parting was final than I recovered with a swiftness that was almost shocking. (Resiliency, let me remind you, is the polite name for this blessed capacity to shake my feathers like a duck.) . . . Why had I been so utterly devoted to Miss Jourdain—so limpet-like in my dependence on her? What was this strangely influential woman like? In appearance she was strictly plain. Her hair just hair-coloured; her chin receding; her small eyes pale—their defective sight necessitating the use of pince-nez. I can still see the queer blurred look of her eyes when these aids to vision were temporarily removed, and the permanent deep rut they left across the bridge of her nose. She had a peculiar trick of giving an exaggerated swallow—a regular gulp— whenever emotionally moved, and, because her Adam's apple was so very prominent, I remember the fascinated way in which, while she read me Holy Writ, my riveted eyes would follow this bony protuberance as it slowly disappeared below the stiffly starched, mannish collar she always wore, and then as slowly reappeared.

Please don't take this list of startling physical attractions as an attempt to analyse my devotion to Miss Jourdain. I can't explain it. I only know that I always found her presence infinitely reassuring. Why did I need reassurance? I can't explain that either, but somehow she seemed, like scaffolding, to hold me together. I suppose her positivity supplied something that my own nature lacked and craved.

She was so single-minded, her sense of direction so strong. Others seemed to "fluctuate without term or scope, and each half live a hundred different lives". She, like the Scholar-Gipsy, was compelled by "one aim, one business, one desire". A vicarious sense of direction she had imparted had lent me confidence, and bereft of it, I felt rudderless—utterly adrift— lost!

To change my metaphor; it was as though the thread that strung the beads of my entity had suddenly been withdrawn and with their scattering I—then, as now, prone to live in some-one *else's* consciousness of myself—felt a disintegration of the whole of my precarious sense of Me-ness. It was, in fact, like dying.

Had the world been searched on purpose, I doubt if a greater contrast to the compelling Miss Jourdain could possibly have been found than her vociferous successor, Fräulein von Moskovicz—a dear, bird-witted little Viennese, of what the

Governess's Agency called "Good Family" ("I did not sink I vould ever be having to earn my own livings"). Under her amiable uncontrol, reacting as widely as possible from the sober little writer of prayers, I now ran completely wild and became an extreme example of what used to be called a tomboy.

"Squidge" (short for squirrel), as because of her bright, shallow, reddish-brown eyes, Fräulein von Moskovicz was nicknamed, did not have it in her to "form" the mind of anyone. Certainly no pupil of hers ran any risk of mental over-strain. However, though her idea of education, so far from being to "draw out", was—for window-dressing purposes—simply to cram in as many mere facts as possible, I do at least owe her the not inconsiderable debt that lessons were never made either oppressive or putting-off and that I was allowed to read during lesson hours the whole (not excluding even Titus Andronicus) of Shakespeare. Another good point was that she shared my own rapturous enjoyment of Dickens, and making her topple off her chair with laughter when I read him aloud was great fun.

Dear Squidge, loving and loved, I am grateful to you for all those untrammelled years in which—a free weed instead of a wired flower—I was left to develop at random, and become in the simplest and most enjoyable sense of the word, excessively naughty.

How clearly this staring back into childhood brings Squidge into my sight and hearing. Seated at the schoolroom table, I see her fling down her loathed darning—"I vas never brought up to be doing my own mendings"—to rub the appalling chilblains—"mes engelures", she called them—on her poor little mittened hands, and I hear her shrill twittering complaints of the atrocity of our climate. Indeed, no English summer was ever long enough to allow those terrible "engelures" to heal.

What besides the eagerly awaited "Elevenses" of milk and Bath biscuits, do I remember of all the thousands of hours spent with Squidge cooped up in that little schoolroom? What were our "studies"? Mental arithmetic, I remember, was a very frequent lesson, one we both enjoyed, for she had the answers in a book, and in so far as my mind worked at all, it worked quickly.

There were also endless written sums, but so mechanically taught was arithmetic that though as often as not my answers would be marked "R" (correct), I seldom had the faintest notion to what my calculations referred. For instance, I would usually manage to put those fascinating little decimal dots in the right places, but had not the remotest idea what they meant!

History? I remember the outsides of several staunchly patriotic books with St. George and the Dragon stamped on their covers, and a fat, completely out-of-date volume called *The Concise History of the World.* Squidge liked me to know plenty of dates—a branch of learning easily shown off—and as my then parrot-like memory found these easy to retain, I was willing to comply. It was wonderfully typical that I would be given quite as high marks if I got the date of the year right and the century wrong as for the other way round! Apart from these dates, my history learning mainly comprised those picturesque anecdotes most obviously suitable for charades. I cannot remember it ever occurring to Squidge that to teach geography in conjunction with history might be a good idea. No, geography was merely the memorising of endless strings of towns, rivers, capes, bays, imports and exports and very occasionally drawing a map— preferably, because of its obliging resemblance to a booted leg— the map of Italy.

The one tenet instilled into my mind by this schoolroom study of history, was the genuine belief that any one Englishman could easily overcome at least four (or was it six?) Frenchmen. I don't remember ever reading of any English defeat—unless perhaps in the case of a battle against the Scots, in which reverse there was nothing to offend a child proud to call herself British. Somehow or other I also imbibed the comfortable notion that history in the sense of any violent events such as big wars, belonged entirely to the past. All that kind of thing had been the long disorderly prelude to the halcyon calm and steady "Progress" of the Present Age.

As for my scientific studies; so far as I remember these began and ended with a brief explanation of the processes respectively called "Evaporation" and "Condensation".

Writing essays—"compositions" they were called—I greatly enjoyed but, of course, Squidge did not know the rudiments of English. Because as with Latin, I thought it a boyish study, I was proud to include Euclid in my time-table. I loved the little box of geometrical gadgets and found it an agreeable relaxation to describe with my compass, taking the tip of her jutting nose for my centre, equilateral triangles on my long-suffering governess's face. Possibly because of this diversion, we never progressed far beyond the *Pons Asinorum*.

My natural passion for learning poetry by heart was encouraged. In fact in every way my memory, but not my mind, was exercised. Opinions were not required. I cannot remember ever being asked to criticise what I read or to try to come to any conclusion on any subject.

In modern languages, after revelling in *Les Malheurs de Sophie*, and other children's classics, we gabbled through all the obvious French and German standard works—Racine, Corneille, Molière, Schiller and Goethe. We were supposed always to converse in French or in German and, speaking each language with a strong Viennese accent, I did arrive at a fair degree of fluency in both.

Music you will, of course, want to know about. Thereby hangs a tale. Though with the vogue for the "Musical Glasses", the era of compulsory "accomplishments"—whether or not assisted by any talent—had passed, and young ladies who had neither ear nor voice, were no longer expected to delight the guests; it was, however, still the custom for the unmusical as well as the musical to learn to play the piano.

Owing, however, to the contiguity of the piano to my father's room, my own music lessons came to an abrupt and early end. One November morning when I was painfully hammering out with cold-stiffened fingers *The Merry Peasant*, the drawing-room door opened, the fat, curly-haired butler appeared and addressing Squidge who, rubbing her perpetual chilblains, sat teed-up on the piano-stool beside my own, delivered himself of the following message: "If you please Miss Frau-leen, His

Lordship says Miss Cincie is to stop playing the piano at once, and needn't never have no more lessons." Owing to my being at that moment—for there was no fire in the drawing-room— quite blue with cold, this arbitrary exercise of the parental veto was not immediately unwelcome. I have never quite made up my mind whether on this occasion my father, whom even at its very best music distressed, was right or wrong. Not that he had weighed the matter. "At all costs this intolerable row must stop at once", was the only conviction that had prompted his intervention.

Since nowadays my mother never by any chance touched the piano, it did certainly seem a waste of time that she, like so many other mothers who also now never played, should for years have devoted four hours a day to its practice. Yet after I grew up, it was a dreadful humiliation to be unable even so much as to play *Three Blind Mice* to my own children. The disability gave me a positively crippled feeling.

Even though there can be no hope of ever becoming a per- former, should one nevertheless learn enough to be able just to read simple music? Perhaps to abstain from this is almost tantamount to not learning to read books because one will never be able to write? I don't know. Anyhow, I found the mortifi- cation of not being able to play so great that it actually goaded me into an attempt to remedy the deficiency by starting to have piano lessons at the age of twenty-six. Once again *The Merry Peasant* was pounded out. But soon—fortunately very soon— for never before or after had my husband been so sorely tried, I returned to my senses.

What did I mean by saying that under Squidge's uncontrol I became thoroughly naughty? Merely the tireless practise of every sort of prank and escapade, such as playing truant by absenting myself from lessons to follow the hounds on foot and staying out the whole day—no one having any idea of my where- abouts or whatabouts; or after placing a successfully deceptive dummy in my bed—next morning Squidge would tell me how sound asleep I had been—stealing out of the house to go for long moonlight walks by myself or with my Chow dog, for as others love sunning themselves, I always loved mooning myself. In London a favourite pastime was to climb from the balcony of our own drawing-room on to that of one of our neighbours; enter their house and after thoroughly exploring every room, escape by way of their front door.

Since you place me on the stool of repentance, I must also confess to an unending succession of practical—strictly practical—jokes. (My father complained that jokes were the only things I *was* practical about.) Not only did I go in for all the hoary old chestnuts of this simple form of humour—stock booby-traps, such as sponges on the top of the door, hairbrushes under the sheet, pepper on the pillow, but others—"original" I claimed these to be—so elaborate that their perpetration involved an amount of trouble worthy of a better cause. Once before a very important game of golf (the then amateur champion of England was one of the players) I stole out betimes and stuffed the last two holes up with sods of turf. This was a great success. The decisive long putt could not be holed.

I even went to the length of procuring a live crayfish—a pond was dragged for the purpose—to put into a governess's (not my own governess) bed. Fortunately, at the eleventh hour, my cousin, Mary Vesey turned King's (Queen's it was then) Evidence in time to save the wretched woman from a shock that might well have driven her off her head.

Another time I put two mice, trapped for the occasion, in the tea-caddy. When the governess, a provocatively hysterical Frenchwoman—again someone else's governess—lifted the lid, her display of excessive femininity surpassed my wildest hopes.

I'll spare you a long catalogue of these atrocities; all merely symptoms of the crude ambition of a child determined at all costs to distinguish herself, to excel at *something*—if it could not be in anything else—at least in mischief. No, I was not a Borstal-bud. There was no malice in my mischief. The excuse a fond stableman makes when his pony kicks you off, "It's only his play", might equally truly have been pleaded in my defence.

But I blush to think what anxiety—she was always so terribly afraid of my hurting myself—some of my more dangerous escapades inflicted on poor little Squidge. However the suffering was by no means all on one side, for this foolish woman had a terrible besetting sin—the blowing of blatant blasts, not on her own, but on her pupil's trumpet. It was a wonder I wasn't lynched by exasperated contemporaries and their affronted governesses, for whenever we went out to tea with other children, she would maddeningly edit her own pupil by extolling the swiftness with which she ran and the agility with which she jumped. Worse still, she would expatiate on the retentiveness of her memory and the quickness of her mind. Worst of all, while I sat dumb as a stone, or merely mumbling of the weather, was the irony of overhearing the stage-whispered words, *"tellement originale"*, or *"si spirituelle"*!

All I could do to try to make amends for my governess was to assure her unwilling audience that to myself she extolled her previous pupil in precisely the same exasperating way. Though these pæans bored me excessively, and also—for had I not seen the suetty girl?—took away any satisfaction her over-praise of myself might otherwise have given me, my assurance did little to placate the children victimised on my behalf.

Worst of all ways of making an utter fool of me, she would advise other governesses against letting their pupils compete against me either at lessons or in games because, so she insinuated, that way lay certain strain and probable mortification! The most glaring instance of this particular folly was when she solemnly warned the governess of—of all children in the world —Violet Asquith, who at that time was delicate, against letting her join my Italian class; the implication being that the strain of keeping up with me might be too much for *her*! My future sister-in-law had already shown the Derby winner form with which she still flashes through life. Just as well might Squidge have warned Mademoiselle Lenglen not to take me on at lawn tennis! Naturally the only inference Violet's governess could possibly draw was that Squidge wanted to save her own pupil from total eclipse.

When, instead of being guests, we entertained luckless children in our own schoolroom, Squidge's ways of showing off her own pupil were far from subtle. One embarrassing dodge was to propose an exceedingly crude game of questions and answers—the germ I suppose of all Quizzes—called "Who Knows?" The winner was whoever correctly answered the greatest number of questions such as "When were needles first introduced into England?" "Who built the Pyramids?" and so on. Since, after playing this game two or three times, no child, not positively deficient, could fail to remember the requisite scraps of knowledge, here was a very easy score over the stranger within the gate. There was also a variety of pencil-games, at which practice, and practice only, gave anyone the knack. Another certain victory for the home team!

After holding this outrageously handicapped tournament, Squidge, smugly muttering, *"Mens sana in corpore sano"*—the only Latin phrase she knew—liked to show that her pupil was active in body as well as in mind. For this purpose, since I really did happen to excel at the high jump, a piece of tape would now be produced and raised inch by inch across the long narrow passage. No attempt whatever was made to conceal her delight when visitors failed to jump the height my own long legs had just cleared. My cheeks still burn at the recollection of such shameless showing-off.

I remember poor Squidge's crazy partisanship meeting with a terrible reverse. During our visits to my aunt, Lady de Vesci, at Abbey-Leix, it was the custom for essays written by my cousin, Mary Vesey, the two other girls who shared her governess, and myself, to be placed in order of merit. Having the disadvantage of being a year and a half older than my cousin, my only chance to save Squidge from disgrace was to head this list. For one of these competitions the theme set was the view from the drawing-room window. Inspired by native love of the landscape—one of the loveliest in Ireland—and gifted with a natural sense of style, my cousin wrote an admirable description quite rightly placed above my own atrociously flowery effort, in which the sun was styled the "Golden Inhabitant of the Sky"! At this judgment Squidge not only burst into tears, but accused the adjudicators of favouritism and of giving a biased verdict.

As I have told you before, I am undyingly grateful to Squidge

for her affection, and all the fun enjoyed during the years spent
nominally under her rule—surely the lightest yoke ever laid on
a child's shoulders. I do, however, sometimes wonder how much
difference it would have made had I been taught by someone
with a mind as well as a heart.

One of my mother's most salient characteristics was her
determination to see—and by seeing to develop—the best in
everyone. A very lovable trait, but not without practical
disadvantages to those in her keeping; for this psychological
"make do and mend" did undoubtedly result in her often
putting up with, instead of discarding, human material when
much better could easily have been found.

The fact was that she saw others through the aura of her own
personality. Indeed her effect—precisely the reverse of a
distorting mirror—on others was to make them so much nicer—
so far above their natural form—that she was apt to have little
or no idea what they were like when not in her enhancing
presence. . . .

I was ten years old when Squidge came and she taught me
until I was sixteen. Did I have any supplemental education in
those years? Not much; but during the many happy weeks
yearly spent at Abbey-Leix, I did English lessons with Miss
Brand, my cousin's governess who, though not an intellectual
woman, did have some method in "grounding" and much more
idea of teaching than Squidge. Accustomed to lonely lessons, I
revelled in the companionship and competition. Like Miss
Jourdain, Miss Brand subsequently, so to speak, took the veil,
for she left the World, the Flesh and the Devil to become a
Deaconess. Why, I wonder, did my cousin and I both thus
affect our governesses?

In London, where we habitually spent May, June and July,
there were occasional French classes and one year an Italian
one. But most extra instruction was in physical exercise.
McPherson's Gymnasium in Sloane Street was bliss. Exhilara-
tingly clad in blue serge tunic, a belt fastened with metal clips
shaped like a snake, knickers and rubber-soled shoes, we
marched, wielded Indian clubs, brandished dumb-bells, swung

on parallel-bars, and vaulted over a contraption called the "Horse"; all these activities carried on to the strains of "Daisy, Daisy, give me your answer, do", "O Flo, why do you go, riding along on a motor car?", and other barrel-organ favourites of those days, strummed out by an unfortunate employee of McPherson's, depressingly described as a "Decayed Gentlewoman". Playing with every inch of her meagre body, this unhappy woman's action at the piano made her look exactly as though she were riding a particularly rough horse, and at the end of her hour's strenuous breadwinning, she was always seen nursing her damaged fingers.

The "Rope", up which I never could learn how to swarm, was my bi-weekly Waterloo; but as I won both the high and the long jump competitions and was also quite successful in other activities, Squidge thoroughly enjoyed my gymnasium classes.

Then of course there was dancing. At what age I first attended the redoubtable Mrs. Wordsworth's class I cannot remember; but it must have been long before the coming of Squidge. I can recall no experience more mortifying. Skipping was my first ordeal. Not one single time did that wretched rope swirl clear of both my large feet. No proficiency afterwards attained with the skipping rope ever made up for that initial discomfiture.

Scarlet-faced, peahen-voiced, the celebrated Mrs. Wordsworth was a truly terrifying woman. One of her eyes was glass, but to make up for this, her black satin back was undoubtedly Argus-eyed. In whichever direction she appeared to be looking, she could simultaneously see every single pupil in her vast class. Anyone starting off on the wrong foot, or in any way outraging Terpsichore, was made the subject of a screamed-out derisive verse, and for these improvised rhymed insults she really had a horrid knack. Whenever, which was often, some Patroness Princess came to inspect the dancing class, Mrs. Wordsworth's favourite pupil a, so the rest of the class considered, quite shamelessly graceful girl always glamorously attired in accordion-pleated skirts, would be picked out to perform a *Pas-Seul*.

I remember my first lessons in the Polka and the Valse, and

what a sad set-back it was, just as I had mastered the steps and begun quite to enjoy galumphing round the room, to be told I must now reverse engines and learn to "Be Gentleman"—a process that made me very giddy. The "Barn Dance" I madly enjoyed. It gave me *joie-de-vivre*. The Highland Fling too I found wildly exhilarating. It made me feel recklessly, headily brave—ready to outdo any Flora MacDonald.

So unforgettable was the overpowering personality of Mrs. Wordsworth—she always reminded me of the Wicked Fairy whose invitation to the christening had been overlooked—that when for the first time I entered the ball-room as a débutante, I again felt her gimlet eye on my fumbling feet and heard the command, "Ladies, take the Fifth Position" shrilled out.

There was a brief glorious phase when a retired army sergeant instructed me in the art of fencing. This ignited quite new ambitions. Stanley Weyman-ish visions of prowess rose before my eyes, and I swaggered about with a buttoned fencing-foil thrust sword-like through my belt. Thus accoutred I proposed to attend Divine Service, but at this even Squidge "put her foot down", and for once kept it there.

When I reached the age of fifteen there must, I think, have been some parental self-questioning about Cynthia's education. Was it adequate? Or was it possible the soil of her mind might be worth just a *little* more cultivation? This family conference led to the insertion of one of the oddest of all the little bits and pieces in the patchwork-quilt of my education. Once weekly, for one term only, Squidge and I made the twelve-mile journey into Cheltenham to attend its famous school. This was my first sight of massed girlhood, and I cannot say that when I came to read Tennyson's "Princess", I found myself reminded of what I had seen at Cheltenham College. The celebrated Miss Beale was already dead, but the first thing I learnt, and the only thing I remember, was the quatrain:

> Miss Buss and Miss Beale
> Love's darts do not feel.
> How different from us
> Are Miss Beale and Miss Buss.

Education?

What else can I remember? The attractive buttery-hatch, called "The Milky Way", to which we went for our "Elevenses" of a glass of milk and a biscuit—and the amphitheatre-shaped classroom, where I attended lectures on Physiography. That, I think, was what the subject was called, but its rather impressive name is all I recollect. I also joined a history class at which on the very first day I scored by being able to supply Kate Barlass's name, because, by a fortunate fluke, I happened just to have read Rossetti's poem, "The King's Tragedy". On this easily gained reputation for scholarship, I was able to rest on my oars till the end of the term. The remainder of my day was taken up with so-called drawing lessons, that for some inexplicable reason (possibly the teacher had veterinary blood) almost immediately devolved into merely learning by heart the name of every bone in the anatomy of the horse. True, at the first lesson—rather puzzlingly called "Drawing from the Life"—I was first set to draw the portrait of a match-box and then to copy a plaster-cast of Cicero; but after this, never again anything whatsoever but various segments of horses! I was very fond of horses, but had no particular wish to be able to put names to their bones. For all practical riding purposes, hocks, pasterns and fetlocks sufficed.

The adventurous to and fro-ing between Stanway and Cheltenham conferred a certain notoriety on the "Once-A-Weeker", as I was called. Indeed, in that very early phase of motoring, the ascent and descent of the spectacularly precipitous Cleeve Hill was no easy undertaking.

In dog-cart days, to lighten the horse's burden, we were always made to get out and walk up the steepest part of the climb.

Our motor-car—what a museum-piece it would look now!—was very primitive. To start its engine, a rope needed to be pulled up, an exertion that knotted the combined muscles of at least two men and a boy. In this machine on an average we usually broke down six times in our ten-mile journey. Once, hailed on our way with ringing cheers, we covered the last two miles in a dairyman's cart full of cans, all dribbling milk.

"Unbeknownst", as Nanny Cliffe used to say, to my parents, I persuaded the chauffeur to teach me to drive. I can still hear

poor Squidge's squeaks of terror whenever I was at the wheel
—or rather at the tiller—for this queer car—in shape like a
double dog-cart—had no steering-wheel.

I don't know why the Cheltenham College phase was so brief.
Probably because it was suddenly remembered that I was now
fifteen, the age at which it was customary "to be brought before
the Bishop to be confirmed".

For this ceremony, I was—a great privilege—prepared by
Cosmo Lang, the future Archbishop of Canterbury, then Bishop
of Stepney, who held a class for girls in a house with the
picturesque address of Amen Corner, Ave Maria Lane. He
became and remained a friend, performed the marriage service
at my wedding and promised, if I would make the date convenient, to bury me.

The outward and visible sign of the religious revival I under-
went, was a violent attack of jaundice. Literally a "golden
girl", I was confirmed with five other girls—pink-and-white
girls—by the future Archbishop in the crypt of St. Paul's
Cathedral.

In those days it was the custom for the daughters of the
"Wicked Rich" to go abroad to be what was quaintly called
"finished" before they "came out". In my case, this idiom
suggested clamping a very flimsy roof straight on to a building,
that consisted of only a ground floor already sadly in need of
repair.

For this "finishing" I was fortunate enough to spend eight
rapturous months in Dresden, where life was one long intoxicating Wagnerian dream.

Indignant and tearful, poor Squidge was left behind to
cultivate the younger children while Bun escorted me into these
realms of gold. My brother Guy, obliged by ill health to leave
Eton, came with me to be the one and only boy among endless
"crocodiles" of "flappers" (a long time since I used those two
obsolete words!) for Dresden was then practically under the
occupation of English schoolgirls. We stayed in a *Pension* condemned with a shudder by the parents of daughters more
conventionally lodged as "very cosmopolitan". My friend,

Eileen Wellesley, was with us and later on we were joined by my
cousin Mary Vesey and her heroic mother. Heroic I call her,
because though at the time the *Pension Wagner* seemed paradisal
to me, I can remember it with sufficient objectivity to know
that I should not now consider either its accommodation or its
food endurable. Also to enjoy the company a robust social
appetite and a simple sense of humour was needed; but I don't
remember Aunt Evelyn ever spoiling our fun by showing she
did not share it.

Several hours daily were spent in a very stuffy studio
disappointingly unreminding of the studios in Trilby. The
drawing-master's method was merely to perch by each easel in
turn, contemplate the charcoal daub in silent gloom, and then
use a vast quantity of bread in rubbing out the entire attempt;
after which, without one word of criticism, he would himself
rapidly substitute a new drawing. After some months spent in
portraying plaster-casts of Julius Cæsar, Socrates, and once
again my old friend Cicero, I was promoted to drawing live
models; but only their heads and shoulders. The study of the
"Altogether" did not form part of a young woman's "finishing".

Apart from the uninspiring nature of the teaching, Eileen
Wellesley's dazzling talent for drawing was quite enough to
discourage the rest of us. To hide talents so tiny under napkins
was surely not a sin?

Besides German and German literature, our studies included
"Kunst-Geschichte". This meant being marshalled round
picture galleries by a voluble and extremely easy-not-to-listen-to
Fräulein while she expatiated on the technique of the Old
Masters.

There was nothing specially good about the teaching at any
of the classes we attended, but formal education was a very
small part of the value of those golden months in Dresden where
for all of us so many magic casements were opening wide.

With Wagner motifs thundering in our ears, we walked
through the days in a mazed trance. Never was the visionary
gleam brighter—the glory and the freshness of the dream more
radiant. To this day I can never hear the clang and moan of an
electric tram without being wafted back to Dresden, and

recapturing something of the rapturous thrill with which we set off for the opera and the tranced state in which, with the fire-music still ringing in our ears, we fell asleep.

How impossible to convey the twofold bliss of that Dresden time; twofold because, while with music, poetry and pictures swimming into your ken, day-to-day life with all its fun and companionship was such delight, there was at the same time still all the thrill of vague expectancy—the sense that, seen through a luminous haze, all immediate experience, however enjoyable, was nevertheless only an intimation of things to come. You had not yet left the shore—but what an entrancing shore! You were still building your boat, a boat about to be launched on trackless, shimmering seas. The mysterious future beckoned.

Not that I ever wanted to grow up. On the contrary I grudged the ending of each year of childhood. I did, however, love the vague sense of expectancy and the uncertainty about my own potentiality. How long, I wondered, might you be regarded as vaguely "promising"? How soon must there be some actual achievement? At what age might you—dread thought—have to reconcile yourself to the fact that you were going to be only just an Ordinary Person?

Besides the discoveries in music and pictures, there was also the discovery of other personalities—the delight of consciously making friends, some of them to be life-long.

A long list would be tedious to you and depressing to me, so—besides Mary Vesey and Eileen Wellesley, both pre-Dresden intimates—I will mention only two. One was Violet Asquith, enthralling company, indeed a verbal Bacchante, and as preternaturally fluent in German as in English.

The other was the lovely Stella, Mrs. Patrick Campbell's daughter, much envied by me not only because of her entrancing nose, that looked as though with a last-minute inspiration the sculptor had chipped a tiny piece off its tip, but also because she was destined to the stage career after which I yearned. Not only was I hopelessly stage-struck, but to me the squirrel-cage of womanhood—by which I meant a life purely domestic and social—seemed a quite intolerable prospect.

Education?

A happy gang (the "Verrückte Englanderinne", we were called), devouring *"Pfankuchen"* and *"Pumpernickel"* as we hurried from class to class, we thronged the streets, humming Wagner opera motifs, declaiming Heine, bandying inane jokes.

Defying the German passion for regulations, we did all manner of things that were "Strengst Verboten". By not keeping off the grass, we played a daily game of Tom Tiddler's Ground with the park-keepers; and by pelting one another with cherry stones between the acts, we outraged the very Opera House itself. In those precincts—so sacred that one was liable to be ejected for a mere cough—I even won a wager by, in the middle of a rather drab overture, extracting a key hairpin from the intricacies of the coiffure of the lady sitting in front of me.

The main object in sending us to Dresden had been that we should learn to speak fluent German; and, although the daughters of the *Pension Wagner* preferred to do whatever language-learning took place themselves, and we were delighted to improve their English, this purpose was achieved.

Personally, I should have liked to work, but it was impossible to contend against the innate frivolity of our guardians. Both Bun and Eileen Wellesley's German governess, a heaven-sent butt—even the least talented could draw a recognisable caricature of her face—were insatiably pleasure-loving, always wanting to break away from routine to take us on some jaunt or other.

During three rapturous weeks of skating, all lessons were let go.

It was on that great shining sheet of ice that for me the future suddenly briefly impinged on the present.

Reclining in a carved and painted chair, constructed in the image of Lohengrin's swan, I suddenly found myself being swiftly propelled over the frozen waters by a tall young man on skates. Not a single word did he say, and it was not for me to break the silence, but I remember a sense of momentousness out of all proportion to the event. Gratified that he should have chosen me out of several other equally buxom and less shy girls, I, with perhaps the vaguest possible sense of premonition, attached greater significance to this silent attention than it warranted. It was—a sensation I have had at a few first meetings and also at the first sight of one or two places—as though just for a flash I remembered the future.

As likely as not it was only the swan-chair that had attracted my silent charioteer, who turned out to be Beb—for by this nickname he was universally called—Asquith, who had come out from England with two of her other brothers to spend Christmas with Violet. Though during our meeting on the actual ice, the social ice remained unbroken, it did not survive my bombardment of cherry stones at the opera that night, and at my very first London ball we danced together several times. Before long we were secretly engaged. That I should meet my husband in Dresden was certainly not according to plan. It would indeed have been thought quite the wrong kind of "Finishing".

It was the custom for the "Finishing" process to be carried out in France as well as in Germany; but my Continental polish was very lop-sidedly applied. My mother took me to Paris. Our intention was to attend lectures at the Sorbonne, but plans cannot have been laid with very much care, for only two days after our arrival the University closed for the summer vacation! Almost at once some family crisis—for the mother of six, few weeks can be without one—took my mother back to England, and I was left in the care of her lady's-maid and a daily French governess. Though an absolute gorgon in appearance—any producer of *Macbeth* would have engaged her on sight to play a witch—my duenna was most good-natured and amenable, in fact a sheep in wolf's clothing.

Having recently read *Trilby* I was pleasurably haunted by Svengali's description of the Morgue, and determined a sight of it should form part of my Paris education. Yes, I *must* see the "slabs of brass all in a row, like beds in a dormitory, where all day and all night from the little brass taps" (so Svengali assured Trilby) "the cold water would trickle down on her beautiful white body." Without much hope of Mademoiselle's consent, I suggested a visit to the Morgue in as casual a voice as I could achieve. To my surprise, this most tractable of dragons promptly acquiesced. *"Oui"*, she blithely replied, *"Oui, chérie, certaine-*

ment, il faut voir la vie à Paris." So off we went to "see life". We did not draw blank.

Beyond the sight of those three corpses, one of them a brutally murdered woman, and an occasional visit to the Louvre, very brief—for my un-reluctant dragon suffered cruelly with her feet—I remember nothing of my Parisian education except the learning by heart of a poem ending with the, to me, then deeply moving verse:

> "*Elle est morte ; elle n'a jamais vécu,*
> *De ses mains est tombé le livre,*
> *Dont elle n'a jamais rien lu*",

a dirge that haunted me as admonishingly as that other schoolroom, "Don't - let - the - grass - grow - under - your - feet" warning, the death-bed wail of the dramatist Greene:

> "Oh that a year were granted me to live!
> And for that year my former wits restored.
> What rules of life, what counsel would I give.
> How should my sin with sorrow be deplored.
> Now must I die of every man abhorred.
> Time loosely spent will not again be won,
> My time is loosely spent and I undone!"

However little I learned in Paris, I suppose my French vocabulary did increase by some few words. One far too frequently on my duenna's lips was the word "*retroussé*". She had a most unhygienic way of caressing my nose with black-kid-gloved hands and bleating out "*Joli petit nez retroussé*". As I then hankered after a far more important nose than it had pleased God to give me, this intended compliment deeply offended me.

Besides our visit to the Morgue, the only other incident I remember is pinning a large label inscribed "FRAGILE" on to my duenna's back before we set out for our morning walk in the Rue de Rivoli. Hearing repeated bursts of merriment from those behind, she remarked, "*Que tout le monde est bien gai ce matin! C'est sans doute parce qu'il fait se beau temps*". . . .

So much for the French polish applied when I was seventeen. On my return to England another family conference was held.

"Whatever is to be done with Cynthia next?"

"Do you mean to say she's not finished *yet*?" exclaimed my father in tones of crumbling patience.

One well-wisher suggested I should go to a housekeeping school. How right he was, I now recognise, but at the time I condemned him as grossly utilitarian. Arthur Balfour's contribution to this conference was to pronounce that I ought to read Froude, and to give me a beautifully bound set of his essays.

· Now followed a very curious interlude in my up-bringing. I was not destined to undergo the metamorphosis quaintly described as "Coming Out", until the following summer when I should be eighteen; but, as my mother must this year present Miss Bullock Webster, the daughter of the Stanway vicar, and did not wish to go to Court two years running, it was characteristically decided that I should make my curtsey to my Sovereign now and then revert to chrysalis-hood.

Since for this purpose I had acquired a real evening dress, it seemed a pity to wear it only once, so the Drawing-room was followed by my going to two balls. After this brief sally into the Beau Monde, I was withdrawn for further cultivation.

My own wish was to go to Oxford; not so much from any particular ambition to take a degree, but because I longed to have what I felt was my almost wicked passion for reading elevated into a duty. As things were, the sight and thought of my mother, so exhaustingly over-occupied with family and household cares, made it impossible for me ever to read a book in the morning without a positive sense of guilt. Recollections of reading parties at Stanway while my brother was working for his Oxford degree, made my mouth water. True, I could not remember the students ever seeming to find either Stubbs's *Charters* or Hobbes's *Leviathan* in the least riveting, but surely these tomes were the thick end of the wedge? How lovely to be able to read and read and read, not as a self-indulgence, but as a bounden duty!

However, in those days, for a girl to go to a university was a deviation from the normal almost as wide as taking the veil, or, by a stride in the other direction, going on the stage. Such a thing could not possibly be done without your getting "labelled". The term Highbrow had not yet come into use, but some other, equally derogatory, would have been applied. Tolerant to a fault, my mother, ever ready to welcome any stranger, be it a human being or a new idea, would not herself have opposed the plan, but the general opinion was overwhelmingly against it.

Was I not to "Come Out"? And what, if one faced facts, was the point of anything so prodigal of parental money, time, and energy as a daughter "Coming Out", unless as the necessary preliminary to her getting married? Would not nearly any so-called—odious word—"eligible" young man be put off a girl with academic aspirations? Yes, to be associated with a university education would undoubtedly be a scandal it would take many seasons to live down. I'm sure my father thought I might just as well be branded on the brow.

A compromise that delighted me was now suggested—I should stay at Stanway and learn Greek ("but don't *tell* any-one!") and English with Mr. Allen, the "Priest" as we always called him. (I'll tell you all about him later on.) This plan suited my genuine hankering after some serious education, and at the same time promised a most enjoyable life, for—pure ecstasy—I was to be allowed to hunt twice a week. The Stanway programme also included keeping up my French and German with Squidge, who was now teaching the younger children.

A few delightful weeks followed. The "Priest", who strongly believed, and how wholeheartedly I agree with him! in the incentive of praise, was an intoxicating teacher. Instead of keeping my nose to the grindstone of grammar, we at once started to read Euripides; his theory being that anyone not positively stupid could in six months' intensive study learn to read Greek fluently.

Such preparation as I had to do at home left me ample time to indulge my gluttony for indiscriminate reading—indeed to become a regular "rake at reading".

I can't remember how long this blissful phase lasted—at most,

I think, only six weeks—not long enough for me to remember much more than its alphabet, but long enough to confer on me the stigma of having *wanted* to learn Greek—in those days a grievous stigma. Modern languages, of course, were an adornment, but the wish to learn a dead language was definitely morbid, if not actually depraved.

The end of this brief episode in my education was very sudden. Mary Vesey was now daily going to a girls' school, and it was thought it would be "nice" for the cousins to be together. So, indeed, despite the initial wrench of leaving Stanway, hunting and Greek, it proved to be.

Thus topsy-turvily, at the relatively mature age of eighteen, and after I had been presented at Court, I, for the first time in my life, became a schoolgirl.

Mary and I were the only day-girls at Northlands, a school near Englefield Green, kept by the remarkable Miss Weisse.

Arriving in a dog-cart at eight in the morning, and fetched away in the evening, we would perhaps feel a twinge of moral discomfort at leaving our school-fellows to darn their stockings, make their own beds, and enjoy their cocoa supper, while we ourselves returned to an excellent "Late Dinner" and every kind of bodily, mental, and spiritual comfort.

I found the first day at school terribly trying. I thought I should never be able to endure the sound of the bell that chivvied me from place to place, the lack of any time to myself—the painful, exhausting "rest", lying, supported only by my reddening elbows, face downwards on a hard parquet floor; but by the next day I had adjusted myself and henceforth greatly enjoyed the rhythmic existence, the companionship, the ravenous appetite I brought to meals, and the sense of being really well taught.

Enshrining its own domesticated musical genius, Donald Tovey, Northlands was predominantly a musical school. My piano-playing having been cut short when I was twelve, I was the only pupil not learning this instrument; but one day, when, because I had a sore throat, I was told to open my jaws and say "Ah-h-h-h", it was discovered that the roof of my capacious mouth, in every way constructed to be an admirable sounding-board, was positively dome-like in its dimensions, that my lungs appeared to be made of leather, while my diaphragm was so powerful that the Peerage experimentally laid on it, fairly leapt into the air at every breath I drew. It had long been the un-realised ambition of this yearningly musical school to produce a singer. Had they at last found her? Excitement was intense; hopes high.

But I was to prove their most bitter disappointment, for though I could emit bell-like single notes of roof-lifting reson-ance, I was unable to sing a note in tune, and alas! no Svengali came forward. After prolonged patient attempts to teach me to sing one song—"Loch Lomond"—the Prima Donna ambition had to be abandoned. I felt bitterly frustrated, for naturally at the mere suggestion that I might become a singer, Grand-Operatic castles in the air had reared themselves sky-high.

The pet educational theory held at Northlands was that the ordinary crudely competitive system prevailing at schools was all wrong. The object of each girl, Miss Weisse contended, should be to compete not against others, but against her own best self. Therefore there was no placing in order of proficiency, or giving of marks. No particular pupil could say she was head of the school or indeed higher up than anyone else. In fact, there was no overt competition; no recognised forms or classes. For girls who were to earn their own living, and were therefore in need of certificates, it was not the right school. For Butterflies-to-Be, it was admirable; delightfully free from any, in the derogatory sense, schoolgirlish atmosphere and an excellent incubator for the appreciation of music and literature, for both of which Miss Weisse had unbounded love and a finely-educated palate.

Besides giving each girl in the school a piano lesson, she daily held classes for the whole school in Literature.

Miss Weisse was a brilliant woman, her gift for teaching out-standing. I have never forgotten her masterly brief summarisa-tion of the Greek Drama. Her passion for, and insistence on the learning of poetry by heart, outdid my own. In fact she con-sidered that not to know every single poem in the *Oxford Book of Verse* by heart was a sign of gross illiteracy.

No one could deny she had her favourites, but, happening myself to be one, I had no particular objection to this not uncommon trait. To make up for the piano lesson for which my father had made me ineligible, she gave me a daily private lesson in literature. I found her a wonderfully stimulating teacher. I have never known anyone possess to a higher degree the power to inspire in others the wish to excel, or anyone whose praise gave greater pleasure. She had a knack of making you feel framed and flood-lit and as though much were at stake. But, if she could be stimulating, she could also be petrifying. Never to me so long as I was her pupil, but when I revisited Northlands as a grown-up girl, how she would pulverise me by her terrible way of in a room full of people suddenly with a pounce, like a cat's at a mouse, darting out the command, "Now, Cynthia, it's *your* turn to say something interesting." Invariably, I failed to take my cue.

Miss Weisse never wore anything that could possibly be described as a dress. Appropriately, she was always "robed". With her strange penetrating feline eyes—she suggested a cat made of steel—she remains an undyingly vivid figure. In the long picture gallery of my memory her portrait still hangs on the line.

What were our physical exercises at Northlands? We did not play *Lacrosse*, whatever that may be. My only game—as I was never there in the summer when lawn tennis was played—was hockey with a soft ball. This took place every morning. In the afternoons there were walks (not in crocodile formation) conducted by one of the teachers; the rule of the road being that we must always talk French, German or Italian, whichever happened to be the language of the mistress in charge of our particular party. This reminds me of an embarrassing incident. On one of these constitutionals, two other girls and myself were justly accused of chattering in our own language. Brought before the High Court of Miss Weisse herself, we were at three o'clock on a lovely day condemned to bed—instantaneous bed. Most awkward for me, since, being only a day-girl, I had no bed to which to go. What was I to do?

My time at Northlands was all too brief—merely two terms,

neither of them complete. I wish it could have lasted longer; for with it ended all the formal teaching I was ever to have. The last stone in the crazy pavement of my education had now been laid.

Without any further shilly-shallying I must "Come Out"!

. . . I have written far more about my young self than I ever intended or, indeed, expected to remember; I had no idea my memory was such a palimpsest. Yet, despite such copious ink-shed, how very few of your questions have I answered!

Except for my attempt at George Wyndham and two or three painters, I have scarcely mentioned any of the "striking, and almost legendary personalities" you asked me to recall. Never mind, I promise you that when I take the pen between my teeth again, I will do my best to describe as they appeared to me, Arthur Balfour, Charles Whibley, Walter Raleigh, D. H. Lawrence, J. M. Barrie and others.

I will try, too, to tell you what it was like to be an Edwardian Girl.

One absurd effect of reliving the long ago is that I have inadvertently slipped back into signing myself Cynthia CHARTERIS!

INDEX

235

INDEX